PUBLISHED BY
gameXplore N.A. Inc
Ottawa ON, Canada

ORIGINAL COVER ART BY Fridtjof Leivestad Olsen (aka Tiftof)

IMAGES REPRODUCED IN THIS BOOK FALL INTO THREE CATEGORIES:
1.Screenshots produced by Game Index Statistics & Analysis AS and used with their permission.
2.Copyrighted material used by kind permission from copyright holders.
3.Press material intended for reprint.

gameXplore® is a registered trademark of
Game Index Statistics & Analysis AS
Oslo, Norway.

Book of Games Volume 2
Printed in Canada
First printing October 2007

ISBN-13: 978-82-997378-2-1
ISBN-10: 82-997378-2-6

BOOKOFGAMES.COM
GAMEXPLORE.COM

LAYOUT AND FRONTISPIECE
Bendik Stang & Bison Design
TYPESETTING
Scala, Klavika

THE BOOK OF

Games

VOLUME 2

gameXplore®

Acknowledgements

An amazing number of individuals have been involved in the making of *Book of Games* Volume 2.

First we would like to thank our outstanding team of game testers and analysts. Playing videogames is fun but also hard work, especially when deadlines loom and late nights turn into early mornings. A special thanks to our lead testers for coordinating and leading the testing process: Joachim Bjørne, Elias Bjørne, Fredrik Enersen, Christopher Køltzow, Erik Staubo, Alexander Holland Jensen, Malene H. Jaeger, Richard Dante, Åshild Amland, Fridtjof "Tiftof" Leivestad Olsen, Magnus Talén, Fredrik S. Baden, Nikolai Heum, Trym Haugerud, Henrik Ræder, Ola Pellerud Hamletsen, and Herman Bergsløkken. Without you guys, we would have not been able to put together the game section of this book.

Book of Games is becoming a very international collaboration with writers from both sides of the Atlantic. Contributors include Jørgen Kirksæther (Oslo, Norway), Eric Segalstad (Boulder, Colorado), David Cole (San Diego, California), Allison Luong (San Francisco, California), Spencer Sherman (Los Angeles, California), Joey Lesh (Seattle, Washington), Scott Steinberg (Atlanta, Georgia), Laura Wampfler (Plant City, Florida), Malene H. Jaeger (Oslo, Norway), Øystein Samnøen (Hamar, Norway), Odd Arild Olsen (Hamar, Norway), Edward F. Maurina III (Hillsboro, Oregon), Luke "Duke" Newcombe (London, United Kingdom), Gareth Williams (Nottingham, United Kingdom), and Robert Hoogendoorn (Holland).

Without them the incredible features, genre introductions, and reference sections would not have been. Special thanks to Ben Furfie and Robert Haxton for their help and insight in producing the Hardcore Territory article, Jun Takeuchi for the action genre, Petter Solberg for the racing genre, Tony Hawk for the sports genre, Al Lowe for the adventure genre, Rob Pardo for the MMORPG genre, Brian Lam for the entertainment genre, Team Dignitas for their insights on clans, Dr. Sarit Ghosh for his candid revelations on the inner workings of guilds, and Andy Schatz, Josh Ritter, and Josiah Pisciotta for sharing their knowledge about indie gaming.

To all our industry and organizational contacts goes a very special thanks. There are way too many to be able to list them all, but we have to mention at least some of you by name: Fredrik Moberg, Daniel Nielsen, Jesper Lund (Ubisoft), Kirsti Danielsen (Bergsala/Nintendo), Michael Auer, Kai Stüwe, Marjon Leenen (Capcom), Peter Jakobsen, Thorbjørn Ingebretsen (THQ Nordic), Jørgen Tharaldsen (Funcom), Silje Thoresen (Microsoft), Ben Schroder (Blizzard Entertainment), Birgitt Berglund, Morten Christoffersen (Nordic Film Interactive/Sony), Jørgen Tharaldsen (Funcom), Hans Moe, Aimar Niedzwiedzki (EA), Kjetil Walseth (Vivendi Universal Games), Petra Tell (Activision), Lars Stuanes, Ørjan Sveen (Panvision), Jens Hvass (KE-Media), David Blundell (NCSoft), Rob Donald (2K Games), Gudbrand Teigen (Innovation Norway), Maud Stevens (PEGI), and Christine Seddon (ESRB).

Thanks again to the wonderful people at Independent Publishers Group, in particular Curt Matthews, Paul Murphy, and Mary Rowles, who all believed in us from the start. And to Barry Friedland and Michele Rivera at Inner Workings for once again turning our electronic files into the beautiful book you now hold in your hands.

A very special thanks to Kasia Piekarz, our wonderful, around-the-clock, tireless copyeditor in chief, who again has edited and re-edited to combine the work of a number of authors form different parts of the world and with varying command of English, into the easy flowing prose you now have before you. This year she was assisted by Spencer Sherman and Christine Luiggi.

Wow, that's more than 80 people—80 of the most talented, knowledgeable, and professional individuals we know!

Last but not least to our investors: thank you for believing in our dreams and making them come true.

Bendik Stang,
Editor in Chief & Designer

Erik Hoftun
Publisher

Morten A. Østerholt
Chief Project Manager

Contents

Preface

Here we go again. With the all-new second volume of *Book of Games* you now hold in your hands, we have established the *Book of Games* as

1.   The only videogame reference series in book form
2.   An ongoing written account about the wonderful world of videogaming

We made a leap of faith when we published *Book of Games Volume 1* last year. There was little or no precedent for what we were doing. This year was very different. The decision to publish Volume 2 was a no-brainer based on the wonderful response we received on Volume 1 both from readers and reviewers. Thank you for receiving our book so warmly and thank you for spending your hard-earned cash to buy it. And last but not least, a great big thank you to all who provided the wonderful feedback that has made it possible to write an even better book this year.

So what's new? The short answer is **everything!**

MORE THAN 100 NEW GAMES! You asked for more information on each game. Done! We have more information about each game we cover while still keeping the full page of gorgeous screenshots you said you loved.

All New Feature Articles—and More of Them! We have more of the feature material you said you enjoyed so much in Volume 1. This year we have some incredible new material on subjects ranging from hardcore gaming to the growing acceptance of videogames as a way to fight obesity and educate kids!

MMORPGs Play a Major Role this year, as they do in the videogaming world we want to reflect. We have in-depth coverage of the biggest games as well as exciting upcoming titles!

Higher-Quality Titles. Choosing which games to cover is the most difficult part of putting together this book. Depending on how you count it, 600 to more than 1000 new titles are released every year. This year we have made it even more difficult to choose by using more stringent criteria and reducing the number of titles. GameXplore keeps a constant eye on the videogame market and is fortunate enough to test the majority of titles that come out every year well ahead of their release. When selecting which titles to include in this book, we considered and weighed each game's audience, quality, uniqueness, as well as average score and popularity—or anticipation if the title has yet to be released.

Game Score. A big change from last year is our new aggregate game score, a brand new variable we have been hard at work developing. It is compiled by averaging the score given by a selection of major review sites and magazines. We will continuously monitor on which reviews we base the aggregated score considering a number of factors like quality, consistency, and credibility of information.

Reach. *Book of Games* is published worldwide, and we monitor all main gaming markets, although our main focus is Europe and North America.

The People Who Play and the People Who Make Videogames. Videogames are made for gamers. A major new section in the book delves into the world of hardcore gaming. We have talked to these guys (they are still mostly guys) to understand what professional gaming means. And we have talked to the people behind the games to understand how some of the all-time great games came to be and what we can expect from the current and coming generations of games.

We do not expect that you will agree completely with all of our choices. We could have made a book ten times the size with no risk of running out of material. But let's face it: there are a lot of bad games out there. And quality is what *Book of Games* is all about.

There are some titles we would have liked to include but could not, either because they were published after this book went to press or because we did not receive copies in time. If you are a publisher reading this, please do contact us and confirm that we receive review copies in time.

Nevertheless, it all boils down to us, the editors. We reserve the right to include or leave out any title. Quality is important, but we do have other criteria, too. Even if the quality is uneven or the game lacks polish, we might include it because it represents something novel, be it in gameplay or player interaction. *Wii Sports* is a perfect example of the latter.

We hope you like *Book of Games Volume 2*. If you enjoy it even half as much as we did putting it together, you will be one happy reader. If this is your first encounter with *Book of Games*, be sure to check out Volume 1 as well. We predict the series will be a major collector's item!

If you have any comments, be it criticism for leaving out your favorite game or suggestions for titles or feature topics you would like to see in Volume 3, we would love to hear from you! Leave us a note at WWW.BOOKOFGAMES.COM!

Enjoy!

Bendik, Hans Christian, Morten, and Erik (the editors)

Disclaimer

As mentioned above, the games in Book of Games have been selected entirely at the discretion of the editors. We have tried to use consistent criteria, some of which are mentioned above. A few games we would have liked to include were simply not available in time to be included.

Although we have tried our best to give every game a fair and correct representation, we take no responsibility for errors in the book.

Some games are published only in North America, others only in Europe. Publishers probably have their reasons for such a practice, but we think you deserve better and thought we would show you a few examples of what you are missing out on. Don't blame us if you can't find a particular title where you live. Contact the publisher!

Please note that, even if Book of Games covers a title as a single entry, graphics and game packaging may vary for different editions of the same game, depending on console and geographic territories. So may the age ratings and parental guidance given by PEGI or ESRB. Therefore, please confirm actual ratings and game capabilities on the game cover.

INSTRUCTIONS ON HOW TO READ THE GAME REPORTS

AVAILABLE ON
Available platforms have a checkmark

PUBLISHER
Tells who is marketing the game

DEVELOPER
Tells who developed the game

FIRST RELEASED
The earliest release date in the western world

GAME GENRE
Defined by the activites in the game like, "Hockey," "Simulation," "Fighting," etc

THEME
The topic of the game like "Sport," "Travel," "War," etc.

TIME PERIOD
When in history does the game play occur?

COMPLEXITY
How difficult is it to play the game? Can children play it?

SIMILAR GAMES
This is based on calculations from our huge database of games and shows the three most similar games, based mainly on gameplay

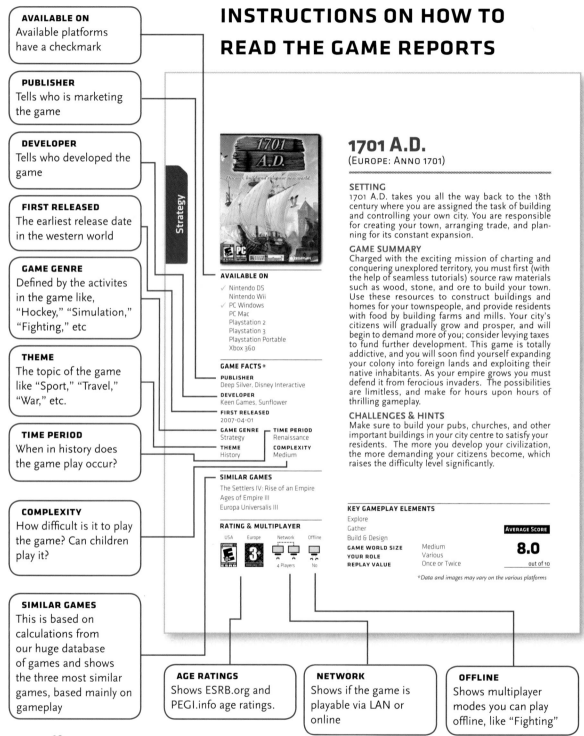

Strategy

1701 A.D.
(EUROPE: ANNO 1701)

SETTING
1701 A.D. takes you all the way back to the 18th century where you are assigned the task of building and controlling your own city. You are responsible for creating your town, arranging trade, and planning for its constant expansion.

GAME SUMMARY
Charged with the exciting mission of charting and conquering unexplored territory, you must first (with the help of seamless tutorials) source raw materials such as wood, stone, and ore to build your town. Use these resources to construct buildings and homes for your townspeople, and provide residents with food by building farms and mills. Your city's citizens will gradually grow and prosper, and will begin to demand more of you; consider levying taxes to fund further development. This game is totally addictive, and you will soon find yourself expanding your colony into foreign lands and exploiting their native inhabitants. As your empire grows you must defend it from ferocious invaders. The possibilities are limitless, and make for hours upon hours of thrilling gameplay.

CHALLENGES & HINTS
Make sure to build your pubs, churches, and other important buildings in your city centre to satisfy your residents. The more you develop your civilization, the more demanding your citizens become, which raises the difficulty level significantly.

AVAILABLE ON
- ✓ Nintendo DS
- Nintendo Wii
- ✓ PC Windows
- PC Mac
- Playstation 2
- Playstation 3
- Playstation Portable
- Xbox 360

GAME FACTS *

PUBLISHER
Deep Silver, Disney Interactive

DEVELOPER
Keen Games, Sunflower

FIRST RELEASED
2007-04-01

GAME GENRE	**TIME PERIOD**
Strategy	Renaissance
THEME	**COMPLEXITY**
History	Medium

SIMILAR GAMES
The Settlers IV: Rise of an Empire
Ages of Empire III
Europa Universalis III

RATING & MULTIPLAYER

USA	Europe	Network	Offline
E	3+		
	www.pegi.info	4 Players	No

KEY GAMEPLAY ELEMENTS
Explore
Gather
Build & Design

		AVERAGE SCORE
GAME WORLD SIZE	Medium	**8.0**
YOUR ROLE	Various	
REPLAY VALUE	Once or Twice	out of 10

Data and images may vary on the various platforms

AGE RATINGS
Shows ESRB.org and PEGI.info age ratings.

NETWORK
Shows if the game is playable via LAN or online

OFFLINE
Shows multiplayer modes you can play offline, like "Fighting"

GAME GENRE
Main game genre

COVER ART
Multi-cover if the game is available on more than two platforms, platform specific if available on only one

GAME TITLE AND SUBTITLE
This is normally the US title, but in cases where the game is big in EU and small in US the EU title is used.

SCREENSHOTS
Mostly in-game screenshots captured by gameXplore to show the true look and feel of the game.

Strategy

1701 A.D.
(EUROPE: ANNO 1701)

SETTING
1701 A.D. takes you all the way back to the 18th century where you are assigned the task of building and controlling your own city. You are responsible for creating your town, arranging trade, and planning for its constant expansion.

GAME SUMMARY
Charged with the exciting mission of charting and conquering unexplored territory, you must first (with the help of seamless tutorials) source raw materials such as wood, stone, and ore to build your town. Use these resources to construct buildings and homes for your townspeople, and provide residents with food by building farms and mills. Your city's citizens will gradually grow and prosper, and will begin to demand more of you; consider levying taxes to fund further development. This game is totally addictive, and you will soon find yourself expanding your colony into foreign lands and exploiting their native inhabitants. As your empire grows you must defend it from ferocious invaders. The possibilities are limitless, and make for hours upon hours of thrilling gameplay.

CHALLENGES & HINTS
Make sure to build your pubs, churches, and other important buildings in your city centre to satisfy your residents. The more you develop your civilization, the more demanding your citizens become, which raises the difficulty level significantly.

SETTING
Tells the background and location of where the game is played

GAME SUMMARY
Tells you the essence of the gameplay and our summary of what to expect

CHALLENGES & HINTS
Tells you what your major challenges in the game will be and gives you hints of what to look out for. (often told in a humoristic way)

AVAILABLE ON

✓ Nintendo DS
  Nintendo Wii
✓ PC Windows
  PC Mac
  Playstation 2
  Playstation 3
  Playstation Portable
  Xbox 360

GAME FACTS *

PUBLISHER
Deep Silver, Disney Interactive
DEVELOPER
Keen Games, Sunflower
FIRST RELEASED
2007-04-01

GAME GENRE	**TIME PERIOD**
Strategy	Renaissance
THEME	**COMPLEXITY**
History	Medium

SIMILAR GAMES
The Settlers IV: Rise of an Empire
Ages of Empire III
Europa Universalis III

RATING & MULTIPLAYER

USA	Europe	Network	Offline
		4 Players	No

KEY GAMEPLAY ELEMENTS
Explore
Gather
Build & Design

GAME WORLD SIZE Medium
YOUR ROLE Various
REPLAY VALUE Once or Twice

AVERAGE SCORE
8.0
out of 10

*Data and images may vary on the various platforms

KEY GAMEPLAY ELEMENTS
Shows the three most frequent gameplay activities

AVERAGE SCORE
This is compiled by scaling the scores of major reviewers based on factors like quality, consistency, and credibility, and then averaging all of these scores together

GAME WORLD SIZE
Tells if you are playing with in a very strict and small world, like a quiz show, or a huge world, like an MMORPG

YOUR ROLE
Who are you in the game?

REPLAY VALUE
Whether the game is fun to play multiple times, like a Sports game, or just once, like an Adventure game

Welcome to the
Greatest Entertainment Industry

WORLD OF WARCRAFT: NO OTHER INDUSTRY PROVIDES A PLAYGROUND FOR MORE THAN 9 MILLION PEOPLE

Since their humble beginnings in the early 1960s, videogames have now become the premier form of entertainment for an increasingly technology-savvy public. More than 69% of Americans play videogames, and the industry continues to grow exponentially, increasing by almost 15 percent in 2006. What had originally been considered a niche market driven by geeks and destined to be a passing fad has turned into a viable business and respected hobby. Youngsters who had once dreamed of becoming rock stars now want to be the next Sid Meier or Peter Moore.

But how did we get here? Without a doubt, we owe a debt to Nintendo for its surprising ability to open up gaming to a wider audience.

When the company launched the Nintendo DS, everyone had their reservations about its potential. Some thought the touch screen was a step in the wrong direction. Publishers thought that high-end graphics supported by Sony's PSP were the future. So without much third-party support, Nintendo set about developing two exclusive titles for the DS that would break open the gaming market to an entirely new audience. *Brain Training* and *Nintendogs* were masterpieces, that offered something new to hardcore gamers while inviting nongamers to participate in games that weren't difficult to learn. This made the DS the most accessible handheld on the market. Both games combined have sold almost 25 million

NINTENDOGS: MORE POPULAR THAN THE REAL THING?

but once again, Nintendo was right. In the space of a year, the Nintendo Wii has outsold both the PlayStation 3 and Microsoft's Xbox 360, and it is expected to lead the current generation of consoles by March 2008. Publishers are flocking to the format after having initially ignored it, while Nintendo continues to maximize their hold on their software market with titles such as *Wii Sports* and *Wii Fit*. For the rest of the industry, it is catching up time, and it needs to do so fast before Nintendo completely takes over the market.

Currently, Microsoft is the market leader for next-generation consoles with its Xbox 360. Launched in November 2005, the hardcore masses have flocked to the console with its exclusive games and affordable price. With almost every publisher firmly behind the sleek white packaging, its success was almost guaranteed when it was the first third-generation console to hit the market. Unfortunately, its rush to be first exposed a serious design flaw: overheating caused fatal errors on the system's motherboard. Microsoft responded with the adoption of a three-year warranty, but the damage to their reputation was already done.

Nonetheless, Microsoft retains the best attach rate for any console, with each Xbox 360 owner owning at least six games. But this success rate has been largely due to games geared to the hardcore audience, such as the groundbreaking *Gears of War* and the recently launched *Halo 3*. In comparison to Nintendo and Sony, Microsoft is having difficulty breaking out of that mold and reaching the mass market. Titles such as *Scene It?* and *Naruto* barely touch the sales of popular games such as Sony's *Buzz!*, *Dance Dance Revolution*, and *SingStar*. *Guitar Hero* and its sequel have both proved popular,

copies between them, the appeal to consumers and the impact on a strictly hardcore-focused publishing sector cannot be underestimated.

While the rest of the industry was removing its collective foot from its mouth, after the runaway success of the DS—which has sold twice that of the PSP—Nintendo dropped another bomb on the gaming world with the Wii and the Wii remote, a single-handed control mechanism purposely designed to be played by anyone. Instantly accessible

"While the rest of the industry was removing its collective foot from its mouth, after the runaway success of the DS..."

when compared to standard two-handed controllers, Nintendo argued that if a parent was used to a remote control, they would quickly be at home with the Wii, therefore bringing videogaming to the entire family. The world doubted Nintendo again,

with sales of more than two million on the Xbox 360 alone, but the games are adored by hardcore followers and the mid-teen male demographic, subsequently lacking the pull power of far-reaching family-orientated titles. Only by learning from Sony and Nintendo can Microsoft truly open up the console race.

Sony, on the other hand, is in very unfamiliar territory these days. Both the PlayStation and its successor have been a genuine success around the world, with the PlayStation 2 making its way into more than 120 million homes and still going strong. After bursting onto the scene in 1994 with one of the most expensive consoles on the market, the original PlayStation won Sony many fans with clever advertising and strong publisher support. Those same loyal fans clamored to own the PlayStation 2, driven by must-have games such as *Final Fantasy* and *Metal Gear Solid*. With so much success, Sony should have dominated the third-generation console war. But so far, this hasn't been the case.

Launching in America and Japan in late 2006, followed by a delayed arrival in Europe the following year, the costly PlayStation 3 is a marvel of modern technology. The console utilized Blu-ray technology and the Cell Processor jointly developed with IBM and Samsung, adding up to almost $800 in manufacturing costs. With an on-sale price of $599, Sony was taking a loss from the very beginning, a loss that looked positive only in the light of the PS3s initial slow sales. The highlight of a poorly performing games division's financial report was the statement that selling fewer than projected meant that the division hadn't lost as much as they had planned.

In spite of the $200 premium the PS3 carries over the 360, it is selling as well as the Xbox 360, a success in and of itself. Where Sony's videogame division is suffering is in its lack of software. Using seven special processing elements and one core controlling processor, the Cell Processor is an ex-

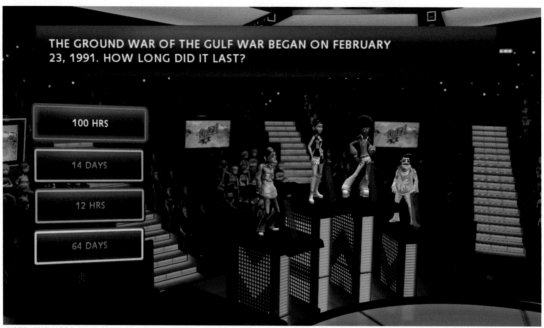

THE GROUND WAR OF THE GULF WAR BEGAN ON FEBRUARY 23, 1991. HOW LONG DID IT LAST?

100 HRS

14 DAYS

12 HRS

64 DAYS

BUZZ: THE MEGA QUIZ: WHY WATCH SOMEBODY ELSE ON A TV-SHOW WHEN YOU AND YOUR FRIENDS CAN PARTICIPATE?

ceptional advancement in computer technology, but developers have had trouble learning how to use the chip, forcing them to take longer to get multiformat code bases to work on the console. In the summer of 2007, developers were falling over themselves to confirm that the Xbox 360 was the choice development platform because, in all simplicity, it was just easier to develop for. With many exclusives coming to the Xbox 360 for Christmas 2007, Sony has been left with no option but to push its few first-party titles. *Heavenly Sword* and *Uncharted: Drake's Fortune* are fantastic fun, but these titles are aimed at the hardcore fan, which can only take the Sony so far in increasing its market share.

Time will tell if Sony has been successful in capitalizing on its technology. A redesigned PSP and the continuing success of PS2 will keep Sony afloat for a while, but without a sharp reduction in price and a more humble approach to marketing,

Sony's position as the market leader is threatened with this third generation of consoles, especially with formidable assaults from both Microsoft and Nintendo.

And with that, the console race continues into 2008. In a year's time, all three consoles could be selling well, or one might be the runaway leader. And this time it might not be unit sales that decide this generation's winner, but a combination of hardware and software sales. Currently, Microsoft is well in the lead in terms of software sold. Nintendo would be on par with Sony, who currently has an attach rate of just over one game per console, if it were not for *Wii Sports* being given away with every Wii sold. And were it not for Sony's recent inclusion of two games and an extra controller, their third-party software sales would be dire. Sony recently announced that PlayStation 3 software had sold in excess of two million copies in Europe, with first-

"Consumers seem ready to accept gaming as a viable pastime, not only for nerds or geeks but for the family as a whole."

party games accounting for less than 50 percent of that figure. This is a figure that, without a doubt, is troubling, especially for third-party publishers. With high development costs for a game that might sell only 80,000 copies per title, this certainly isn't good enough. Over the lifespan of the PlayStation 3 this may improve, but only with unique and compelling content that is only available on Sony's platform.

Adding to all of these changes are the changes in the average gamer. Each console manufacturer is catering for an increasingly aging consumer who brings their family into their gaming life as much as possible. But creating a market where gaming is open to everyone isn't something that can be done overnight. Microsoft's much-lambasted target of reaching one billion consumers with the

Xbox 360 could be achieved but not in a single generation nor with a single console. And crafting an install base of more than 110 million with the PlayStation brand isn't so much of an achievement but a start. With new initiatives such as PlayStation Home and massively multiplayer online role playing games coming to all consoles, even the PC market is beginning to converge with consoles. And new avenues for entry-level gaming are opening all the time, with the advancement of mobile gaming continuing apace.

Whether mobile gaming will ever reach a position where it can compete with handheld consoles is another discussion entirely, but with the tempo of technological change moving faster than ever before, the gaming industry is at a crossroad. Do they embrace new ideas and forge new sectors of the market or continue on the current path, pleasing a hardcore but niche market? The answer, of course, is a mixture of both, embracing change at a pace that is sustainable but fast enough to keep up with consumer demand. As a new generation of consoles enters its second year, the growing audience will ask for more creativity, newer ways to play, and the ability to play on their own terms. Content on-demand is becoming more popular than ever, as is downloadable content, but both are at the mercy of platform holders. How fast do they want the industry to evolve, and are they ready for what the future holds? And what do gamers want? Will the release schedule for publishers be decided by the fads of 9–14-year-olds or by what the 35–64 demographic wants to experience that month? Consumers seem ready to accept gaming as a viable pastime, not only for nerds or geeks but for the family as a whole. But is the industry ready for them?

GAMES ARE FOR
Everyone

The biggest console war since the rise of video-game culture is happening at this very moment as three factions battle it out for market share: Microsoft's Xbox 360, the Nintendo Wii, and the Sony PlayStation 3 (PS3). Complicating this fight for the top is the videogame industry's recent infiltration into the mass market. This potential to reach an entirely untapped market has led many industry analysts to believe that the console that most successfully penetrates the mass market will ultimately win the console war. And so, all three of these companies have locked their eyes on the mass-market prize, adopting the mantra that everyone—men and women, young and old—is a possible gamer.

Back in the late seventies and early eighties, games were mostly played by boys in the basement of their parents' homes. Even though arcade games like *Pac-Man* brought games to a broader public, computer games were mostly the toy of young adolescent males. Lately, this stereotype has changed to include a much wider audience. Thanks to the efforts of the gaming industry and the growing

"...a gamer is no longer only a young male. Nowadays grandfathers can be gamers too."

influence of gaming on our culture, more people are joining the culture of videogames. Research by the British BBC in 2005 provides solid evidence that even grandfathers are gamers, mothers are playing games when their sons are at school, and girls are taking

It's well documented that playing videogames can improve hand–eye coordination. This can have many practical uses. Medical research by the Beth Israel Medical Center in New York, for instance, showed that people who played Super Monkey Ball in advance to operating on a patient made 37% less mistakes during the operation, were 27% faster, and performed 42% better in a chirurgical test.

Not only can your hand–eye coordination be improved, but playing videogames might also enhance your actual sight. According to research conducted at the University of Rochester, playing a first-person shooter for 20 minutes a day can improve your sight by 20%. Researchers explained that these types of videogames in particular train your eyes to focus faster.

Games can even be good for your mind. In Japan, Brain Training on the Nintendo DS is used in homes for the elderly to reduce dementia. People who work in Japanese nursing homes believe that playing simple games like Brain Training helps keep their patients mentally active by stimulating their brain.

And there are many more examples of the physical benefits of game playing. The GetUpMove.com website tells success stories of people who play dancing videogames like Dance Dance Revolution (DDR) or Dancing Stage to lose weight. Seventeen-year-old Tanja Jessen, for instance, lost more than 70 pounds playing DDR, reducing her weight from 230 pounds to 140.

While some have speculated that game playing has a negative effect on the libido, research by Gametart and Breeze showed that among 200 women, those who played games regularly were also having sex an average of four times a week, while nongamers were having sex an average of only two times a week.

over and beating the boys in the expanding range of videogames now available in the market.

One way that Sony and Microsoft have tried to expand their audience is to promote their consoles as multimedia hardware that can become the center of family entertainment. With one machine for everything, families can seamlessly transition from watching a movie to playing a game.

"Bring your Wii to a boring birthday party and you will have the most fun in your life guaranteed,..."

But in terms of a console that has wholeheartedly embraced this new demographic, the Nintendo Wii stand outs as the machine to beat. Unlike the PS3 and the Xbox 360, the Nintendo Wii wasn't designed with hardcore gamers in mind. It has a cheaper price tag, it doesn't require an expensive television, and most of all, the games are easy to pick up and play. *Wii Sports*, which is sold with the console, is tailor-made for the entire family and has successfully brought a wide audience into the fold. Moving your arms to hit a ball isn't as arbitrary as moving an analogue stick and pushing several buttons on a controller. In a scenario that would have been unthinkable 20 years ago, now you could bring your Wii to a birthday party, watch your mother play tennis against your grandfather, and witness the whole family have the time of their lives.

Running right alongside the Nintendo Wii is the PlayStation 2 (PS2). The PS2 has sold more consoles than any of its competitors in the world. Even at this very moment, Sony is selling thousands of PS2s

SCENE IT? LIGHTS, CAMERA, ACTION

along with hundreds of games that have become fan favorites. So instead of discontinuing development for the PS2 after the release of the PS3, Sony is using the PS2 to reach out to families with affordable games. Titles like the karaoke game *SingStar*, the quiz show *Buzz!*, and several *EyeToy* games appeal to a wide audience that includes children, parents, and even grandparents. *Konami's Dance Dance Revolution* for the PS2 has families around the world dancing together. Pink versions of the PSP, PS2, and Nintendo DS were released to attract female gamers.

Microsoft's intention to compete with Sony and Nintendo in the casual gaming market was recently showcased during the 2007 Electronic Entertainment Expo (E3). Defined by people who play easy-to-pick-up games at infrequent intervals, the casual gaming market attracts families in need of games that are simple and fun, and it has potential to become a large, mass-marketbaudience. In an obvious attempt to compete in this market, Microsoft

announced the release of the highly popular trivia game *Scene It?* for the Xbox 360 as a direct competitor with the PS2's *Buzz!*

Third-party software developers like Electronic Arts, Ubisoft, 505 Gamestreet, and Eidos are also getting in on the action. Ubisoft's bestselling titles aren't Ghost Recon: Advanced Warfighter 2 or *Splinter Cell* but casual virtual pet games like *Horsez*. With successes like these, third-party developers have recognized that the audience for videogames is much bigger than previously thought possible. Who is the potential buyer of casual games? Any person on the planet, they hope.

WHO IS PLAYING WHAT IN 2007?

To put it simply, people like to play games. Research by the BBC Audience Research (December 2005) among residents of the United Kingdom showed that 98 percent of all children ages 6 to 15 years old play videogames. In the 16 to 24 group,

WHY BOOKS ARE BAD FOR YOU?

After conducting research on a group of boys aged 7–10, Arlette C. Perry of the Miami School of Education stated the obvious: playing videogames burns more calories than reading a book.

But this statement is only one aspect of a larger question: how might children benefit from playing videogames instead of reading books? Marc Prensky is a famous researcher of videogames and educational tools, and he claims that books are on their way out as a form of education on many levels. Because children often have a difficult time getting interested in books, books can be very ineffective learning tools. Videogames, on the other hand, are efficient and stimulating, which helps students more fully engage in what they're learning. Several researchers like Hans Christian Arnseth from the Institute for Educational Research of the University of Oslo (Norway, Europe) want gaming to be considered as a serious tool for the future of our educational system. Although he admits that the impact of gaming should not be overestimated and that further research is needed, he states that "what [the research] do[es] tell us is something about how learning environments might be organized in order to enable students to make sense of various school subjects" (Arnseth, 2006).

Researchers who study the effects of videogames in learning environments argue that instead of making a reader active, books actually provide a passive environment, where the reader takes no part in the storytelling but is "being told" how the story unfolds. This passivity contrasts with the way people play videogames. Arnseth notes that active gamers are engaged and motivated to complete the task at hand and their actions affect how the story unfolds. Still, this doesn't take into account the amount of imaginative activity involved in reading. While gamers watch events unfold like a movie, readers must use their imagination to depict visual descriptions of a book.

Similar to reading a book, a certain amount of immersion occurs when playing videogames. But playing a videogame has greater consequences for the player because he or she is acting as the protagonist of the story. A reader has no say in what happens to the protagonists of a book. Arnseth notes that, while we might feel empathy for the protagonist of a book, emotions run higher for videogames. By controlling the protagonist in a videogame, we become an active participant in the story. We are no longer passively being taken for a ride, but have to process information actively, make decisions and respond to stimuli from the game. Thus videogames are the stronger medium playing to a broader register of the human mind.

the percentage of gamers decreased to 83 percent, while approximately 60 percent of people ages 6 to 65 play videogames. This data prove that games have become a broadly used medium for our spare time.

The main reason we play videogames is to be entertained. Playing a game lets us escape everyday life in an environment that is safe and controlled. Research has proven that people choose gaming as a relaxing way to spend time, even though it doesn't necessarily relax the mind and body. Games also provide an opportunity for gamers to do what they can't do in everyday life. Playing games can offer a sense of achievement that watching television shows cannot.

SCENARIO: GAMING IN THE FAMILY

Let's take a look at a "typical" family household and how the recent influx of causal games has changed their entertainment habits. Peter is the man of the house. He is 57 years old and works as an assistant manager at a local computer shop. Peter and his wife Megan, who is 52 years old, have three children together. Tom, 23, is the oldest. He is studying chemical sciences at a respected university. Chrissy is the middle of the three children. She is

HORSEZ

17 and just loves hanging out with her friends. The youngest of the bunch, Kevin, has just turned 12 and will go to middle school next year. What kinds of games might this kind of family play?

Chrissy and her friends crowd in her room to sing along with *SingStar*. To them, their scores aren't important. It's all about having fun. When her friends aren't over, she often borrows Kevin's Nintendo DS to play some simple and fun minigames. She likes *Brain Training*, but her favorites are *Nintendogs* and *Mario Kart DS*. She dotes on her puppies in *Nintendogs* and enjoys annoying her brother by beating his high score in *Mario Kart DS*.

Now that the oldest, Tom, has moved out, Kevin has access to Tom's gaming paradise. Tom left behind his mounted HD LCD television and Xbox 360.

Kevin is awestruck by the incredible graphics of the Xbox 360. Playing mostly sports games, Kevin wants to learn how to beat all the kids at school. When not playing as his favorite sports team, he enjoys the heart-racing speed of *Project Gotham Racing 4* and the tense, atmospheric environments of Bioshock and *Halo 3*. Even when Kevin is not at home he wants to play games, which is why he bought the Nintendo DS as soon as it was released. But after seeing his high scores in *Mario Kart DS* disappear (Kevin suspects that his sister Chrissy plays the handheld more than he does), he's now switched to the PSP. The PSP has all kinds of cool functions: you can watch movies, listen to music, and even steal cars in *Grand Theft Auto*!

Tom doesn't mind that his brother is using his TV back home. He is far away studying and partying

BIOSHOCK - NOT FOR THE FAINT-HEARTED

with his friends. But this doesn't mean he's stopped gaming. In fact, it's just the opposite: when he got to university, he treated himself to a PlayStation 3. He likes the intense graphics and wants to see his new HDTV with Dolby surround sound used to its fullest capacity. He is waiting in anticipation for the new *Metal Gear Solid*, but until then, he plays *Resistance Fall of Man* online. He is getting really good at it—his username is at the top of the PlayStation Network's rankings.

But he doesn't only enjoy hardcore games. He still loves games that are simple and playful. Tom can't wait for the special Home feature on his PlayStation 3. As soon as LittleBigPlanet is downloadable online at the PlayStation Store, he'll get it. Software like LittleBigPlanet is made with an emphasis on socializing. Instead of killing people, Tom can invite friends into his PlayStation 3 Home, where they can watch movies he's made himself. If he's feeling

homesick, he can even invite his little brother to this virtual house to chill out.

In addition to playing by himself, sometimes Tom and his friends organize LAN parties where everyone brings their computers and links them over the local area network (LAN). They'll play games until the early hours of the next morning...until one of the players realizes he has an exam in two hours and starts to go crazy! With the help of his friends, though, he thinks up an elaborate excuse to skip his test. Typical...

Tom's father, Peter, never really understood the obsession his kids had with games. But in recent years, his fascination for this phenomenon has grown. It all started a couple of years ago when the family was on holiday. Lying on the beach, Peter got bored and turned on his son's Gameboy Advance. That triggered something inside Peter. Ever since then, he's become fascinated by everything with awesome, high-definition graphics. Peter does not yet own his own console but sometimes plays with Kevin on Tom's Xbox 360. He even bought some Microsoft Points to spend on Xbox Live Arcade games. Xbox Live Arcade games are simple and don't require extensive gaming knowledge to play. This new fascination of Peter's even got the attention of his wife, Megan. Megan plays *Brain Training* on the Nintendo DS because she heard it helps fight the negative effects of aging. The game obviously won't stop her from being 52 instead of 39, but Peter knows better than to tell her this. She can tell her neighbor Charlotte that her *Brain Age* is 24, and that's all that matters.

On rare occasions, like holidays or birthdays, when the whole family comes together, there are always games in the house to entertain them all. Family gatherings now follow a new tradition. First, people come by the garden to drink and chat. After a while, Peter puts on the barbecue and Megan serves some wine. When the party's really roaring, Megan's asked to "get that singing game" from her room.

Tom drunkenly sets up the Nintendo Wii in the living room and soon everyone's moving about playing *Wii Sports*, singing songs with *SingStar*, and laughing at each other. Although initially met with skepticism, Grandma and Grandpa prove to be competitive Wii Sports players—especially in bowling.

While this scenario may seem foreign to some, it's not fictional. Games are reaching a wider audience and finding greater acceptance in a variety of social situations. To follow this trend, companies like Nintendo, Sony, and Microsoft are adjusting their strategies and incorporating more mass media and public events for exposure. Video games are reviewed alongside other respected media, like film and music. They have become a serious and widely accepted phenomenon and integral part of our culture, breaking down social boundaries in an entirely new way. The immediate future seems clear, but once videogames have infiltrated every family's living room, where can gaming go next? Only time will tell...

PROJECT GOTHAM RACING 4

Asian
Game Markets

With a market worth more than $8.5 billion in 2007, the Asian countries of Japan, Korea, China, and Taiwan are some of the largest and most avid gamer markets in the world. In Asia, gaming is so popular that top professional gamers in Korea can earn hundreds of thousands of dollars a year playing games for a living. In addition, popular game characters from Blizzard's *World of Warcraft* and *Nexon's Kart Rider* are so beloved and recognizable that Coca-Cola prints their images on Coke bottles.

NEXON'S KART RIDER

Japan Hardware Total for 2006

PS2	1,547,866
PS3	466,716
GameCube	89,775
Wii	989,118
Xbox 360	208,697
GBA SP	275,779
GB Micro	157,557
PSP	1,946,911
DS	1,336,931
DS Lite	7,526,038

Asia, though, cannot be treated as one monolithic region. Japan, Korea, China, and Taiwan all have unique cultures with different gaming preferences.

JAPAN

Home to gaming behemoths Nintendo and Sony, Japan is a hotbed of innovation with cutting-edge games. Japanese designers have created some of the world's most iconic videogame characters such as *Super Mario*, *Sonic the Hedgehog*, and *Donkey Kong*, along with evergreen franchises such as Square Enix's *Final Fantasy*, Capcom's *Street Fighter*, and Konami's *Metal Gear Solid*.

The Japanese videogame market is significantly different than that of the U.S. or Europe. Japanese consumers tend to prefer locally developed content, much of which tends to have a cuter graphic style compared to U.S. games. A glance at the top

20 titles in Japan in 2006 includes titles such as *Pocket Monster Diamond/Pearl*, *New Super Mario Bros.*, *DS Brain Age*, *Animal Crossing: Wild World*, and *Tetris DS*.

Overall, 2006 was a stellar year for the gaming markets in Japan. The Japanese gaming industry was worth an estimated 625 billion yen ($5 billion), according to researcher Famitsu, largely driven by the runaway success of the Nintendo DS. This allowed 2006 to be the gaming market's best year ever, breaking the previous record year 1997. The Nintendo DS sold an impressive 8.8 million hardware units, four times more than its closest competitor the Sony PSP, which sold close to 2 million hardware units.

CONCEPT ART FOR WORLD OF WARCRAFT: DRAENEI MALE

FRAN "FINAL FANTASY XII"

ONE OF THE HEROINES IN FINAL FANTASY XII;
FRAN IS VIEWED AS A GODDESS IN THE JAPANESE
MARKET DUE TO HER ROLE IN THE POPULAR GAME
SERIES PRODUCED BY TOKYO BASED SQUARE ENIX.

Nintendo took a different marketing approach with the DS, targeting a more mass-market audience, including females, senior citizens, and other dormant gamers. This strategy paid off handsomely for Nintendo as the DS has revitalized the games industry in Japan with nearly 8 of the top 10 titles in Japan being on the DS. The top-selling title in 2006 was *Pocket Monster Diamond/Pearl*, which sold an impressive 4.3 million units.

The future for gaming in Japan looks bright as Japanese consumers continue to satisfy their entertainment needs by purchasing console, mobile, and online games.

CHINA

China is well known for many things, including its large 1.3 billion–person population and its status as the "factory" of the world. Surprisingly, China is also the world's second-largest Internet market, just behind the U.S. More than 137 million Chinese citizens go online and 59 million PCs are connected to the Internet at any given time. And games are the primary reason many young Chinese go online, with 62% of Internet users citing games behind news and general browsing. As a result, the games market in China is expected to exceed $1 billion in 2007.

Although the numbers may mislead you into thinking gaming did not exist in China prior to the adoption of online games, China's gaming culture has in fact been evolving over the past 20 years. As 8-bit red-and-white Nintendos were brought to China in the late 1980s, gaming started to become an integral part of entertainment for young people in urban China. Most people who grew up during that period remember the most popular neighborhood kid they used to bribe with popsicles in exchange for some Nintendo playing time. Over the years, as PC penetration grew, gamers in China embraced popular Western titles such as Blizzard's *StarCraft* and Valve's *Counter-Strike*, as well as various Asian RPG and strategy titles.

SCREENSHOT FROM STARCRAFT II

However, nearly 90% of packaged PC and video games sold in China are pirated copies that consumers pay $1 or less for. Thus, the popularity of gaming initially amounted to little revenue for game publishers. It wasn't until the introduction of online games in 2000 that China has seen significant financial growth in its games industry. Online games differ from packaged games in that game operators control access to the game. Players have to pay a fee to gain access to the game, making piracy difficult.

In late 2001, Shanghai-based game operator Shanda launched *Legend of Mir II*, a game it licensed from Korea. This game transformed the Chinese online games industry as gamers could spend less than five cents an hour to play an ex-

ARTWORK FOR STARCRAFT II FROM BLIZZARD ENTERTAINMENT

citing and well-made MMORPG game. By 2004, Shanda had generated $165 million in revenue, an incredible amount for a company that just started operating games in 2001. Following the success of that title, more game operators targeted the Chinese market as they recognized its huge potential.

AUDITION

While MMORPGs represent the largest segment of the market, casual games are growing rapidly. Games such as *Audition* (an online dance and music game) and *Freestyle* (an online basketball game) are among the top 10 online games in

"While 5 cents per hour does not seem like a lot, World of Warcraft was able to generate close to $120 million in China in 2006 with this low hourly rate."

China, capturing up to 780,000 peak concurrent users. In addition, free-to-play, pay-for-virtual-item games have also gained a foothold in the MMORPG segment in recent years. Free games such as MMORPG Zhengtu thrived on that busi-

FREE MMORPG: ZHENGTU

to the hospital after days of intense gaming. Some parents are now renting apartments near their children's college to make sure their sons and daughters are not skipping classes and spending their food budget on a cool virtual sword.

Faced with increasing criticism over the addictive nature of online gaming, the Chinese government felt that it had to regulate the gaming industry. In 2005, the General Administration of Press and Publication, a Chinese government agency responsible for regulating games, issued a rule requiring game developers to include an antifatigue system in their online games.

According to the rule, three hours of gaming per day is considered "healthy" for minors while gaming beyond five hours is "unhealthy." The system cuts minors' in-game gains to half after their third hour and decreases gains to zero after the fifth. However, the effect of such a system remains unclear as players, Internet café owners, and even game operators are finding ways to cheat the system.

ness model, accruing 870,000 peak concurrent users within a year of launch.

However, despite numerous free titles on the market, players in China are still willing to pay for high-quality content. For example, Vivendi's *World of Warcraft* charges approximately 5 cents for each hour of playing time while operator Netease also charges players by the hour. While 5 cents per hour does not seem like a lot, *World of Warcraft* was able to generate close to $120 million in China in 2006 with this low hourly rate.

FATIGUE SYSTEM

Some in China may even say the popularity of online gaming has spun out of control. China is unique in that is has a "fatigue system," which is aimed at controlling the amount of hours gamers can play online games. The fatigue system is a result of growing pressure from parents concerned that their kids spend too much time and money playing online games. It is not unusual to read horrifying stories about college kids getting sent

THE POPULARITY OF QQ

TENCENT'S INSTANT MESSENGER: QQ

HALF LIFE 2: EPISODE TWO

Imagine one day your fashionable friend comes to you bragging about his new AIM logo jacket. Whatever your reaction might be, it is probably safe to assume you are most likely not going to your neighborhood AOL store and getting your share of AIM fashion. Well, things are a little different in China. With nearly 28.5 million peak concurrent users, QQ is China's most popular instant messenger tool. QQ is virtually unheard outside of China, but it is China's most popular instant messenger program, eclipsing Yahoo Messenger and Microsoft Instant Messenger by a wide margin.

In 2000, QQ's operator Tencent licensed its IM logo QQ penguin to apparel maker Donice to develop the Q-Gen brand and a full line of fashion products. Six years after the launch of Q-Gen, there are now more than 200 stores across

the nation, and consumers can find Q-Gen in department stores among Levi's jeans and Nike shoes.

The popularity of QQ resulted from Tencent's early market entry and dedicated effort in the IM business. Launched in 1998, QQ faced little competition as other prominent IM software such as Yahoo Messenger and AIM (ICQ) did not have a Chinese version, and local Internet companies such as Sina did not aggressively pursue the IM market. By May 2000, IM had more than 100,000 peak concurrent users, and that number quickly grew to 1 million by February of the next year.

As QQ continued to attract users, Tencent saw the opportunity to capitalize on its vast user base by launching numerous online games. Starting with chess and board games, the company quickly moved on to offer more elaborate content such as the MMORPG *QQ Fantasy* and the casual racing game *R2Beat*. As of Q4 2006, while QQ received 24.5 million peak concurrent users, QQ games also enjoyed 2.7 million concurrency and $17.4 million in revenue. It is likely that QQ will continue to grow in popularity because the company has such a streamlined distribution platform through its messenger service.

INDIA

Compared to other Asian countries such as China and Korea, India has a much smaller gaming market valued at less than $30 million in 2006. India, however, could emerge as a potential leading gaming market as gaming companies are just starting to invest heavily there.

With the console and software piracy at more than 80% and low PC penetration, India's gaming market has always lagged as game publishers and distributors struggled to find a niche for the gaming market. Part of the reason might be cultural since India traditionally has not had a strong gaming culture. This is slowly changing, though, as income levels rise in India and as Indian youth take a greater interest in the Internet and in entertainment.

Similar to Korea and China, one of the most

RAGNAROK ONLINE BY LEVEL UP

significant trends is the growth of online games. There are an estimated 35 to 50 million Internet users in India, many of whom are hungry for entertainment content. Many game operators are excited about the prospect of online gaming in India since online games circumvent piracy. Traditionally, piracy has been one of the major issues with growing the gaming market in India.

In October 2005, game operator Level Up brought the first massively-multiplayer online game (MMOG) *Ragnarok Online* to India. This was followed by Sify, a media company, with *A3*. Both of these games are from Korean publishers, with some local flavor added to appeal to an Indian audience. These games have accrued a loyal base, but the amount of concurrent users is relatively modest, often at fewer than 10,000. With increasing investment and the right content, online games are expected to be a significant driver for the Indian gaming market.

> **"India has more than 100,000 Internet cafés and nearly 40% of Internet cafés are used for online games."**

MMORPG A3 BY SIFY

MMORPG A3 BY SIFY

INTERNET CAFÉS

Supporting this interest in online gaming is an increasing number of Internet cafés. India has more than 100,000 Internet cafés and nearly 40% of Internet cafés are used for online games.

Games play a pivotal role at Internet cafés, helping to attract customers who tend to spend more time and money compared to general users. Games are a "sticky" activity, meaning that users will spend 30 minutes or more playing games, compared to general users that spend a few minutes checking e-mail or surfing the Internet. Internet café owners are capitalizing on this trend and responding to the needs of their users by stocking more games.

Indian Internet cafés also serve as important marketing vehicles, providing gamers a venue to demo the latest games and participate in promotions and contests. An example of this was when Sify hosted a national *Counter-Strike Condition Zero* tournament across 202 Gamedromes in 60 cities over a period of 45 days in September 2006. Sify said around 10,000 gamers participated in the tournament with total prizes worth more than

one million rupees ($22,000), including cash and phones from Sony Ericsson. The tournament was supported by a tie-in with Animax for TV coverage and was also heavily promoted in Sify's Internet cafés.

Similar to China and Korea, Indian Internet cafés serve as a popular place for youth to hang out, chat, play games, and check e-mail. Other than going to multiplex cinemas, India's urban youth lack entertainment options, making Internet cafés one of the "cool" places to hang out.

Popular games at Indian Internet cafés include packaged PC games such as VUG's *Counter-Strike* and *Half-Life 2*, EA's action games, Ubisoft's *Tom Clancy* series of games, cricket games, casual Web games, and MMOGs. Overall, shooters are one of the most popular games played at Indian Internet cafés.

In the next few years, even more Internet cafés are expected to open up, pointing to the Indian government's decision to allow Internet café con-

COUNTER-STRIKE SOURCE

cession stands at train stations and in the country's rapidly growing shopping malls, as well as new competitors in the Internet café market . This continued growth is expected to bolster consumer access to PCs and the Internet, which is necessary for gamers to go online and play games.

GAMING PREFERENCES

Gaming preferences for Indian consumers are very unique. India has a rich cultural heritage and booming film (Bollywood), TV, and music industries that can be tapped into to create game content that resonates and appeals to Indian consumers and to help drive the popularization of games.

In order to achieve mass-market appeal, online games in India will most likely be tailored to Indian gamer preferences, including themes, characters, and storylines based on Indian culture, traditions, mythology, and history. And these localizations cannot be just cosmetic or language based but must resonate on a deeper level to gain wider acceptance.

CONCLUSIONS

In conclusion, the vibrant games market in Asia is driven by both an avid gamer base and increasing development capability in the region. While solid infrastructure allowed Korea and Japan to brew a strong gaming culture over the years, rising income levels and Internet penetration are boosting the online games market at unprecedented rates in less-developed countries such as China and India. The emergence of these new markets is likely to add an interesting twist to the dynamics of the Asian games industry as companies compete to come up with more diverse offerings for gamers around the world.

A Market

IN TRANSITION

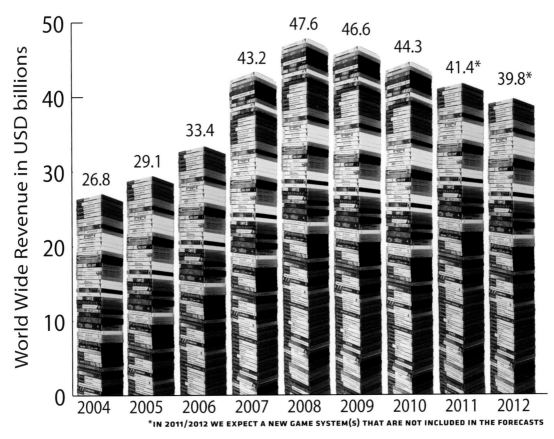

World Wide Revenue in USD billions

- 2004: 26.8
- 2005: 29.1
- 2006: 33.4
- 2007: 43.2
- 2008: 47.6
- 2009: 46.6
- 2010: 44.3
- 2011: 41.4*
- 2012: 39.8*

*IN 2011/2012 WE EXPECT A NEW GAME SYSTEM(S) THAT ARE NOT INCLUDED IN THE FORECASTS

The video game industry is exploding worldwide. (DFC Intelligence defines the video game and interactive entertainment industry as including console hardware and software, portable hardware and software, PC game software, online game subscription revenue, digital distribution of games, and advertising revenue for games.) In 2006 this market passed $30 billion in worldwide revenue and is forecasted to reach about $45 billion by 2012. This will make the video game industry about as large as the global music business.

The interactive entertainment market has traditionally been dominated by the video game console systems that attach to a television set. Furthermore, for the past decade the console market has been dominated by the two PlayStation platforms from Sony Computer Entertainment. The PS One and PlayStation 2 each shipped over 100 million units worldwide. This huge installed base of systems

"This will make the video game industry about as large as the global music business."

created a steady market that allowed numerous third-party software developers to build their own megahit franchises. To put the enormity of the success of the PlayStation systems in perspec-

MICROSOFT XBOX 360 ELITE

systems have been released from Sony, Microsoft, and Nintendo, and Microsoft and Nintendo are both hoping to offer more mass market alternatives. To extend the soft drink analogy, the soda wars are heating up, with Microsoft hoping the Xbox 360 can be a Pepsi to Sony's Coke. And, with the Wii, Nintendo is hoping to offer a mass market alternative to cola with a radical new control scheme—sort of an "uncola," like 7UP or Sprite.

It's unclear how the market will shake out among the three major players. Consumers will be making that decision in the 2007–2010 time frame. What we can say with confidence is that over the next few years consumers will be replacing their console systems en masse. It is expected that overall sales of the new systems will equal those of the past generation, though it seems unlikely that any one platform will have the sheer dominance of the first two PlayStation systems. Developers must have a multiple console platform strategy. Furthermore, console system revenue as a percentage of overall interactive entertainment revenue is expected to decline significantly. In 2003 console system revenue accounted for 67 percent of overall interactive entertainment revenue. However, DFC Intelligence forecasts that by 2011 console systems will account for only 42 percent of overall revenue. The big revolution in the game industry is all the new ways consumers will be able to purchase and consume games.

tive, it can be compared to the Apple iPod this way: the first iPod launched in 2001, but it wasn't until April 2007, after five generations of basic configurations (plus spin-offs like the nano, mini, and shuffle) that the iPod passed the 100 million unit sales level.

Another way to understand the recent dominance of the PlayStation 2 is to make an analogy to the soft drink industry. The PS2 was like the industry's Coca-Cola—but without a competitor like Pepsi. At best, Microsoft's Xbox could be considered a Mountain Dew and Nintendo's Game-Cube an A&W root beer. However, the exciting thing about the video game console market is that even established players must start from scratch every five years or so. From 2005 to 2007 new

In a sense, the traditional video game model has been rather limited. The average new game sells in the $30 to $60 range--a pretty big investment for an entertainment product. Considering that there is a vast difference in not only the quality, but also

SONY PLAYSTATION 3 (40 GB VERSION)

the quantity of entertainment time provided, it is clear the industry is leaving a great deal of money on the table. Indeed there are some that argue that consumers actually spent more per capita putting quarters into machines back in the arcade days of the late 1970s and early 1980s.

In many ways the video game market is analogous to the movie industry of fifty years ago. At that time the only way for the most people to see a film was to go out to a movie theater. Today people still go to theaters and multiplexes, but only at a fraction of the rate they did before television. Still, Hollywood exploded despite the rise of television, cable television, home video, international markets, and multiple viewing and payment options. The box office is only a small portion of today's filmed entertainment business.

The video game industry could experience similar trends as consumers' increased access to broadband connections and the rapidly decreasing cost of storage technology become greater factors in their gameplaying habits. The big console manufacturers are clearly looking at new business models. Microsoft has implemented subscription services, and, with the Xbox Live Marketplace for the Xbox 360, they offer users the ability to purchase point cards at retail to download products and to make purchases that cost as little as a quarter. Nintendo has a similar feature called the Virtual Console that allows consumers to download classic titles for prices as low as $5. For the PlayStation 3, not only can consumers purchase products online, but Sony has also created Home, a virtual, 3-D world.

When it comes to online games, most consumers think of the expensive subscription games like *World of Warcraft*. However, there is growing interest in business models like the ones found in East Asian markets such as China and Korea

where consumers are usually billed in much smaller increments. It may surprise some people to learn that the largest market for online games has been South Korea. In a country of 47 million people, a single game, called Lineage, has been known to attract as many as two million users in a given month. This is six percent of the country and would be comparable to 18 million people playing a single game in the United States.

The Korean game market started with online game play in Internet cafes known as PC bangs. Through this forum Lineage and other massively multiplayer online games (MMOGs) became huge. Recently, virtual item purchase games, in which consumers pay for items that can be used "in-game," have emerged as the most popular game type in Korea. The diversity of genres available to Korean gamers has exploded in the last few years.

Following the Korean example, China's online game market has emerged as one of the world's largest, spawning several companies listed on the NASDAQ stock exchange. The Chinese market has largely followed the same path from pay-to-play MMOG to virtual item purchase~powered games. Chinese games are also notable for their sheer size: the country's most popular game, NetEase's *Fantasy Westward Journey*, has been known to draw over one million users at the same time.

The difference between Korea and China and the American model is that users pay in small increments, often paying only pennies per hour or playing for free and buying premium in-game items. *Nexon's Kart Rider*, a game similar to Nintendo's *Mario Kart* series, is the defining game for what is known as the "virtual item sales" model. Essentially, players pay for upgrades to their cars, guns, character skills, etc., depending on the game. The prices are low, usually between $1 and $10 depending on the virtual item. *Kart Rider* has been a big success, and Nexon claims over 25 percent of South Korea's population has played the game.

As their respective home markets mature, Chinese and Korean companies are looking to bring their games to North America and Europe. These companies will bring to the traditional video game market an entirely different understanding of what can work with consumers, an understanding that could help drive video game innovation over the next decade. Already games such as Jagex's *Runescape* and Sulake's *Habbo Hotel* are attracting significant usage by offering free gameplay with the ability to upgrade to a premium level by paying.

Then there is the hottest segment of the video game market, the portable systems. It is impossible to consider the portable game market without highlighting the efforts of one company: Nintendo. Since the 1989 launch of the original Game Boy, Nintendo has driven the direction of the portable game market. Many companies have released portable systems, but none of these systems have had anywhere near the impact of the Nintendo Game Boy, Game Boy Advance, and the Nintendo DS.

Nintendo's current success story in the portable game market is the Nintendo DS. This system, launched in late 2004, is unique in that it comes with two screens, one of which is a touch screen. This has allowed for an entirely new style of game play that has expanded the audience for games into the "Touch Generation." The DS is on track to become

the most popular game system ever in Japan and in 2006 started to take off on a worldwide scale.

However, Nintendo is no longer the only major player in the portable market. Sony launched the PSP (PlayStation Portable) in Japan in late 2004. The system went worldwide in 2005, and by 2007 Sony had shipped over 25 million PSP systems. This has clearly made the PSP the strongest challenger Nintendo has ever faced in the portable market. Still the PSP targets a very different demographic from the Nintendo systems. It's aimed at a more adult audience that traditionally plays mainly console games, along with being a true multimedia device that can play music and movies. So far, it appears that, by going after this new demographic, Sony has expanded the overall portable market. Considering that portable game systems have only recently started to go online so that users can share data and play with others, the opportunities are just beginning.

As we can see, the video game business is exploding on a global scale with a wide range of platforms and products to choose from. Video games are no longer just a toy for children. The adults that grew up playing video games in the 1970s and 1980s are now continuing to play alongside their own kids. In this way, it's similar to how the music industry exploded in the 1980s. Respectable adults in the 1950s and 1960s didn't listen to rock and roll, but as the members of the rock and roll generation grew up, they continued to listen to the music of their youth. As a result the music industry more than tripled in size in the 1980s, a trend that is repeating itself today in the video game business. Not only that, but the real growth is just starting. Video games are truly an entertainment industry of the future.

DANCE DANCE REVOLUTION UNIVERSE 2

VIDEO GAMES AT
School

VIDEO GAMES – A NEW MEDIUM IN EDUCATION

To many leaders in education, videogames are dismissed as distractions and hobbies, rather than potential educational tools. Few educational games exists, and those that do have gained little recognition in the education field. The potential,

> **"...A closer bond between the gaming industry and education could lead to a whole new approach to education. "**

though, is limitless. A closer bond between the gaming industry and education could lead to a whole new approach to education while opening up the videogame industry to mega markets it has only dreamed of.

Until recently, most titles and marketing cam-

paigns for videogames have been tailored for young and middle-aged males. The last few years, however, have seen game titles targeting new demographics: women, families, and older people. Rethinking basic game concepts to target these new demographics has opened up the video game industry to even more new audiences, including schools:

Physical Education and Motor Development
- Eyetoy
- Dance mats
- Wii Sports

Music and Rhythm Development
- Donkey Konga
- SingStar and Karaoke Stage (European titles)
- Guitar Hero

Logic Training
- Brain Training
- Big Brain Academy

Memory Training
- Mind Quiz

Social Training
- The Sims

Knowledge Development/Imparting Knowledge
- Buzz!
- Back Packer

Language and Reading Development
- Talkman

Expanded multiplayer functionality has also made gaming more attractive in education. Entire classrooms can connect and play together with the

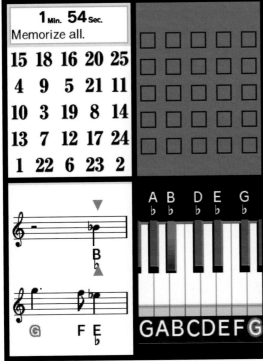

BRAIN AGE 2: MORE TRAINING IN MINUTES A DAY

DANCE DANCE REVOLUTION HOTTEST PARTY

expansion of broadband Internet connections. For educators afraid their students will all load up *Grand Theft Auto* instead of *Brain Training*, the parental control functions on the PlayStation 3, Xbox 360, and Nintendo Wii help them prevent unwanted games from being played.

Although the ability of videogames to reinforce negative behavior in children is well-documented, not many have studied the medium as a potential teaching tool. "Computer games improve children's abilities to solve problems," says professor Jon Martin Sundet at Oslo University, Norway. Sundet says this especially applies to logical and geometrical problems. In an interview with the Norwegian Daily Verdens Gang last year, Norway's minister of education Øystein Djupedal issued this declaration: "I call on schools to use games as a teaching aid." He went on to say that he believes schools need to study the positive effects of videogames, and he isn't alone.

"Because of their interactivity, videogames provide deeper levels of immersion than television and film," agrees Stanford University psychologist Don Roberts . As a balance to all the intellectually vapid games being released, Roberts also believes it is important to provide children with the opportunity to play the well-made games that reinforce positive values.

The benefit of games in school isn't limited to the cerebral, however. Now that games are more physically interactive, studies are being conducted as to their use as an effective exercising tool for children. In the United States, West Virginia has the highest incidence of obesity amongst children and young adults. To combat this problem, local authorities have begun offering Konami's *Dance Dance Revolution* as an alternative choice in gym class. While old-fashioned jumping jacks might illicit apathetic shrugs from students in West Virginia's 157 middle schools, jumping on a Dance Pad to the catchy rhythms of *DDR* has been met with enormous success.

Vear Elementary School was the first school in Norway to introduce videogame dance as a part of the school day. School physiotherapist Inger Marie Solberg discovered the game when she visited a fair and initiated a pilot project at the school. "We want the students to become more physically active in school, and dance mats speak the language of the

BOOGIE

Where can I find a duty-free store?

TALKMAN FOR PSP

young." According to Solberg, the program offers a great alternative for students who don't participate in organized sports.

Students are able to master the challenges quickly and compete only against themselves. This builds self confidence, says Solberg. School inspector Christi Jørgensen has no doubt that the dance mats have a positive effect: "Students expend their energy in a positive way. And they improve their motor skills. We can even see a change in how they write. Their writing has improved after they began videogame dancing!"

Educators are basing the implementation of games in schools on a variety of recent studies. According to Reuters, one study was conducted on 50 children between 7 and 12 years old over 24 weeks. Results showed that children who played physically active dancing games 30 minutes or more per day maintained or reduced their weight. If this routine were implemented in the long term, it would result in fewer incidents of obesity, heart disease, and diabetes. A control group did not have access to the game during the first 12 weeks, and their weight increased an average of 6.6 pounds (3kg). For the last 12 weeks, the control group began participating in the dance program and their weight stabilized.

In the future, children and youth will continue to play games and will undoubtedly be influenced by this medium. The games we feed their consoles with will decide what these influences are. As children and adolescents become more serious about their gaming, and the line between movies and games disappears, it is increasingly important to train both parents and children to think critically about games. A better understanding of the medium ensures that gaming becomes a positive, constructive, and engaging exercise.

Closer cooperation between education and the industry is a way to meet this need. In Great Britain, Sony is now working with the Ministry of Education to develop a special version of their *Buzz!* title especially targeted toward schools. More relationships like this are likely to develop as both educators and

GUITAR HERO 3

videogame corporations benefit from mutual cooperation. Schools provide the gaming industry with a wider audience and demand for new products, while educators adapt to, rather than compete with, the broadening stimuli that today's children have at their fingertips.

Traditional teaching methods now compete for their student's attention in a world of Multimedia Flash, YouTube, and MySpace. The goal of education isn't to be senselessly fun or overwhelmingly boring but to provide children with the tools and opportunities they'll need to become productive members of society. Games can become one of these tools if both educators and videogame developers realize this necessity.

While today's schools have gyms, music rooms, art studios, libraries, and computer labs, tomorrow's schools may combine all of these into one multimedia classroom. The classroom will become a room for learning and development where broadband, game consoles, and sound and video equipment are ready to be used at any time. Instead of hall passes and passing time, students could spend their entire day in one classroom with schedules like this:

- 30 minutes of concentration exercises with handheld consoles
- 30 minutes of PE on the dance mats
- An interactive science session using touchscreens and simulated dissections
- 20 minutes of graphic design drawing on a graphic tablet
- A history quiz in the Buzz! format
- 20 minutes playing The Sims version of a French court in the time of Louis XIV
- Music lessons including karaoke songs and electronic instruments
- A project where students build their own virtual business with a special software package developed to teach macroeconomics and business terminology

Who could say no to a school day like that? Our guess is that everyone, including students, teachers, principals, parents, and future employers would welcome the multimedia classroom.

A multimedia classroom will provide an interactive environment, using technology as a bridge from students to one another and their teachers. As more and more schools upgrade to broadband Internet technology, students can use computers to communicate locally in the classroom and worldwide to other nations. Levels of difficulty for task-based games can be tailored to individual abilities and allow everyone to feel the satisfaction of mastering a challenge. In videogames, everyone can be a hero.

A classroom like this creates a natural framework for teaching critical thinking and safe digital behavior. Is it true? Is it healthy? Is it relevant? Is it constructive, positive, challenging, and developing? The school of the future must provide children with healthy digital habits and attitudes, not only IT knowledge.

Beyond producing just software, the videogame industry has the potential to actually change the landscape of classrooms. But is it willing to deliver games and teaching tools adapted to the wishes and needs of schools? Can it deliver equipment that can sustain the kind of heavy use at a school? And will it be affordable?

The industry must adapt to educational plans and develop products that make everyday school life better for both teachers and students. The possibilities are fantastic and limitless. Further research is needed, but games may revolutionize the way schools of the future look. History lessons can be visualized and actually experienced by students, the future can be simulated and tried before it becomes reality. The biology and geography of the whole world can unfold in front of you and be studied in minute detail. The possibilities ought to challenge every publisher of traditional school books, entice all publishers of videogames, and inspire future educators.

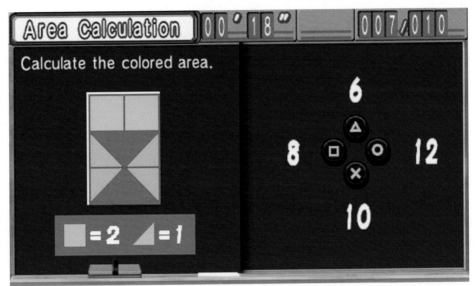

MIND QUIZ: YOUR BRAIN COACH

CONCEPT ART FOR AGE OF CONAN

Games as
Art

With more than 50 years of history, it is no wonder the once humble videogame is catching the interest of the art world, not only for its inherent coolness and chic factor, but as an art object in and of itself.

In the new millennium, electronic games have been the subject of exhibitions as well as popular and academic research and books. They are often reviewed alongside literature, music, and film. In some countries, game development even receives governmental grants, not as industrial products, but as bearers of cultural meaning and national heritage.

Like its older sibling the motion picture did in the mid–20th century, electronic games have come a long way in the public's view over the last few

CONCEPT ART FOR GEARS OF WAR

decades. Throughout the progression from blips in remote computer labs to today's global mass medium, the general public's perception of games has been one of bewilderment, indifference, or ridicule. But over the last couple decades, videogames have silently snuck up on us as a major cultural and economic force worldwide. Now both genders, all age groups, and all levels of society play electronic games. Games are everywhere, as is their influence.

Therefore, it's no wonder that artists working in other disciplines are influenced by electronic games. They grew up playing videogames, and many continue to play videogames well into adulthood. The influence of electronic games can be seen in movies such as the Matrix trilogy, graphic design, and fine arts, and most pervasively in popular television and music. Games culture is everywhere, popping up wherever and whenever. The player's dreaded "Game Over" has become a standard phrase used by everyone from school kids to presidents.

But what about the games themselves? Is it possible for several hundred people to work on an object within a strict economic framework with tight deadlines and arrive at the end with something that

can be called a work of art? The notion of the lone artistic genius is still quite pervasive and clashes with what the collaborative effort producing a game is. Then again, very few people make movies all by

"...over the last couple decades, videogames have silently snuck up on us as a major cultural and economic force worldwide. "

themselves, most music is touched by at least a couple of hands before it reaches its listeners, and even books have editors that snip, cut, and suggest alterations. Similarly, producing a commercial game takes a planned and tightly executed effort from a team of skilled individuals. With the exception of some independent game efforts, very few games are the product of one single mind. Even with games where the single idea maker—the auteur—is highly visible, such as Kojima Hideo and his *Metal Gear Solid* games, the creative process is still a collective one. Yet, within this collective the art in the work can easily be seen.

The immediately apparent artistic factor is, of course, how these games look. Although they are considered pop culture icons today, it would be a stretch to call the severely pixelated images of yellow pizza pies and jumping plumbers from the

CONCEPT ART FOR OKAMI

1980s "artistic." However, looking at the production models and graphic sheets from recent games *Doom III* and *Half-Life 2* inspire comparisons to classical artists such as Rembrandt, Hieronymus Bosch, and Salvador Dali. For example, the use of lighting in the various set pieces in *Doom III* rivals the Dutch master's mood-enhancing techniques and mimics film director Ridley Scott's best efforts—all while the virtual game world is moving in real time and reacting to player input. For the majority of games, one can also see strong ties to three-dimensional art forms, such as sculpture. Building an in-game object is quite similar to a classic sculptor's work, the only difference being that videogame designers use digital instead of solid tools and materials.

For years, the holy grail of video games was to create something that mimicked film, by creating game worlds that resemble the real world but give the player new ground to explore within that familiar setting. Huge online role-playing games *World of Warcraft* (WoW) and *Age of Conan* are prime examples of this, where familiar physics are offset by fantastic creatures and superhuman endeavors. Here the game designers have taken

what we know and remixed it into something that works even better within the game. Just like Jerusalem in Ridley Scott's *Kingdom of Heaven* movie isn't really that close to the real medieval city, the orcs in WoW move like earth bears but look more like something that makes sense within the world of the game.

Dramatic computer technology advances in recent years have completely changed the range of possibilities for game makers. A computer's speed is no longer a bottleneck for visual output, allowing game graphics to approach photorealism and achieve what had been a long-standing goal: to make videogames look like film, both with photorealistic images and real-world physics. Having achieved these advances, some game developers have taken this creative freedom beyond a cinematic look. Recent games *Okami* and *Crackdown* are examples of this. The former draws its inspiration

"...Doom III and Half-Life 2 inspire comparisons to classical artists such as Rembrandt... "

from the culture the game is based on and aims for the look of classic Japanese sumi-e watercolor paintings. The graphics thus underpin the story and draw the player into the *Okami* universe. This technique was so effective that *Okami* won IGN's Game of the Year award in 2006. The game *Crackdown* for the Xbox 360 uses a similar strategy. With urban violence as its core theme, the game emphasizes its futuristic comic-book framework by employing a graphic look called cel-shading, where computer graphics are made to look hand drawn and flat. By consciously opting for a nonphotorealistic look,

CONCEPT ART FROM GOD OF WAR II

CELL SHADER IN CRACKDOWN

the game's exaggerated feel is strengthened, while providing players with graphics that evoke feelings beyond the basic drive, run, and shoot premise.

There will, of course, always be technological boundaries to what is possible, but one thing is clear: the hunt for the real world has now taken a back seat in favor of artistic expression. There is a world of difference between the gritty and downright dirty visuals of action classics *Gears of War* and *God of War II* and the funky beat detectives in *Elite Beat Agents*, but the basic premise is the same: with a multitude of choices available, games are more a product of the imagination than an expression of technology's limits. In the end, the real artwork lies in the creation and facilitating of a game experience. Perhaps that is the core of games as art: their ability to facilitate something outside of themselves, to transcend the basic object. This they have in common with all other art forms.

Game making is a craft as well as an art form, calling on videogame designers to create games that work on several levels: entertainment, enjoyment, engrossment, and involvement. Game makers need to be true renaissance men and women, with skills from many creative toolboxes. Combining theoretical skills such as higher mathematics and physics with a sense of visual and aural communication is essential to creating dynamic games that many different people can enjoy. Who possesses these skills? Only a few decades ago, people working on games were either self-taught or came from quite different disciplines. Now, partly due to the medium's increased recognition, the creation of games has become part of the academy as something to be studied, taught, and learned on its own terms. The future lies with these educated game makers who can only raise the bar even higher, giving us gaming moments tomorrow that we can only dream of today.

VIDEO GAME
Music

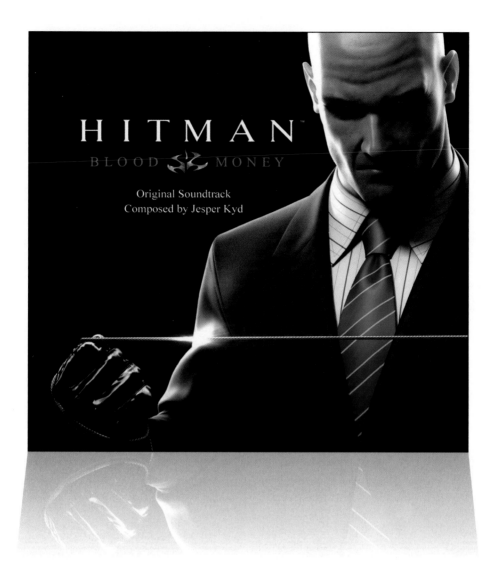

Playing video games is one of the world's most popular leisure activities, and although everyone talks about how graphics and game play have evolved over the last couple of decades, it's easy to forget that video game music has developed as well—from monotone beeps and simple melodies to full-fledged orchestral scores, no-holds-barred guitar rock, electronica mixes, and much more.

Most of us might not think about the music

we hear while playing video games unless it's *Guitar Hero* or *Dance Dance Revolution*, but subconsciously we're aware of it. Clever sound design and effective music help draw us in, heighten the

Most of us might not think about the music we hear while playing video games unless it's Guitar Hero...

TOP FIVE VIDEO GAME SOUNDTRACKS

BY GREG O'CONNOR-READ

Greg O'Connor-Read is a prolific video game music promoter and founder of the leading resource on the topic, Game4Music.net. We asked him to list his Top Five Video Game Soundtracks. *(O'Connor-Read has worked with Jesper Kyd, Michael McCann, and Richard Jacques)*

"SPLINTER CELL: DOUBLE AGENT"

ARTIST: MICHAEL MCCANN

This is one of my favorite scores of 2006 and was initially a bit of a dark horse since it was Michael McCann's first game score. Working as lead composer and musician, Michael spent almost 10 months on the soundtrack to the game. From massive action sequences to subtle ambient tracks, the score for *Splinter Cell: Double Agent* includes over three hours of music! The dramatic story of the game takes players to locations all over the world—from Iceland to Shanghai, Africa to New York City, and beyond. This is an ambitiously dynamic and epic original score. And the implementation was superb! Michael's score won the IGN Xbox 360 Award for Best Original Score and was nominated for Best Original Score at the Academy of Interactive Arts & Sciences Awards.

tension, and set the mood for different rooms, levels, or missions. In this article, we take a closer look at this little-heralded part of video game development.

> ## "It builds suspense or can give a sense of exploration, which helps the game become something deeper, almost emotional."
> *-Jesper Kyd*

The first video games were quiet, but it didn't take long for programmers to augment their games with otherworldly bleeps and bloops. Although few would classify *Space Invaders* from Taito and Asteroids as having soundtracks per se, the sounds, which pick up speed as enemy invaders cut closer, definitely added tension for early gamers. In the years that followed, games emitted piercing laser shots, crude explosions, racing engines, jet plane swooshes, and the ubiquitous sound of an 8-bit car crash.

In racing and sports-driven games music is still used to increase adrenalin, whereas soundtracks for story-driven games tend to pull elements from the story into the music. "The music has more than function," says composer Jesper Kyd, who is known for his work on the Hitman series. "It builds suspense or can give a sense of exploration, which helps the game become something deeper, almost emotional."

But not all games have budgets for custom scores, so like their colleagues in the movie business, many game directors have chosen to license existing tracks from record companies. To the casual gamer it might seem like licensed tracks started to pop up in games ten years ago, the tradition stretches back a little further than that.

In 1989, the 16-bit Sega Genesis system sported an unprecedented six-channel stereo sound, and the company teamed up with the eponymous pop star to produce Michael Jackson's Moonwalker. In the game MJ searches graveyards and pool halls for children kidnapped by mobster Mr. Big. Instead of weapons or violence, MJ busts out dance moves to sideline the bad guys. Not only did the game have hilarious game play, it was also one of the earliest to feature licensed pop music with strange electronic versions of MJ hits "Beat It" and "Billie Jean."

With the advent of CD-quality sound chips and a growing market for video games, Psygnosis took music in video games to another level by successfully capturing the hip clubbers of the mid-nineties with Wipeout. The game's antigravity racing featured commissioned work and remixes by such electronica groups as Orbital, Leftfield, and the Chemical Brothers. Players could even choose a track to race to, making the music as important as selecting the ride. Psygnosis equipped select clubs with PlayStations so patrons could play Wipeout, and they released a soundtrack that featured songs from the game.

Four years later Rockstar Games came in with Trasher: Skate and Destroy. The soundtrack is peppered with old school hip-hop luminaries such as Public Enemy and Grandmaster Flash. The competing Tony Hawk Pro Skater went the punk and hardcore route licensing tracks from Primus and the Dead Kennedys.

"HITMAN" (THE SERIES)
ARTIST: JESPER KYD

Jesper Kyd's music for the Hitman series (and other games such as *Freedom Fighters*) is so immersive it gets inside your head and refuses to let go. There's so much going on beneath the surface in his tracks. I do believe he is an artist in the true sense of the word.

Jesper's most recently released project, the stylish musical score for *Hitman: Blood Money*—recorded with the 90-piece Budapest Symphony and 60-member Hungarian Radio Choir mixed with contemporary electronic music—received IGN's Xbox award for 2006 Best Original Score and was nominated for Best Original Video Game Score at the 2006 MTV Video Music Awards.

Kyd's distinctive fusion of DJ-style and minimalist electronica, surreal choir vocals, and foreboding percussion grooves featured in *Hitman: Contracts* also garnered global attention as a truly groundbreaking original soundtrack. In 2005 he won Best Original Music from the British Academy of Film and Television Arts at the BAFTA Games Awards, as well as Best Cinematic/Cut-Scene Audio at the Game Audio Network Guild (G.A.N.G.) Awards.

"HALO" (THE SERIES)

ARTISTS: MARTY O'DONNELL & MIKE SALVATORI

The surreal mix of Gregorian choral chant with Celtic, symphonic, and synth music elements makes this one of the most instantly recognizable game scores of all time, not to mention the bestselling video game soundtrack in North America.

"HEADHUNTER"

ARTIST: RICHARD JACQUES

I attended the recording session for *Headhunter* at Abbey Road Studios and it literally changed my life. (I was crossing over from working in the music industry to starting out in the video games industry.) In my opinion "Jack's Theme" is still one of the most powerful anthems ever written for a video game and was a major inspiration during the development of Music4Games. Just don't play it while you're driving!

Those early efforts were prodigious since most label executives were skeptical about these unusual licensing deals. Licensing is typically a model of payment that incorporates the number of plays for any given track, but video game deals are different. After all it's difficult to monitor how many times a track is played, so video game licensing deals come in "all sorts of wacky forms," to quote music producer Nile Rodgers. The music industry's attitude toward video games has changed, though, says Steve Schnur, Electronic Arts' worldwide executive of music and music marketing.

Take California punkers Green Day. In 2004, the multi-platinum band was busy recording American Idiot, but the members made sure to ask Schnur about deadlines so the album's title track could make it onto *Madden NFL 2005*. The band worked hard to complete the track, and *Madden* players heard it before the album, which won a Grammy for Best Rock Album later that year, was officially released.

It's difficult to find a band that has made it solely from contributing tracks to a video game, but MorissonPoe has come close. The band contributed two tracks that were used for *Perfect Dark Zero*, a 2006 Xbox 360 first-person shooter.

"*Perfect Dark Zero* was an extraordinary opportunity," says vocalist and eager gamer Jean Morisson. "The feeling of knowing that we are a part of something bigger than ourselves is overwhelming."

Although the game failed commercially, the band gained fans from their cameo and even landed a record deal from *Perfect Dark Zero*'s soundtrack producer Nile Rodgers' label Sumthing Distribution.

Rodgers is a legendary musician and

producer whose credits include the number one disco hit "Le Freak" with his band Chic, production for Madonna's "Like A Virgin," numerous Duran Duran singles, and soundtracks for *Resident Evil* and *Halo 2*.

"Like the rock 'n' roll business, the video game industry is interesting, frustrating, and always changing," Rodgers says. "It feels just as revolutionary as rock 'n' roll used to feel."

His job as a video game producer includes working as a middleman between game developers and artists, coaching composers, inviting musicians for studio work (such as guitar ace Steve Vai for *Halo 2*), and finding and executing licensing deals where he sees fit. "MorissonPoe contacted me through my website and invited me to check out their show. I showed up not knowing what to expect and was blown away," Rodgers says. He thought some of their work would fit *Perfect Dark Zero*, and the rest is history.

Although Rodger enjoys working with the artists, he argues that the industry still has to overcome a few challenges.

"I look at it as art. The problem is that it's called a video game. Make music for film and it's art. And that's frustrating to me. The geniuses that I work with—it's amazing what they do, but it's not regarded as highly as the work of film composers," he says. The lack of regard for video game composers is strange, considering the difficulty in composing for today's non-linear games—and the money involved. Technicalities aside, video game composers often outsell their movie score colleagues.

The average movie soundtrack with an original score might sell 10,000 copies, while the average video game soundtrack can sell 20,000

"MEDAL OF HONOR"
ARIST: MICHAEL GIACCHINO

Inspired by Steven Spielberg's movie Saving Private Ryan, the original Medal of Honor is one of my personal favorite orchestral scores from a game and, along with the Headhunter soundtrack recordings at Abbey Road Studios, motivated me to focus the website Music4Games.net on promoting composers of original music for video games. Michael Giacchino has since gone on to score the hit TV shows Alias and Lost and such blockbuster movies as Pixar's The Incredibles and Star Trek XI

copies, according to Greg O'Connor-Read, an industry promoter and founder of Music4Games. net. "The first *Halo* soundtrack sold 150,000 units," he adds.

"Gamers sit there for maybe 100 hours, so they grow attached to the music," Kyd says. Kyd spends most of his time scoring video games and has several successful soundtracks on his résumé.

"The first Halo soundtrack sold 150,000 units"

O'Connor-Read agrees. "Music is an auxiliary product that increases exposure for the game. Look at Japan: soundtrack sales [there] are tremendously successful and have been for many, many years." He points out that the Japanese gaming market sees dozens of soundtrack releases every month. Compare that to the U.S. market, which saw about 80 releases for all of 2006.

When the now-legendary video game creator Shigeru Miyamoto composed a ditty on an electronic keyboard in 1981 for *Donkey Kong*, he created one of the first video game scores. Four years later the revolutionary *Super Mario Bros.* was released. Referring to *Super Mario* might seem like a cliché, but Miyamoto's game deserves credit for its music in addition to the game itself. Koji Kondo's score blended with the game play like no other game that came before it, moving from the background to the foreground and becoming an inseparable part of the game. If you don't believe it, play with the sound muted and try to figure out when the power from *Mario*'s immunity star wears off.

A testament to the quality of today's game music is the larger budgets soundtracks have been given. Major titles often spend a few hundred thousand dollars on custom scores, which attract top-of-the-

food-chain–type composers such as Kyd.

"If my current score isn't my favorite, I'm doing something wrong," says the 34-year-old composer whose career echoes the growth of the industry. " I started on the Commodore 64 when I was 13. About a year into it my interest totally peaked, but I never expected it to become my profession." Kyd immersed himself in the European demo scene

"It could be an Aerosmith concert, but it's not. Up on stage are chairs for a full-fledged symphony."

and founded a game company with a few friends that produced Subterrania, a game Sega eventually purchased from the young game designers.

Kyd now lives in the U.S. and has made music for 33 games, 15 movies, and an assortment of trailers and commercials over the last 14 years. His credits include the *Hitman series, Dance Dance Revolution: Ultramix 2, Splinter Cell: Chaos Theory*, and *Unreal Tournament 3*. Creating game scores takes anywhere from two months to two years, he says, and it can be a lonely process. At least rock musicians get to have fun when they go on tour, right?

Until now. Imagine this scene. A giant stadium with a massive stage illuminated by rows of par cans, a gigantic video screen, and colorful, sweeping lasers. People of all ages cram the turnstiles to get in. The venue fills up quickly. It's a sold-out show.

It could be an Aerosmith concert, but it's not. Up on stage are chairs for a full-fledged symphony—not stacks of Marshall amps—and the fans aren't all greasy rockers with black T-shirts, although there are a few of those in the audience as well.

VIDEO GAMES LIVE

PERFECT DARK ZERO'S SOUNDTRACK PRODUCER, NILE ROGERS - HERE WITH FRIENDS

Video Games Live began in 2005 and is now selling out shows in the U.S., Brazil, Korea, Sweden, and beyond, and it's a phenomenon that makes so much sense many wonder why no one hadn't thought of it before.

"A lot of people think video games are just for kids. We show just how culturally significant they are," says *Video Games Live* founder Tommy Tallarico, who is also Aerosmith singer Steven Tyler's cousin.

Video Games Live embraces the culture and music of video games and offers people a rare chance to hear it live, performed by soloists, bands, or symphony orchestras, and supported by choirs in a rock show, multimedia format.

One of the regular soloists at *Video Games Live* is Martin Leung, better known as the Video Game Pianist. Leung is 20 years old, placed third in the prestigious Oberlin International Piano Competition in 2002, and has made a career from touring game conventions where he is hired to play video game classics such as "*Super Mario*," "*Zelda*," and the "*Halo 2* Main Theme" on the piano, often blind-folded and at breakneck speed. In 2005, at a concert in Austin, Texas, he received multiple standing ovations and played 21 encores until the audience was satisfied. Instead of touring with a regular symphony, *Video Games Live* collaborates with orchestras in the cities it tours, such as the Los Angeles Philharmonic Orchestra and the Edmonton Symphony.

It's not difficult to find pompous cultural snobs with a disdain for renting out the local symphony to play music composed for video games, but these concerts expose gamers to classical music in an unpretentious setting. Composer Chance Thomas recently told AOL's Game Daily that game music concerts had, in effect, "countered the counter-culture with culture."

"It's coming full circle," Thomas says, "back to a time when orchestras played the popular music of the day."

The future of video game music is obviously hard to predict, but one creative direction could be paved by legendary producer and self-styled "non-musician" Brian Eno. Famous for working with Roxy Music, Talking Heads, David Bowie, and U2, Eno is generally lauded as the father of modern ambient music. With the exception of writing the 3.25-second startup sound for Windows 95 and a ditty heard in Microsoft XP's setup, Eno has been remarkably absent from projects in the computer world. But his influence on video game musicians such as *Splinter Cell: Double* Agent composer Michael McCann is hardly surprising.

SPORE: Procedural music

VIDEO GAMES LIVE

Eno's sense of futurism must have piqued *Sim-City* and *The Sims* creator Will Wright. Wright's highly anticipated game *Spore* turns traditional follow-the-leads-to-the-next-level game play inside out, offering players an open-ended game that tackles user-guided evolution. And this revolutionary game requires a revolutionary soundtrack.

During a lecture last January at the University of Arts in Berlin, Eno said Wright "wanted a sound that is just as procedural as the game itself." Instead of using pre-composed loops for specific parts of the game, a special piece of software baked into the game will use sampled fragments to compose the game's soundtrack on the fly. Eno says the Shuffler will never create "the same composition twice within a lifetime." Sounds wild, huh?

Although the 8-bit bleeps and bloops from *Asteroid* and other early arcade classics sound today like expired sonic curiosities, they were revolutionary when first heard. Video game music, like the games it accompanies, keeps pushing boundaries, and one thing is certain: it's only going to get better and better.

WWW.BEHAVIORMUSIC.COM
WWW.MUSIC4GAMES.NET
WWW.JESPERKYD.COM
WWW.PDZSOUNDTRACK.COM
WWW.SPORE.COM
WWW.SUMTHINGMUSIC.COM
WWW.VIDEOGAMESLIVE.COM
WWW.VIDEOGAMEPIANIST.COM

Game Heroes
THE LIFE CYCLES

There are a lot of interesting game heroes. Some come about by accident, some by necessity, and many by careful design, but only a few achieve truly iconic status. Lara Croft, Tomb Raider, and Solid Snake are two of those who embody the best in videogame character development.

"...and there she was, the perfect poster girl for the new wave of gaming. "

Lara first appeared in 1996 and was quickly catapulted into the limelight. In the mid nineties, gaming was poised to recover from a slump in public interest, and there she was, the perfect poster girl for the new wave of gaming. Until then, female game characters had usually been assigned to backup or sidekick duties. Ms. Pac-Man and some combatants from the *Street Fighter*, *Virtua Fighter*, and *Mortal Kombat* series were minor exceptions to the rule, but as a whole, few games featured female leads. Lara's arrival on the gaming scene, then, was aptly (and advantageously) timed, but she certainly brought some depth of her own to the party as well.

The first thing everyone notices about Lara Croft are her quite obvious physical attributes. According to creator Toby Gard, the decision to amplify the character's female shape was a conscious one. Built to cater the tastes of what was assumed to be the core audience for games, the Lara we met in 1996 looked like something approaching a parody of the female form. Interestingly, this became quite irrelevant once one sat down to play the game. The combination of skill testing, puzzle

LARA CROFT FROM TOMB RAIDER: LEGENDS

LARA CROFT TOMB RAIDER: THE ANGEL OF DARKNESS

solving, and remarkable on-screen agility hooked players of all ages and genders. Even those who didn't play *Tomb Raider* quickly became familiar with Lara; she turned into a public persona of sorts, gracing the covers of fashion magazines in all her computer-generated glory.

As the Lara Croft phenomenon gained momentum, CGI Lara's development was mirrored by a series of flesh-and-blood incarnations. Angelina Jolie's portrayal of Lara Croft in two blockbuster action movies probably marked the culmination of the character's fame. In addition, Lara appeared in all sorts of pop-cultural places; her image has sold lunch boxes, coffee mugs, T-shirts, and other paraphernalia.

The tomb-raiding Lara has developed substantially over the course of the last decade. The character's visible changes are due partly to advances in CGI technologies, but are mostly a function of game designers fine-tuning the character herself. Even in the first game, Lara was given a background story. As the abandoned only child of a British aristocrat, she spent her time hunting ancient artifacts from around the world. In her spare time, she relaxed in a grand mansion, complete with a private gym, luxurious bedroom, and butler. Gamers could actually guide Lara around the mansion and its outdoor grounds and could even annoy the elderly butler by somersaulting over him. Throughout the game series, this background story has evolved, and Lara herself has evolved with it. In comparing the seven versions of the character, one can watch a slightly pixelated hyper-sexualized Indiana Jones clone turn into a brooding action heroine with a troubled past and a thoughtful present. She still looks like a million bucks, but gamers no longer need to be lured with

LARA CROFT TOMB RAIDER: THE ANGEL OF DARKNESS

eye candy into picking up the controller. Her appearance now adds to her character's complexity, as her battle skills aren't far removed from those of her sisters (and brothers) in fighting games such as the *Tekken* series, but her on-screen presence far exceeds that of comparable characters. This winning combination makes Lara Croft particularly interesting as both a game character and global phenomenon.

METAL GEAR SOLID 3: SNAKE EATER

Today's other big "human" game hero is pretty much Lara's polar opposite. Solid Snake, star of the *Metal Gear* series, is a secret agent who executes clandestine missions on behalf of various organizations. Unlike Lara, we know very little about Snake's background. Other than revealing his first name at the end of *Metal Gear Solid*, this series keeps its main character as much of a mystery as his missions.

The character's mystique enhances players' involvement in the game and intensifies the sense of trickery and deception that *Metal Gear* works hard to cultivate. Casting backward glances at neoclassic antiheroes such as Clint Eastwood's nameless gunslinger in Sergio Leone's spaghetti

westerns and his later alter ego, "Dirty" Harry Calahan, Solid Snake has managed to capture the imagination of generations of game players. Because the game series has kept secret much of Snake's background information, he remains as fresh a character today as he was 20 years ago.

First appearing in *Metal Gear* in 1987, Solid Snake is an amalgam of a handful of classic action heroes. By creator Hideo Kojima's own admission, the early versions of Snake were based on movie stars Michael Biehn and Mel Gibson, while his namesake is Kurt Russell's character Snake Plissken from John Carpenter's film, *Escape from New York*. Visually, it is quite obvious that later incarnations of the character borrow more than just the name from Carpenter. While concept designer

Yoji Shinkawa cites actors Jean-Claude Van Damme and Christopher Walken as his main inspirations, it is equally obvious that Plissken's rough looks and world-weary attitude have shaped Snake's development.

Naturally, in the early games, our sense of Snake's appearance depends mostly on box and poster art. The in-game character was pretty pixelated, thanks to technical restrictions. Even so, Snake's personality was always more than evident. While his looks change throughout the early part of the series, Snake's trademark bandana is always in place, as are his sneaky but powerful stance and gaze. After the release of *Metal Gear Solid*, however, the character's basic appearance stayed relatively uniform, though game designers have taken pains to age him appropriately. This is perhaps the most interesting aspect of the Solid Snake persona: when looking at the series as a whole, we can watch a young, reckless action hero gradually become a haggard old man. With only one good eye left, Solid Snake appears in *Metal Gear Solid 4* as a dusty

"...when looking at the series as a whole, we can watch a young, reckless action hero gradually become a haggard old man."

secret operative found at the back of a storage cupboard. For players that have stayed with the series throughout its development, this amplifies involvement with the character; gamers gradually come to understand and sympathize with Snake. His visual aging suggests a life lived, whether we know anything definitive about it or not.

Snake regularly makes appearances in games outside of Kojima's main storyline. In the *Metal Gear Acid* series for the PSP he is portrayed

METAL GEAR SOLID

more as a mercenary than a secret agent, while his cameo roles in *Evolution Skateboarding* and *Ape Escape 3* are rather more comical. He is perhaps more at home in the fighting game *Super Smash Bros. Brawl*, but his appearance is still quite tongue-

in-cheek. Even so, in the above games he is obviously Solid Snake, with very few departures from the hard-nosed character we see in the *Metal Gear*

METAL GEAR SOLID 3: SNAKE EATER

games. Despite strange surroundings, Snake himself remains constant.

Because of Solid Snake's mystique, every player walks away from the *Metal Gear* games with their own personal opinion of him. Therein lies one of the series' main strengths: instead of constructing a complete picture, it invites player involvement in terms of storytelling and character development.

Both Lara Croft and Solid Snake have benefited from advances in CGI technologies. Once pixelated stick figures, these now fully-rendered computer models showcase game-making as a craft and an art form. Even though their evolutionary paths have been quite different, both Lara and Snake are now canonical fictional characters. Their credibility as characters has less to do with true-to-life visual realism than with the fact that their chosen appearances correspond to their respective game universes. Obviously over-the-top, they both *work*. Whether the result of a sudden stroke of genius or systematic designer development, they are perhaps the best examples of contemporary game stars—or better put, heroes.

Hardcore Territory

WATERCOOLING AN OVERCLOCKED PC

The advent of online gaming has led to a dramatic increase in the amount of time gamers spend sitting in front of their computers by themselves. An avid gamer might spend hours in a single sitting trying to pull off the coolest headshot or finish a quest that was a month in the making. To make up for this decrease in personal social interaction, gamers have created LAN events: in-person gaming competitions that bring people together while retaining the competitive edge that makes online games so much fun.

A LAN (Local Area Network) is defined by a network of computers connected together via Ethernet cables so that participants can play one interconnected game at the same time. LAN parties can vary, from two or more close friends that get together in someone's basement, to large events that attract thousands of people from all over the world. The common element is that everyone congregates in the same physical space limited by the length of Ethernet cabling. Originally limited only to PCs, LAN parties have recently expanded to

THE GATHERING: WAITING TO ENTER THE VIKING SHIP, HAMAR 2007

consoles with the introduction of Dreamcast, the first console with online networking access, and the Xbox and Xbox 360.

No matter what the setup, the gamers that attend LAN events all have one thing in common: an enthusiasm for competitive gaming. LAN events take this enthusiasm and provide gamers with the opportunity to meet new friends and take part in competitive tournaments in the hopes to be crowned the world—or the basement's—best gamer.

THE GAMING CALENDAR

What started as small, isolated events, have now become large-scale entertainment events that attract thousands of people from around the world.

Event	Location	Website
Centralan UK	United Kingdom	http://www.centralanuk.co.uk
DreamHack	Sweden	http://www.dreamhack.se
LANWar	Dallas, Texas USA	http://www.lanwar.com
The Gathering	Hamar, Norway	http://www.thegathering.org
Multiplay iSeries Newbury	United Kingdom	http://multiplay.co.uk
QuakeCon	Dallas, Texas USA	http://www.quakecon.org

Over the course of the gaming calendar, there are a number of large events that are worth noting. Here are just a few examples:

LAN events contain a vast range of games and in most cases are playable on attendee computers, although many major LAN events include sponsor booths that showcase each sponsor's game and allow players to play on their machines. The games vary from LAN to LAN, but the most popular games are *Counter-Strike*, *Command & Conquer*, *World in Conflict*, and *World of Warcraft*.

DREAMHACK

DreamHack is the world's largest LAN with more than 10,000 people attending each event. Held twice a year just outside Stockholm, Sweden, the event attracts gamers of all ages, as well as numerous game publishers and sponsors. Massive Entertainment participated in June 2007 and had a number of computers running *World in Conflict*.

Clans or Teams play a very important role at this event. Most members of a clan like to play as part of a team and play for fun. However, in the realm of e-sports there are a number of clans that play professionally and in most cases can earn a good living just by playing videogames. The competition at these events is fierce as there are usually cash prizes or hardware bundles up for grabs.

THE GATHERING

The Gathering started more than a decade ago and has since become an annual LAN event held in the Vikingskipet Olympic Arena in Hamar, Norway, over a five-day period every Easter weekend. Gamers traveling from as far as Japan, the United States, and across Europe descend upon this LAN. The event itself is a surreal experience as people bring with them all types of computer hardware, wooden racks for storage, and music systems. The Gathering is also a unique social experience as more than 5,000 people make a giant stadium

THE GATHERING: INSIDE THE VIKING SHIP

I-SERIES, NEWBURY 2007

their home for five whole days. The event features a wide variety of activities ranging from the world's first official *Command & Conquer 3* tournament to seminars on copyright issues. Overall, the Gathering is a unique social experience that any serious gamer should attend at least once.

I-SERIES

Multiplay hosts the I-series of LAN events and is the United Kingdom's largest LAN event, pulling in 1,500 gamers from across Europe. The event hosts tournaments, and in 2007, *World in Conflict* and *Quake Wars: Enemy Territory* took the spotlight. The presentations alone drew in hundreds of gamers, all eagerly awaiting news of the games. The LAN took

place over Easter Weekend and lasted for four days. The event itself is held on Newbury Racecourses and is housed within three buildings.

XL

The XL LAN is a series of LAN events run by Xbox community website Matchbox360. The first XL LAN was held on the 25th and 26th of November 2006 at the Birmingham NEC arena and saw more than 300 gamers from across the UK and Europe competing across six titles including *Halo 2, Gears of War*, and *F.E.A.R.* While organizers Matchbox360 were new to the LAN scene, they brought with them decades of experience from various parts of the events industry as well as an enthusiasm rarely seen in LANs of this scale. Spread over two days, the event complete with over 200 Xbox consoles each with their own 28-inch TV, as well as 16 Xbox 360 pods, had the unique feeling of a huge, professionally run tournament but with a sense of community.

CHIPPING

The popularity and visibility of LAN parties has led to several negative repercussions for the integrity of the gaming world. One of those repercussions is referred to as chipping: the use of illegal computer chips in a console. Chipping allows gamers to bypass many security features, such as those that prevent owners from running copied games on their consoles. While many of these chips do nothing but bypass the console's security system, the mere fact that these consoles are "compromised" means there is no guarantee that gamers with chipped consoles will not use them to cheat.

MOD CHIP: ILLEGAL IN MANY PLACES

Many countries have laws pertaining to the ownership, use, and sale of such chips. While most countries do not class it as illegal to own them, the sale and purchase of these chips often is. There is also no clause in the law that says the use of these units at events such as a LAN is illegal, so it is up to the event to determine what restrictions they want to place on the use of chipped consoles. A group of friends having a house party might not scorn at the use of a chipped console, but large-scale, organized events with prizes usually ban them outright to prevent possible cheating.

These events are also likely to ban chipped consoles because those consoles may be running illegal copies of the games. Some of the more professionally run events are often sponsored by major companies and offer significant prizes to gamers, either in the form of games or cash, so using a chipped console completely compromises the integrity of the event and its sponsors. Events such as the World Cyber Games and Cyber Professional League (CPL) go as far as to supply their own hardware to prevent any form of cheating.

HACKING

Hacking has also existed at LANs almost from their inception. Using either external programs or flaws in the software to gain an unfair advantage, hackers are considered the lowest of the low both in LAN parties and in traditional online gaming. Many events, PC- and console- based, expel gamers found hacking or manipulating a game in an unfair way to gain an advantage.

There are many things that can be considered as hacking. Some involve using glitches or bugs that developers failed to find or remove during the development and testing stages of a game. Others involve the use of cheats. Cheating codes or com-

COUNTER-STRIKE: SOURCE

mands are often leftover after the development and testing stages of a game. While there is no standard set of cheats, many games, in particular the first-person shoot-'em-ups that are popular at LANs, have cheats such as "no clip," which allows gamers to "fly" both over land and through walls; god mode, which makes players invincible or at the very least gives them extra health; and cheats that allow hackers to see through walls and have instant headshots. No matter what the cheat, it is clear why organizers and other gamers have great disdain for those that use them.

In fact, the hatred for hackers can be seen in popular game culture. Dozens of YouTube videos show gamers receiving harsh treatment when suspected of or caught cheating. In one well-known, exaggerated sketch, a gamer is "found" to be hacking what appears to be a game of *Counter-Strike*. As soon as he is singled out, he is thrown out of the room with his machine, which is smashed into little pieces. Even though it's staged, the video sends a strong message to gamers about what happens to those who decide not to play by the rules.

MODDING

In comparison to hackers, modders—people who modify their hardware or favorite games—are held in the highest regard at LAN events for their ingenuity and creativity.

Owing to the fact that the majority of LANs (especially those involving PCs) are large events requiring a high level of technical knowledge, many of the attendees tend to be experienced gamers who have either attended previous LANs or know people who have and are attending one with them. With so many experienced gamers as attendees, both in terms of playing as well as building equipment, a subculture of hardware modders has risen around LAN events. At many large events such as the World Cyber Games, part of the fun is in walking around the event hall admiring the work of other modders. Some of their creations are truly spectacular, with the more experienced hardware modders building PCs that resemble other icons of "geek" culture such as the Millennium Falcon from Star Wars.

Most modders, though, follow a fairly standard pattern that is strikingly similar to that of car modification. Glow rods, Perspex covers offering a view into the innards of a gaming PC, case modifications, and so on are common among LAN attendees. Some events even have awards for the best modified machines.

CONSOLE MODDING

Consoles aren't excluded from modding, either, as long as it is only the casing that has been modified. Console modding is nowhere near as developed as PC modding, but many people see the Xbox 360, with its emphasis on personalization as a feature of the console, as a driving force

MODDED PC BY 3XS SYSTEMS

that could lead to more console gamers competing for the modding attention of gamers at large LAN events.

SOFTWARE MODDING

At the other end of the spectrum are software modders. Unlike their hacker cousins, software modders only have the intention of adding an unobtrusive feature to a game such as new maps or gameplay modes like the famous Zombie mode in *Counter-Strike: Source*. Because of the nature of these modifications, many events often see no problem with allowing this; however, some events only allow the "vanilla" or original version to be used for competitive purposes. It is common for modders to be greeted as celebrities at these events, mainly thanks to the fact that they have given the community something fun—and often useful—for nothing.

> ## "Unlike their hacker cousins, software modders only have the intention of adding an unobtrusive feature to a game."

LAN events also play an important part in the launch of new modifications to popular games, as well as being a place where modders can gain valuable first-hand feedback. As such, software modders in PC LAN events have become a permanent feature of this part of the gaming landscape.

ESL EUROPEAN NATIONS CHAMPIONSHIP 2007 (PHOTO: FRAGBITE.COM)

Game Communities Worldwide

Intrinsic to the nature of online gaming is a sense of community. Although communities that coexist with an online game are themed around the game, they also provide players with a means to socialize with other players. Gamers discuss their latest game-based ventures and often form virtual friendships as they play these games together.

As in other online social activities, gamers rarely use their real names when playing games. Instead they'll use tags. These "gamer tags" represent their online persona and are often associated with profiles. Profiles include games-based information like stats, games they've played, and friend lists.

CLANS

One way that online gamers often enhance their gaming experience is to form what are known as clans: a group of friends that play with each other on a regular basis. Clans are made up of gamers who share a passion for playing a particular game as part of an elite fighting unit.

Clans were first associated with PC first-person shooter games, but as consoles developed online capabilities, cooperative play quickly crossed over to consoles as well as a wider variety of games. The introduction of Xbox Live on the Xbox and online components to Sony's PlayStation 3 and

ESL EUROPEAN NATIONS CHAMPIONSHIP 2007 (PHOTO: FRAGBITE.COM)

the Nintendo Wii introduced clan-based play to everything from racing games to real-time strategy games.

PROFESSIONAL GAMING

As the sophistication of LAN events has increased, so has the level of clan- and team-based competitions at those events. This has led to the development of professional gamers and clans, like the 4Kings and Team Dignitas, who win coveted sponsorships from large corporations and can even make a living competing at large gaming events.

Any major LAN distinguishes itself as a leading hub of gaming when it holds premier international e-sport competitions. The 2007 summer Dream-Hack event displayed glittering credentials when it hosted the CPL World Tour, Electronic Sports World Cup (ESWC), World Cyber Games (WCG), and the World GameMaster Tournament (WGT). These events not only attract the world's leading players and clans but dedicated e-sport competitors from across the globe.

Pro-gamers (a name associated with those in a professional clan) spend countless hours of training before they even entertain the notion of competing in the international arena. Any person watching a premier e-sports event should have no doubt that they are witnessing only a tiny fragment of what forms a Herculean investment of time from each competitor.

Most nongamers struggle to understand how anyone could commit themselves so wholeheartedly to such a singular activity. Traveling the globe and competing in competitions for major cash rewards obviously motivates these players, but such opportunities come with sacrifices. The number of gamers who earn a living wage from playing videogames is pitifully small. It is fair to assume that 99% of gamers competing in e-sports would reap a greater financial reward if they had spent the number of hours practicing a videogame on a minimum- wage job instead!

HTTP://WWW.THECPL.COM
HTTP://WWW.CPLWORLDTOUR.COM
HTTP://WWW.WORLDCYBERGAMES.COM
HTTP://WWW.GGL.COM
HTTP://WWW.THEPGL.ORG
HTTP://WWW.JOYSTIQ.COM

CLANS FROM THE PERSPECTIVE OF A PRO– ROBERT HAXTON OF TEAM DIGNITAS

What can you tell us about your clan Team Dignitas?

The clan was formed in 2003 with the aim to become one of the best professional gaming teams in the world. We maintain our high standards through the dedication of both our players and staff. We are always looking to attend major e-sports events worldwide so that our players can show off their skills.

What is your role within the clan? And how many hours do you spend practicing per week?

Within the *World in Conflict* team, I take a leading role in ensuring that we are properly organized on a day-to-day basis. The complexities of which are vast given our numerous commitments, both personal and game related, all of which are pleasantly

TEAM DIGNITAS

exacerbated by our current prominent position within the community. In fact it is fair to say that coordinating and promoting the team can approach the same amount of time as our practice! Given that we usually practice at least five of the seven evenings in any one week (20 hours), you quickly appreciate the significant commitment undertaken when becoming a team leader.

What is your primary goal for the clan?

I joined Team Dignitas solely to help establish a pre-eminent *World in Conflict* team. As a team we entered our first international event in Verona having little knowledge of one another and even less experience with *World in Conflict* itself. Fortunately, this was the same situation many of our early competitors found themselves in and we emerged on top of the pile and have remained there ever since. The primary goal for the clan is now to maintain our position of excellence and be at the forefront of the *World in Conflict* competitive community.

What is your greatest achievement in the clan?

Since Team Dignitas formed a *World in Conflict* team we haven't looked back, traveling to and winning CPL World Tour stops in Italy and Sweden for a combined sum of $18,000. This total excludes our online cup victories during the same period, but combined they add up to a fearsome record of success in these early competitive days of *World in Conflict*. Currently, our greatest achievement was our first CPL World Tour win in Italy. The game was still in an alpha state and virtually no one had had any time with it before the event itself. Success at the event came down to who worked and learned best together as a team on the day.

By the fall of 2007 I'll have hoped we have surpassed this achievement by winning the grand final of the CPL World Tour... a first-place prize of $60,000!

Which games do you play, and which one is your favorite?

I have and always will be a strategy player. I am passionate about games that force you to use your brain beyond what you can simply see visually on the screen at the time.

I have pursued a long line of popular real time strategy (RTS) games in particular over the years, ranging from *Warcraft, Command and Conquer, Age of Empires, Supreme Commander, Empire Earth, Blitzkrieg, Close Combat,* etc. Variations on this theme, but titles that remain very close to my heart, would be the *Total War* series, *Theme Hospital, Aces of the Deep, Pizza Tycoon, ATrain, SimCity, Battle*

Isle, Space Quest, Colonization....the list really is long...and quite eye opening when I consider how many titles I have played over the years!

How would someone new to gaming get involved with a clan like yours? And how can they take part in competitive competitions like the CPL World Tour?

Anyone "new" to gaming wouldn't get into a clan like Dignitas. When you first compete online there is a significant learning curve that a player must follow before reaching the top. Today's professional gamers would list a number of previous games that contributed to their current success. Just like any profession, you seldom reach the top without spending time learning the ropes.

Player character is also important in determining whether a professional clan signs and retains you. In Dignitas we place great importance on player conduct. Whilst gaming excellence is of core importance, we also expect our players to act as gaming ambassadors, remaining conscious of their cutting-edge position in promoting e-sports.

Events like the CPL World Tour should not be understood as being exclusive to professional clans. The nature of the competition (usually for significant cash prizes) does attract competitive gaming's biggest names, but ultimately each event is open to everyone, and just one good result could get you noticed by an established team. The tournament visits regions across the globe, and I would encourage anyone with a desire to compete to explore the event.

Any tips for budding gamers that are keen to expand their portfolio like you have?

If someone was looking to establish themselves as a serious gaming contender, I would immediately say prepare for a marathon, not a sprint. Recognition, dare I say "fame," takes time to attain, but if you have the passion and commitment then you have a chance. As you develop your skills, you should monitor and engage with Internet gaming sites, especially those that cover major e-sports. They will allow you to keep up-to-date with competitive events across the world, and the sooner you learn of these, the sooner you can begin your own preparation.

As you develop your gaming skills and overall community awareness, you will increasingly establish contacts with influential gaming figures. Inevitably, doors will open for you. It then boils down to how effectively you seize these opportunities.

HTTP://WWW.FOUR-KINGS.COM
HTTP://WWW.TEAM-DIGNITAS.ORG/

TURN YOUR GAMING PASSION INTO A CAREER

Surprise! Despite what you've seen on TV, turning your passion for interactive entertainment into a career isn't as easy as pressing start. But chin up: It's easy to break into the biz with these simple tips, sure to help you go from enthusiast to expert overnight:

• Game On – Don't just sit there – get creative! Start a fansite. Use WordPress to blog. Build a podcast using a USB microphone and free programs, i.e. Audacity. Design a homebrew game modification (a.k.a. "mod") using titles like Half-Life 2's built-in toolkits. Join Major League Gaming or The CyberAthlete Professional League, which offer cash for tournament wins. The power to create cool projects or become part of movements that shape the industry has never been easier, or more accessible.

• Make the Connection – You are who you know: It's essential you attend tradeshows, contribute to industry forums and become a familiar presence around sites like Gamasutra.com and IGDA.org. Local colleges and professional organizations can also help you build contacts, and provide the educational background you'll need to succeed. Added bonus: The more people hear your name, the more value placed upon it – with thousands of others competing for industry jobs, make certain you're not just another face in the crowd.

• Play Hard – Shine through inspiration and work ethic. Anyone can construct cool games with XNA Game Studio Express or Torque Game Engine and publish coffee table books or even cool t-shirts with the help of providers like CafePress and Lulu.com. But ultimately, it's your uniqueness and dedication to the craft – hint: successful gaming insiders grind 24/7 – that'll really help you land a high score.

WWW.GETRICHGAMING.COM

Largest Guilds in World of Warcraft

Guild Name	Members
Danes of Honor	670
The Core	513
Silver Oak Guardians	304
The Legacy	280
Angry Mob	237
TTH	231
Rancid	226
Cantonium Elites	217
Playboyz	217
The End	198
Knight of The Temple	187
No Win Scenario	185
Aetas Exordium	184
Turul Legion	182
The Moo Mafia	179
Aloria	179
ConFused	169
Kalevlased	166
eXistenZ	166
Storm Guard	164
Marauding Camelids	157
Furies	154
The Alterac Deviants	154
Mercury	154
Order Of The Hammer	149
Most Wanted	148
Nemetos Order	148
Most Wanted	148
Elemental Gankery	147
Kinsmen	146
Inquisition	145
Undecided	143
Semper Danica	142
DUSK	142
Black Division	138
Ring of Shadows	136
FauleStudis	136
Drunken Dragons	135
Sauna	135
Evil Inc	132
Avatars of Vengeance	130
Forsaken	130
Neophyte	130
Forsaken	130
irishclan	129
Tharaka	129
Redeemed	128
iO	128
Oni	128
Justice League	127
The Lords of Kobol	126
Ambassadors of Truth	125

GUILDS

Like clans for first-person shooters, guilds are the single best way to stay in touch in and enjoy an MMORPG. In a game such as *World of Warcraft*, not a lot of fun can be had running around the hills and dales of Azeroth on your own, but throw a few players into the mix, and things get a lot more interesting. Having someone there to watch your back, a team for support when you're raiding a high level dungeon, or even just a friend to sit and talk to as you down a pint of virtual ale is part of what makes MMORPGs as popular as they are today.

Guilds cater to all types of players, from small groups of friends who want to stay completely in character to large groups of players from around the world. For a small group of friends, a guild allows you to see when your other pals are online, as well as speak to each other no matter where you are in the game. For those who are more serious about progressing through the game and leveling up their character, though, guilds are an essential component. Many MMORPGs have been designed to foster the creation of guilds and nurture team spirit, requiring players to band together to defeat certain enemies. The further you go in the game, the more necessary it becomes to join a larger guild.

Large guilds can range from 50 members to thousands of players and come complete with a whole host of benefits for the player. There's an air of companionship and loyalty present across all large guilds, and more established members are never too busy to help novice players out. Whether it's giving you a rare item to bolster your skills, or helping you out if they see you in trouble, seasoned members of a large guild can bring a certain amount of protection—a feeling that if you ever get into trouble with an enemy creature or another player, someone will be there soon to help. The extra strength in numbers also means that raids on dungeons are more likely to be successful, thanks to the greater likelihood of getting a respectable number of players together.

THE GUILD STYLE

Guilds can often be identified by their styles of clothing, as they often wear a similar pattern or design. In *World of Warcraft*, guild leaders can design and sell their own tabards to new recruits, helping players to easily identify the guild's members by simply looking at their clothes. Other guilds may choose to have distinctive identification in their username, such as -=TehRoxxor=- followed by the player's name. In certain games, guilds may even have their own guild hall at a prominent location in town where their members can meet before events and new members can go for help. The bigger and better the guild, the bigger and better the guild hall, which can lead to heated competition among large guilds.

"Members of an überguild are required to dedicate an incredible amount of their time to help their guild succeed in being the first guild to complete certain tasks."

Of course, advancing through the levels in an MMORPG is not the objective of all players. In *Guild Wars*, there is a guild known as "The Ladies Rhythm and Movement Club [MADE]", which is famous for the bizarre events they organize. From a naked race across the country to a hide-and-seek game where

Danes of Honor (Shadowsong) Highest ranking officers

NAME	LVL	RACE	CLASS	RANK
Aldebaren	60	Human	Paladin	Guildmaster
Zendium	18	Night Elf	Druid	Colonel
Kraus	60	Human	Rogue	Captain
Cayle	60	Night Elf	Druid	Captain
Hoshek	60	Human	Warlock	Captain
Torris	60	Human	Paladin	Captain
Ilia	60	Night Elf	Warrior	Captain
Thorbjoern	60	Night Elf	Hunter	Captain
Eagleeyes	60	Night Elf	Hunter	Captain
Kraus	60	Human	Rogue	Captain
Matok	60	Night Elf	Druid	Captain
Ilia	60	Night Elf	Warrior	Captain
Riis	60	Night Elf	Rogue	Captain
Waussauski	60	Gnome	Warlock	Captain
Beavis	60	Dwarf	Hunter	Captain
Reallic	60	Dwarf	Priest	Captain
Torrid	60	Dwarf	Hunter	Captain
Thorbjoern	60	Night Elf	Hunter	Captain
Matok	60	Night Elf	Druid	Captain
Torrid	60	Dwarf	Hunter	Captain
Sigmar	52	Gnome	Mage	Captain
Froren	49	Human	Warrior	Captain
Zendium	48	Night Elf	Druid	Captain
Lorel	44	Human	Mage	Captain
Lailah	37	Night Elf	Rogue	Captain
Cornhoolio	35	Gnome	Rogue	Captain
Gisla	35	Dwarf	Paladin	Captain
Betelgeuse	17	Dwarf	Hunter	Captain
Poke	16	Gnome	Rogue	Captain
Dohbank	1	Human	Priest	Captain

GUILD WARS

their members had to solve a series of riddles that were posted on their website, the guild has quickly gained many followers, despite their relatively few members.

Staying true to the principals behind MMORPGs, certain guilds (and entire servers) have dedicated themselves to role-playing, requiring their players to speak entirely in character. While this type of clan is certainly not for everyone, many role-playing guilds are incredibly creative, and even write their own storylines for the game, creating heroes, villains, and folklore to enhance their members' experience. It goes without saying that talk of the weather, sports, or anything else relating to the "real world" is banned, although the rule usually isn't strictly enforced.

The final category of guild, the überguild, is present in many MMORPGs and consists of the most powerful and dedicated players across the server.

Members of an überguild are required to dedicate an incredible amount of their time to help their guild succeed in being the first guild to complete certain tasks, such as defeating a new boss or finding the rarest weapon. Upon completion of a task, many überguilds post screenshots over the Internet bearing their guild logo to ensure that they get the necessary bragging rights. Überguilds are extremely selective in whom they let join, even going so far as to conceal the identity of their members from the general public. Because of the amount of dedication they require from their players, only the most serious of gamers receive an invite.

RAIDS

Of all the activities a guild can take part in, dungeon raids are by far the most common. An all-out assault on a specific dungeon in the game world, with the intent of defeating as many bosses as possible, is usually impossible without the cooperation of several players working together. Guilds take these raids very seriously, scheduling them several weeks, if not months in advance to give guild members sufficient time to arrange to be online at the specified time.

A large amount of time is spent in the game world prior to a raid organizing exactly what's going to happen, discussing strategies for the different bosses, briefing their new members on what to expect, and ensuring that everyone is properly equipped. Having a decent selection of character classes in your guild, as well as a healthy air of teamwork is essential to any successful raid, especially in a game such as World of Warcraft where certain bosses can take hours to defeat.

Of course, the reach of a guild doesn't always stop in a game. Many guilds around the world organize fan get-togethers for their members, or arrange to meet up at a specified event. Seeing what similarities players bear to their avatars is always a popular activity for guilds, and some players even go as far as to dress up as their character wearing custom-made costumes.

The appeal of being a member of a guild cannot be overestimated. Through the strengths of guilds, people have fallen in love, best friends have been found, and millions of friendships formed. Whether you love them or loath them, the guild is here to stay.

INTERVIEW WITH A GUILDMASTER

Full Name: Dr. Sarit Ghosh
In-Game Tag: Raon
Guild Name: Ashes
URL: ashesbh.guildportal.com

THE LURKER SLAIN BY ASHES

Being a Guild Master must be time consuming. How many hours do you spend running your guild weekly?

The answer to this question will vary with size and ambition of guilds. We are a medium size (75 plus accounts) casual raiding guild and so I can only give you an impression of what it's like for us.

Well, I'm on every day for usually anywhere between two to six hours. I know some of my fellows are on for much longer, but my work keeps me busy. Of the time I'm on, the amount of whispers and issues I have to deal with do take plenty of time. Luckily, I have an able-bodied bunch of great officers helping me, and I often point people to them. Like any organization, communication and delegation lighten the workload. To answer your question, it's difficult to assign a time as I'm often doing two things at once, but really, every minute I'm on there is something actively being discussed to move the guild forward. Running the guild structurally happens mainly on our forum where active discussion between all members and officers is the norm. So I'd say I spend at least three to four

ART: WORLD OF WARCRAFT

hours a week actively discussing problems and theories in this way.

What do you see as the primary purpose of forming a guild?

To gather a group of like-minded players for a common purpose and a sense of community. The game has both social and gameplay aspects, and the perfect guild probably blends both of these to achieve an eclectic mix of happy players. The integration of different cultures across Europe gives people an insight on how people interact in various parts of the world and, therefore, has some real-life connotations. My personal goal for the guild is to progress in the game and have fun doing it. Often these two are interlinked in themselves.

What are your most important tasks as a Guild Master?

To keep things together. Sometimes it is a real fight to keep people happy. If anything, I feel more like a politician than a game player. My main tasks are to overview, delegate, and make sure everything is running smoothly. I have officers to take care of, raid leading, recruitment, and personnel. Thankfully, I don't have to look after the minutiae.

If you were to describe your most memorable moment as a Guild Master, what would it be?

Most memorable moments come from a particular raiding success of the guild. One in particular, I remember, is our first Gruul kill. This is probably the first 25-man raid boss instance in the *Burning Crusade* expansion to *World of Warcraft*. Gruul is the final boss of this instance. We had been struggling for a few raids on this encounter. It involves players running and dodging while fighting/healing, so it takes a fair amount of skill. We went in with 25 men and women into the boss's lair—we had just wiped twice, and there was a timer soon to be up for a trash mob respawn, which meant we would have to clear all those mobs again. The hour was late, close to midnight game time, and people had work the next morning. The boss "grows" at specific intervals and hits the tanking warrior harder and harder. In addition, his ranged area of effect abilities of Shatter and Cave is hit harder. So the aim is to damage the boss to kill him really before 12 grows. So we started dpsing (damaging) and lost about three to four people in the first shatter. Knowing that this would be the last attempt for the night, we carried on. People died at regular intervals, and we thought all was lost when our tanking warrior died at the ninth grow! However, Morfea, our skilled feral druid, took over and managed to tank him to 16 grows when we took him down with perhaps a quarter of the raid group up. The reward for that moment made all the hard work worth it.

What is the greatest achievement of your Guild?
Well, we have completed Karazhan with two raid groups in four hours. However, every guild is measured in success by their last boss kill. Currently, for us, this is Gruul, and we hope to look forward to more success shortly.

Your Guild has been very successful and become one of the more famous ones. What are the secrets behind a successful Guild?
Organization, teamwork, and communication: attributes that are probably important for success in all aspects of life. As long as you listen to your peers, you won't go far wrong. I personally believe foresight is also particularly effective—heading off problems before they have a chance to arise. A guild is only as successful as its members, so listen to them!

COMMUNITY INTERACTION

Community interaction is now viewed by many games publishers as an essential tool in yielding a games success. A game without a community presence can easily disappear into the shadows. Gamers really appreciate the personal interaction and rely on the community management of a game to keep them apprised of the latest news, tournaments and real world events.

PRO GAMER CHAMPION

The 21-year-old Norwegian student, Olav Undheim, took a year off from school to compete professionally in videogames. After winning a competition in *Warcraft III* at the huge Gathering 2007, he qualified for and was sponsored to go to the World Cyber Games in Seattle, Washington. Olav took the trip as a "vacation," but he left the competition a top player and $20,000 richer. Now he is back at the university in Trondheim, where he is studying for a Master's Degree in Computer Science.

Action
Games

An Interview with Jun Takeuchi

DEVELOPER: JUN TAKEUCHI

You are the creative force behind some of the greatest action/horror games ever created. How did you get into these kinds of scary games?

Well, I started out as a designer, doing illustrations, etc. I have also always loved movies, even back when I was in design school, especially horror movies. I started working at Capcom as a designer right after graduating and continued to watch a lot of movies while working there. During that time, Shinji Mikami had the idea of creating a horror game. There was this idea of making the game very cinematic, and I felt like it was a chance to really put my talents to use. The films of directors like Romero and Hitchcock have always fascinated me, and I felt it would be a great title for me to work on. Even when working on other titles such as *Lost Planet*, I always am trying to find ways to make these games more cinematic.

Even though Jun Takeuchi is relatively young, he is still regarded as a veteran in the video gaming industry. His career started immediately after he graduated from design school when he landed a job at one of Japan's major videogame publishers, Capcom Entertainment. Takeuchi's sense of style stems from his love of movies and the cinematic feel for the horror genre in general. All this helped him show his talents when he started on Capcom's *Resident Evil* in 1996. Even to this day, he tries to incorporate his love of movies into his games.

Takeuchi-san has over the years worked on many famous titles, including *Street Fighter II* (1992), *Resident Evil* (1996), *Onimusha: Warlords* (2001), *Lost Planet: Extreme Condition* (2006), and many more. He has now returned to the *Resident Evil* franchise where he is currently serving as the Chief Producer for the highly anticipated, *Resident Evil 5*.

TAKEUCHI-SAN AND HIS TEAM AT CAPCOM

What do you think has been the greatest achievement in the action genre so far?

Well, there have been quite a lot of incredible games in the action genre, but I think that the greatest achievement was *Super Mario Bros.* This game, created by Shigeru Miyamoto, really laid down the control fundamentals of action gaming. Mr. Miyamoto really understood the importance of the feeling of responsive controls when designing action games and put incredible effort into creating his control schemes. Pressing the jump button too early or too late is no good, you have to be precise with *Mario.* This is something fundamental that has stayed with action games up to this point.

Which is more important in creating successful games: brand building and franchises or original content?

Well, Capcom is creating the fifth *Resident Evil* game right now, and I think that series is very successful, but personally, I feel that the ideal length for a series is three games. When you make any new game, there are always things that you want to do that you are unable to that first time around. When creating the second game in the series, you have a chance to go ahead and make these additions, as well as improve things based on user feedback. With the third game, you can further perfect your vision of the series and bring it

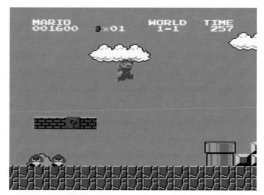

SUPER MARIO BROS.

to a satisfying close. That would be the ideal balance for me. First, create original content, perfect it through the course of a trilogy, and then create something else completely new. Of course, this is a business, and business considerations are very important when creating games. In the case of *Resident Evil*, we created the first three games, (along with quite a few games branching off from the main series), and then with *Resident Evil 4*, the series underwent a complete renewal. I think this is one of Shinji Mikami's great achievements. If you can find a good way to do it, it's absolutely possible to continue a series and keep it successful.

We are seeing a new trend in gaming: more girls and older people are picking up games as entertainment. How do you think this game genre will develop from here in regard to this demographic shift?

The action-horror genre is a kind of game that has a lot of public relation challenges associated with it. Even now, in today's society, there are a lot of things that we see in movies that are still unacceptable in games. There

ART: RESIDENT EVIL 4 CHARACTER, ADA WONG

could be a game and a movie that have very similar content, yet a 15-year-old is allowed to see the movie, while the game player must be 18 before he can play the game. The rating systems are simply stricter for games right now. I think that the acceptance of games not just as entertainment but as art in the same way that a medium like film is accepted as art is a necessary step we need to take as a society before younger women and older gamers really start to get excited about playing these kinds of games as entertainment. I think this is an important goal as a game developer. I want to create games that are accepted by people as art and entertainment in the same way that movies are.

What is your all time favorite game?

That is a very difficult question to answer! If I was forced to pick, I think that I would have to say that *Wizardry*, which I played on the NES, would have to be my favorite game.

Playing that game really showed me how much fun games could be. I won't ever forget that game. I also really love *Metal Gear Solid*, if we're talking about more recent games.

Lastly, what can you tell us about your latest endeavors, such as Resident Evil 5?

Of course, we haven't made too much information about this game official yet, so I can't say very much. I can tell you that we are trying to do some new things that you haven't seen in a *Resident Evil* game before. So far the series had been known for a very dark atmosphere. There hasn't been much daytime action in *Resident Evil* before now. We are trying to put a lot of new environments and a new look into this game, as well as some other new interesting game systems. There are some things that you might have seen in other games, but with a *Resident Evil* twist added. I hope that you are looking forward to playing the game!

ASSASSIN'S CREED

AVAILABLE ON

Nintendo DS
Nintendo Wii
PC Windows
PC Mac
Playstation 2
✓ Playstation 3
Playstation Portable
✓ Xbox 360

GAME FACTS *

PUBLISHER
Electronic Arts

DEVELOPER
EA Games

FIRST RELEASED
2007-11-13

GAME GENRE	TIME PERIOD
Shooter	Present
THEME	**COMPLEXITY**
War	Medium

SIMILAR GAMES

Stranglehold
Call of Duty 4
BioShock

RATING & MULTIPLAYER

USA	Europe	Network	Offline
		Yes	Yes

Army of Two

SETTING

Army of Two combines coordinated gameplay with an interesting plot. As part of a Private Military Corporation, you and your partner form a deadly Army of Two to fight a conspiracy that is threatening the whole world.

GAME SUMMARY

The politically charged storyline revolves around the ethical issues of Private Military Corporations, making Army of Two very different from other combat games. Choose between AI partners and live partners online and travel all over the world to carry out dirty deeds on behalf of your various employers. Army of Two offers two dozen weapons that can be upgraded and shared with your partner. You will have access to a GPS that serves as the map you follow throughout. Working closely with your teammate, you can climb walls and make your way through enemy fire. Your "aggro" level measures how much of a threat you are to the enemy and the level of aggression with which you are met accordingly in combat. To reduce one player's aggro level, the other must build up his own. The cash you receive for successfully completing your missions can be used to buy weapons from weapon dealers. Duct-tape weapons to your body, but remember to use your weapons tactically.

CHALLENGES & HINTS

The game focuses on players' aggro levels, and you will only survive fights by balancing yours with your partner's. You can easily identify who has the most aggro as that player is surrounded by a red glow. Cooperation is the key to victory.

KEY GAMEPLAY ELEMENTS

Attack/Fight
Steer/Maneuver
Tactics/Plan

GAME WORLD SIZE	Large
YOUR ROLE	Mercenaries
REPLAY VALUE	Once or Twice

AVERAGE SCORE

NA

out of 10

Data and images may vary on the various platforms

AVAILABLE ON

✓ Nintendo DS
  Nintendo Wii
✓ PC Windows
  PC Mac
  Playstation 2
✓ Playstation 3
  Playstation Portable
✓ Xbox 360

GAME FACTS *

PUBLISHER
Ubisoft

DEVELOPER
Ubisoft

FIRST RELEASED
2007-11-06

GAME GENRE	**TIME PERIOD**
Action	Medieval
THEME	**COMPLEXITY**
War	Medium

SIMILAR GAMES

Prince of Persia: Sands of Time
Thief: Deadly Shadows
Onimusha: Dawn of Dreams

RATING & MULTIPLAYER

USA	Europe	Network	Offline
MATURE M	18+ www.pegi.info	No	No

Assassin's Creed

SETTING

Assassin's Creed is set in 1191 AD as the Third Crusade is turning the people of Jerusalem against each other. As Altair, you intend to put an end to these hostilities as you shape the events and the future of the Holy Land.

GAME SUMMARY

You work as an assassin for a man named Hashshashin who assigns you different killing targets within the city. The game gives you total freedom to do whatever you wish, whenever and wherever you please. Set in Jerusalem, you explore the detailed and historically accurate city and are witness to the goings-on of its inhabitants. With realistic graphics and gameplay, you can run from rooftop to rooftop, ride horses, or blend in with crowds as you escape from enemy guards or head out in search of your next target. To avoid being seen by the guards, simply use the game's "blend" mode so you don't attract attention. If, however, you do find yourself being followed, you have two options: fight or flight. In fight mode, you can fend off enemies with either a sword, daggers, a hidden blade, or fists. You can also grab an enemy and push or pull him off a building. After an assassination, Altair is required to wipe the victim's body with a feather and bring it to Hashshashin at his hideout; first, though, you must lay low until you are no longer a wanted criminal.

CHALLENGES & HINTS

Remember that this game is not only based on combat. Much of the time you will be attempting to outrun the enemy or finding a hiding place, and as much as you would like to chop people up as you pass through crowds, all your actions will have consequences. Stay out of sight!

KEY GAMEPLAY ELEMENTS

Attack/Fight
Steer/Maneuver
Tactics/Plan

GAME WORLD SIZE	Medium
YOUR ROLE	Assassin
REPLAY VALUE	Once or Twice

AVERAGE SCORE

NA

out of 10

Data and images may vary on the various platforms

Action

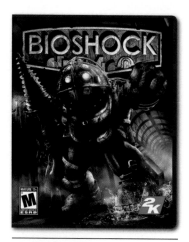

BioShock

AVAILABLE ON

Nintendo DS
Nintendo Wii
✓ PC Windows
PC Mac
Playstation 2
Playstation 3
Playstation Portable
✓ Xbox 360

GAME FACTS *

PUBLISHER
2K Games

DEVELOPER
2K Australia, 2K Boston

FIRST RELEASED
2007-08-21

GAME GENRE
Shooter

TIME PERIOD
Recent History

THEME
Horror/Thriller

COMPLEXITY
Medium

SIMILAR GAMES

Halo 3
Enemy Territory: Quake Wars
Half-Life 2: Episode One

RATING & MULTIPLAYER

USA	Europe	Network	Offline
		No	No

SETTING

Experience Rapture, an underwater utopia filled with art-deco nostalgia and colorful neon. You will soon realize that this deceiving facade is hiding a living hell filled with twisted plots and mutant creatures.

GAME SUMMARY

After crashing your plane in the ocean, you find yourself in Rapture, though spending some time in the city starts to make drowning seem a better choice! There's no way back home, so you search for Rapture's creator, Andrew Ryan—a crazy scientist who created a place where science and capitalism could develop without the interruptions of ethics. You will quickly be in need of a weapon, and later on will start to use genetic enhancements called plasmids. Plasmids allow you to use mutation to your advantage, equipping you with different magical abilities that help you to survive the attacks of the city's aggressive inhabitants. Rapture's citizens are varied and surprisingly intelligent; featuring their own agendas and behavior, they force you to come up with countless combat strategies.

CHALLENGES & HINTS

It's often safer to avoid certain creatures, such as the giant diver Big Daddy, although harvesting others for genetically modified material (ADAM), like the Little Sister, will pay off and even prove necessary for survival. Bioshock's intense encounters are both challenging and frightening. The ambient sound keeps you immersed while exploring Rapture's nerve-wracking environs.

KEY GAMEPLAY ELEMENTS
Attack/Fight
Steer/Maneuver
Gather

GAME WORLD SIZE	Large
YOUR ROLE	Plane Crash Survivor
REPLAY VALUE	Once or Twice

AVERAGE SCORE

9.4

out of 10

Data and images may vary on the various platforms

BlackSite
AREA 51

SETTING
In Blacksite: Area 51, an extraterrestrial infestation is breaking out in the Nevada desert. Your character is a U.S. military commando on a mission to save the world from ferocious alien species.

GAME SUMMARY
Playing as a military veteran in charge of a Special Forces unit, you need to lead your team with proficiency and strategy. Battling giant aliens can be nerve-racking, so your team of soldiers will get anxious and unfocused if the unit's morale is low. Their insecurity results in shaky aim and unreliable behavior. These human elements help the player get closer to his teammates and to the storyline. It's easy to order your squad around, issuing commands to unlock doors or plant explosives, but the game's levels can follow multiple paths requiring different strategies. In multiplayer you can play online modes for up to 16 players, or can cooperate on the main campaign.

CHALLENGES & HINTS
Some of the giant bosses are bigger than any of the buildings in Blacksite's small-town setting. These hideous creatures can kill you with any number of terrifying attacks, including giant laser beams and acid-spewing mortars. So grab a rocket launcher, use your squad for distraction, and aim at an enemy's weak point to maximize damage.

AVAILABLE ON
Nintendo DS
Nintendo Wii
✓ PC Windows
PC Mac
Playstation 2
✓ Playstation 3
Playstation Portable
✓ Xbox 360

GAME FACTS *
PUBLISHER
Midway
DEVELOPER
Midway
FIRST RELEASED
2007-11-12

GAME GENRE	**TIME PERIOD**
Shooter	Present
THEME	**COMPLEXITY**
Horror/Thriller	Medium

SIMILAR GAMES
Half-Life 2
Perfect Dark Zero
BioShock

RATING & MULTIPLAYER

USA	Europe	Network	Offline
		Yes	No

KEY GAMEPLAY ELEMENTS
Attack/Fight
Steer/Maneuver
Gather

GAME WORLD SIZE	Large
YOUR ROLE	Military Veteran
REPLAY VALUE	Once or Twice

AVERAGE SCORE

NA
out of 10

Data and images may vary on the various platforms

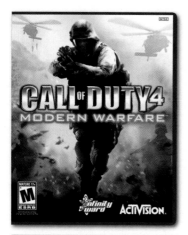

Call of Duty 4
MODERN WARFARE

SETTING
As either a U.S. marine or British SAS soldier you are transported to some of the most remote and dangerous locations in the world to defeat a growing threat of nuclear war.

GAME SUMMARY
Although you will be fighting with either the U.S. marines or the British SAS, both armies share a common goal of dismantling a plot that is threatening world security. No matter whom you choose to fight for, you use all means necessary to prevent the nuclear war that is about to erupt. Victory depends on how effectively you combine speed and communication. Various cut scenes guide you through the storyline and your missions. You crawl through fields and seemingly deserted towns until shots are fired at you from an unexpected enemy. You have many chances to plan assaults, and air support is critical in this version of Call of Duty. Armed with a large arsenal of modern day weaponry including sophisticated technology and great firepower, you are more lethal than ever. Weapons such as the Javelin antitank weapon can lock onto enemy armor and launch rockets directly upward that eventually plummet down and destroy the enemy.

CHALLENGES & HINTS
It is now possible to coordinate land and air strikes on the battlefield, and using the two forces correctly together is the key to defeating the enemy. Don't forget to use gadgets such as night-vision goggles and ghillie suits for maximum camouflage in the field.

AVAILABLE ON

✓ Nintendo DS
  Nintendo Wii
✓ PC Windows
  PC Mac
  Playstation 2
✓ Playstation 3
  Playstation Portable
✓ Xbox 360

GAME FACTS *

PUBLISHER
Activision

DEVELOPER
Infinity Ward, n-Space

FIRST RELEASED
2007-11-05

GAME GENRE	**TIME PERIOD**
Action	Present
THEME	**COMPLEXITY**
War	Medium

SIMILAR GAMES

Tom Clancy's Ghost Recon: A.W. 2
Resistance: Fall of Man
Haze

RATING & MULTIPLAYER

USA	Europe	Network	Offline
MATURE M	16+ www.pegi.info	32 Players	No

KEY GAMEPLAY ELEMENTS

Attack/Fight
Steer/Maneuver
Tactics/Plan

		AVERAGE SCORE
GAME WORLD SIZE	Large	**NA**
YOUR ROLE	Soldier	
REPLAY VALUE	Several Times	out of 10

*Data and images may vary on the various platforms

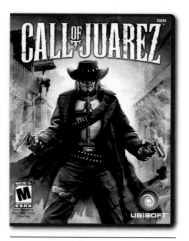

Call of Juarez

SETTING
Take in vast scenery, experience saloon brawls, and brandish the authentic weapons of the Wild West. Immerse yourself in the cat-and-mouse game of hunter and fugitive by playing as either character.

GAME SUMMARY
The young Billy Candle is wrongly accused of his parents' murders and consequently becomes the main target of the priest and bounty hunter Reverend Ray. Play as Billy and use your wit and whip to survive. You will climb mountains, sneak past threats, and disarm adversaries. Use brute force and powerful weapons when playing as Ray, a gunslinger who can shoot from horseback and batter down doors. This ex-outlaw wields two powerful six-shooters, which you can aim by targeting both crosshairs in slow-motion, and takes out a whole army in no time. Call of Juarez also features a Duel mode, where precision and reflexes can make you "the fastest shot in the West." In the multiplayer mode, 2-16 players can duke it out with authentic guns and maps and carry out a brutal bank robbery.

CHALLENGES & HINTS
Billy's whip is often hard to target correctly while you have a horde of bounty hunters after you, which can get really frustrating after falling off a cliff for the fifth time. The world of Call of Juarez is a ruthless one, so playing as a professional gunslinger feels a little safer than playing as a farm boy equipped with bow and arrow.

AVAILABLE ON
Nintendo DS
Nintendo Wii
✓ PC Windows
PC Mac
Playstation 2
Playstation 3
Playstation Portable
✓ Xbox 360

GAME FACTS *

PUBLISHER
Ubisoft

DEVELOPER
Techland

FIRST RELEASED
2006-09-15

GAME GENRE	**TIME PERIOD**
Shooter	Renaissance
THEME	**COMPLEXITY**
Western	Medium

SIMILAR GAMES
Medal of Honor: Airborne
Call of Duty 3
Brothers In Arms Hell's Highway

RATING & MULTIPLAYER

USA	Europe	Network	Offline
	18+ www.pegi.info	16 Players	No

KEY GAMEPLAY ELEMENTS
Attack/Fight
Steer/Maneuver
Gather

GAME WORLD SIZE	Medium
YOUR ROLE	Hero
REPLAY VALUE	Once or Twice

 AVERAGE SCORE

7.0

out of 10

Data and images may vary on the various platforms

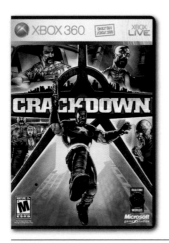

Crackdown

AVAILABLE ON

Nintendo DS
Nintendo Wii
PC Windows
PC Mac
Playstation 2
Playstation 3
Playstation Portable
✓ Xbox 360

GAME FACTS

PUBLISHER
Microsoft Game Studio

DEVELOPER
Realtime Worlds

FIRST RELEASED
2007-02-20

GAME GENRE	TIME PERIOD
Action	Present
THEME	COMPLEXITY
Crime	Medium

SIMILAR GAMES

Gears of War
Lost Planet: Extreme Condition
Kane & Lynch: Dead Men

RATING & MULTIPLAYER

USA	Europe	Network	Offline
	18+ www.pegi.info	2 Players	No

SETTING

Three criminal gangs have seized control of the city's downtown area and the police are implementing super-agents in the fight against the mob. Prepare for a high-paced action game with very open-ended missions. There's a serious (and bloody) storyline behind the cartoon graphics.

GAME SUMMARY

Hired as a super-agent for the police, you are assigned the task of removing the three criminal gangs that control parts of the city. The city's downtown core is a large area, and you are given the freedom to explore its every corner. How you decide to complete the missions is up to you and your actions will affect your abilities as a super-agent. You will have to use this freedom to find creative solutions to succeed in this game. Dynamic surroundings allow you to flip cars and form blockades, and you can use garbage bins and debris as weapons in capturing the gang members. Your superpowers work to your advantage since they can be developed however you choose. Make sure to increase your physical strength so you can jump from rooftop to rooftop. Collect orbs that are hidden on top of buildings around the city for bonus points. Coordinated play with a friend is possible with Xbox Live; work together in co-op mode to execute attacks on the gangs.

CHALLENGES & HINTS

The only way to catch the mob is to be faster, stronger, and smarter than them. Why not build muscle by lifting a couple of cars? All of your agent's abilities can be developed. If, for example, you always choose to shoot rather than fistfight, you will have problems when you run out of ammo.

KEY GAMEPLAY ELEMENTS
Attack/Fight
Tactics/Plan
Steer/Maneuver

		AVERAGE SCORE
GAME WORLD SIZE	Large	
YOUR ROLE	Hero	**8.5**
REPLAY VALUE	Once or Twice	out of 10

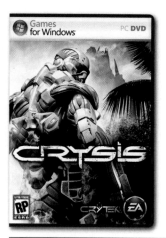

Crysis

SETTING

In 2019 a massive asteroid lands on Earth. It contains a giant alien ship whose force-field freezes parts of the island. Your task is to confront the aliens and defend Earth from invasion.

GAME SUMMARY

Crysis is an engrossing three-act story that assigns you the all-important role of saving mankind by ridding earth of alien invaders. Even before the asteroid breaks open to reveal the alien ship, however, a conflict arises between North Korea and the United States, with each country claiming the right to study the asteroid. This means that you must contend with both parties in order to complete your task. Your most important piece of equipment is probably your suit. It acts as a cloak and shield and has futuristic features that boost your strength and speed. Crysis gives you the freedom to explore the North Korean jungles and to decide how to complete your missions. The aliens have extremely well-developed AI, making it challenging to reach the alien spacecraft. Your human enemies will use military tactics to try and stop you from completing your task. Due to the climate changes that the aliens brought with them, you will also encounter life-threatening natural catastrophes including earthquakes, landslides, and tornados.

CHALLENGES & HINTS

In order to handle North Korea's rugged landscape, use the equipment available to you (including vehicles such as trucks, tanks, boats, and helicopters) for easier transportation and navigation. In this constantly changing world, you will need to adapt your methods and tactics over and over again.

AVAILABLE ON

- Nintendo DS
- Nintendo Wii
- ✓ PC Windows
- PC Mac
- Playstation 2
- Playstation 3
- Playstation Portable
- Xbox 360

GAME FACTS

PUBLISHER
Electronic Arts

DEVELOPER
Crytek Studios

FIRST RELEASED
2007-11-16

GAME GENRE	**TIME PERIOD**
Shooter	Present
THEME	**COMPLEXITY**
Horror/Thriller	Medium

SIMILAR GAMES

BioShock
Halo 3
Far Cry

RATING & MULTIPLAYER

USA	Europe	Network	Offline
		32 Players	No

KEY GAMEPLAY ELEMENTS

Attack/Fight
Steer/Maneuver
Tactics/Plan

GAME WORLD SIZE	Large
YOUR ROLE	Hero
REPLAY VALUE	Once or Twice

AVERAGE SCORE

NA

out of 10

AVAILABLE ON

Nintendo DS
Nintendo Wii
✓ PC Windows
PC Mac
Playstation 2
✓ Playstation 3
Playstation Portable
✓ Xbox 360

GAME FACTS *

PUBLISHER
Activision

DEVELOPER
id Software, Splash Damage

FIRST RELEASED
2007-09-28

GAME GENRE	TIME PERIOD
Shooter	Future
THEME	**COMPLEXITY**
War	Medium

SIMILAR GAMES

Battlefield 2142
Star Wars: Battlefront
Crysis

RATING & MULTIPLAYER

USA	Europe	Network	Offline
		32 Players	No

Enemy Territory
QUAKE WARS

SETTING

The year is 2065 and a conflict is brewing in the Quake universe. You are forced to take a stand and choose who to fight for: the barbaric alien Strogg armies, or the humans defending planet Earth. Whichever you choose, prepare yourself for some serious team-based multi-player action!

GAME SUMMARY

Play in one of five character classes for either the Global Defense Force or the rising Axis of Evil. Each class has a unique look, as well as its own movements and behavior. A wide arsenal of weapons and more than forty futuristic vehicles and structures are available in this high-tech war. During combat, players will have to use their own fighting skills as well as directing teamwork to destroy the enemy. Plan and complete strategic missions to capture and secure enemy territory, and you will gain skills and rise in rank. Try to gain tactical advantage by establishing bases and deploying defense structures, such as artillery and radars, in your enemy's midst. The authenticity of the enormous battlefields is remarkable, with great visual detail and realistic lighting, and battles will be fought both during the day and at night. As you move through mountains, deserts, and glaciers, accurate atmospheric conditions for each location add to the game's realism.

CHALLENGES & HINTS

Constant character growth and achievement on and off the battlefield will be rewarded, and your selection of weapons, vehicles, and other equipment is integral to the team's success. Keep in mind that this is a game where good teamwork is necessary to defeat your enemy.

KEY GAMEPLAY ELEMENTS

Attack/Fight
Tactics/Plan
Steer/Maneuver

GAME WORLD SIZE	Large
YOUR ROLE	Soldier
REPLAY VALUE	Infinite

AVERAGE SCORE

8.5

out of 10

*Data and images may vary on the various platforms

Gears of War

SETTING

Follow the human coalition soldier Marcus Fenix on his mission to defeat the Locust Horde and save the planet Sera—and the human race—from total extinction.

GAME SUMMARY

Gears of War's gameplay modes are heavily focused on cooperative play. You can either play with AI-controlled computer teammates or invite friends (or foes) to play with you. Unlike games of this sort, Gears of War features only a few, but powerful, weapons ranging from sniper rifles and pistols to shotguns and assault rifles. These guns work very well in combination with other weapons and tools—one rifle, notably, has a chainsaw attached to it. In order to make progress in the game, you have to successfully complete missions that are handed to you, such as getting from one point to another while taking out specified targets along the way. So take up arms and prepare for some hardcore shooting action!

CHALLENGES & HINTS

This game differs from other first-person shooter games as the player can withstand a barrage of bullets. However, you will be in serious danger if you take more then a few shots. To stay alive take cover, remain focused, and strategically plan your next move.

AVAILABLE ON

Nintendo DS
Nintendo Wii
✓ PC Windows
✓ PC Mac
Playstation 2
Playstation 3
Playstation Portable
✓ Xbox 360

GAME FACTS *

PUBLISHER
Microsoft Game Studio

DEVELOPER
Epic Games

FIRST RELEASED
2006-11-07

GAME GENRE
Shooter

TIME PERIOD
Future

THEME
War

COMPLEXITY
Medium

SIMILAR GAMES

Lost Planet: Extreme Condition
Crackdown
Earth Defense Force 2017

RATING & MULTIPLAYER

USA	Europe	Network	Offline
	18+ www.pegi.info	8 Players	2 Players

KEY GAMEPLAY ELEMENTS

Attack/Fight
Steer/Maneuver
Tactics/Plan

GAME WORLD SIZE	Large
YOUR ROLE	Soldier
REPLAY VALUE	Once or Twice

AVERAGE SCORE

9.4

out of 10

*Data and images may vary on the various platforms

Geometry Wars
GALAXIES

SETTING
What happens when you place colorful geometric shapes into space and order one of them to shoot down the others? You get Geometry Wars: Galaxies!

GAME SUMMARY
In Geometry Wars: Galaxies you fight enemies in a variety of galaxies and work to upgrade your battle drone. For the first time in a Geometry Wars game, you can play through a single-player campaign where your single objective is to survive as long as possible and score as many points as you can. There is also a multiplayer mode where you can play with or against friends. A new currency allows you to upgrade and personalize your battle drone. You can also connect to the Nintendo Online service and put your high score on the leader board or link up with the Wii or DS versions of the game for new content. The game also features a full version of Geometry Wars: Retro Evolution.

CHALLENGES & HINTS
It may seem simple to shoot down basic geometric shapes, but eventually there will be a lot of them coming at you all at once. Once they explode, they shoot out a lot of colored fragments, which will confuse you and make you lose your position. On top of that, the battle grid warps, so stay focused!

AVAILABLE ON

✓ Nintendo DS
✓ Nintendo Wii
  PC Windows
  PC Mac
  Playstation 2
  Playstation 3
  Playstation Portable
  Xbox 360

GAME FACTS*

PUBLISHER
Vivendi

DEVELOPER
Kuju Entertainment

FIRST RELEASED
2007-11-06

GAME GENRE	**TIME PERIOD**
Shooter	Future
THEME	**COMPLEXITY**
Sci-Fi	Low

SIMILAR GAMES

Geometry Wars: Retro Evolved
Blazing Lazers
Astroids

RATING & MULTIPLAYER

USA	Europe	Network	Offline
	3+ www.pegi.info		
		Yes	No

KEY GAMEPLAY ELEMENTS
Attack/Fight
Steer/Maneuver
Build & Design

GAME WORLD SIZE	Medium
YOUR ROLE	Geometric Fighter
REPLAY VALUE	Several Times

AVERAGE SCORE

NA

out of 10

*Data and images may vary on the various platforms

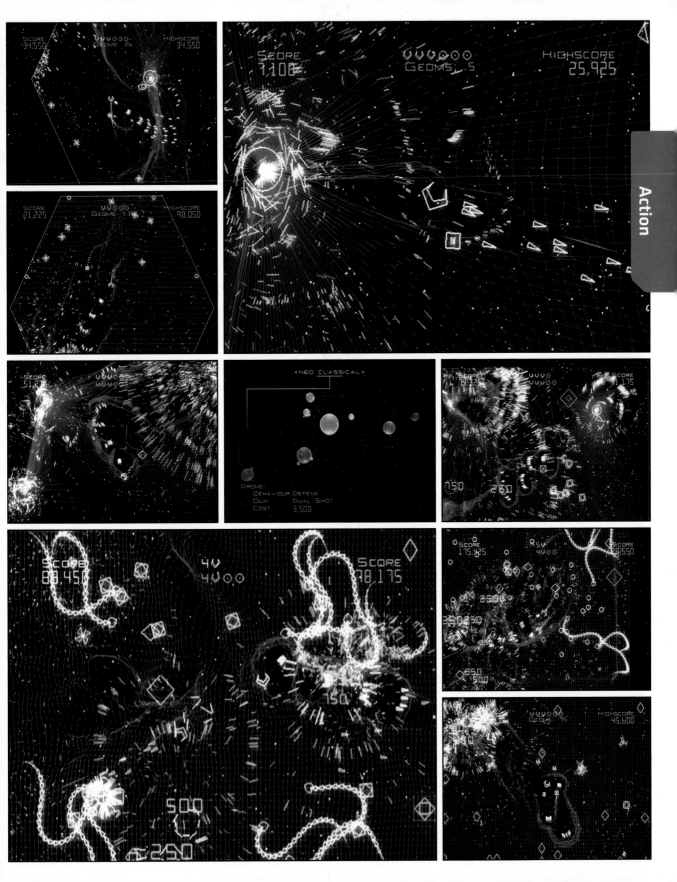

God of War II

SETTING

Continuing the story of God of War I, players once again assume the role of the bloodthirsty man-god Kratos from ancient Greek mythology. More ruthless and power hungry than ever, Kratos sets out from his throne on Mount Olympus to end his torment and find a temple that can alter what no mortal before him has changed—destiny.

GAME SUMMARY

Determined to find the remote temple that houses the Sisters of Fate, Kratos will kill anyone who stands in his way. Kratos's journey leads him to the edge of the earth and reminds him of the horrors from his past. Every creature Kratos encounters is determined to stop him from reaching the temple, and his only option is to destroy everything that gets in his way. The brutality of this game is evident throughout. Equipped with new barbaric combat moves, Kratos cannot simply kill his victims: he has to torture and deform them in order to continue. He fights the usual assortment of cyclopes, Minotaurs, and zombie warriors, but there is also a cast of new creatures and figures from Greek mythology. Among the new weapons are winged creatures that fly to your next killing destination. You can also utilize magic that is based on natural elements. Kratos's signature weapon, the dual blades, is an all-purpose weapon that does massive damage every time, especially if upgraded. As the journey continues, you must solve intelligent and progressively more challenging puzzles to move on and string together the full story.

CHALLENGES & HINTS

Although the puzzles may seem illogical and random at times, it is important to remember that Kratos has everything working against him, and that some things are there simply to mess with him. God of War II is a thrilling action adventure for those who enjoy blood and gore as well as challenging mind puzzles.

AVAILABLE ON

Nintendo DS
Nintendo Wii
PC Windows
PC Mac
✓ Playstation 2
Playstation 3
Playstation Portable
Xbox 360

GAME FACTS

PUBLISHER
SCEA, SCEE

DEVELOPER
SCEI

FIRST RELEASED
2007-03-13

GAME GENRE	**TIME PERIOD**
Fighting	Ancient
THEME	**COMPLEXITY**
War	Medium

SIMILAR GAMES

Shadow of the Colossus
Prince of Persia: Warrior Within
Devil May Cry

RATING & MULTIPLAYER

USA	Europe	Network	Offline
		No	No

KEY GAMEPLAY ELEMENTS

Attack/Fight
Steer/Maneuver
Tactics/Plan

GAME WORLD SIZE	Medium
YOUR ROLE	Protagonist
REPLAY VALUE	Once or Twice

AVERAGE SCORE

9.0

out of 10

Halo 3

SETTING

The final chapter of the epic Halo trilogy is here! The year is 2552 and the survivors of the human race are fighting desperately against the terrifying alien civilization that collectively calls itself the Covenant. The second Halo has been activated, and an all-consuming, intelligent parasite, known as the Flood, transforms all living creatures into giant puppets. The faith of the Galaxy once again lies in the hands of Master Chief.

GAME SUMMARY

The Halo series is famous for its story-based campaigns, as well as its multiplayer battles. The exhilarating story continues when Master Chief returns to fight the Covenant. Joining him this year is the Arbiter, the honorable leader of the newly formed alliance the Elites, who accompanies you on several missions. The game graphics have improved, and an upgraded AI plays a significant part in the outcomes of battles. Halo 3's co-op mode allows four players to cooperate for the campaign mode, controlling Master Chief, the Arbiter, and two brand-new Elites: N'tho 'Sraom and Usze 'Taham. The game's multiplayer mode introduces several new maps, including Sand Trap and Last Resort, as well as new vehicles like the monstrous Elephant, which can carry a Scorpion Tank, and the Brute Chopper antigravity hover bike. All battles can be recorded and uploaded on Xbox Live.

CHALLENGES & HINTS

The expanded four-player co-op mode, new combat vehicles, and an upgraded AI add to the complexity of this game and intensify the battles. More than ever, your success depends on your tactical decisions and ability to coordinate offensive strategy with your team.

AVAILABLE ON

Nintendo DS
Nintendo Wii
PC Windows
PC Mac
Playstation 2
Playstation 3
Playstation Portable
✓ Xbox 360

GAME FACTS

PUBLISHER
Microsoft Game Studio

DEVELOPER
Bungie

FIRST RELEASED
2007-09-25

GAME GENRE	TIME PERIOD
Action	Future
THEME	**COMPLEXITY**
Sci-Fi	Medium

SIMILAR GAMES

TimeShift
Metroid Prime 3: Corruption
BioShock

RATING & MULTIPLAYER

USA	Europe	Network	Offline
	16+ www.pegi.info	16 Players	Yes

KEY GAMEPLAY ELEMENTS

Attack/Fight
Steer/Maneuver
Tactics/Plan

GAME WORLD SIZE	Large
YOUR ROLE	Hero
REPLAY VALUE	Once or Twice

AVERAGE SCORE

9.6

out of 10

AVAILABLE ON

- ✓ Nintendo DS
- ✓ Nintendo Wii
- ✓ PC Windows
- ✓ PC Mac
- ✓ Playstation 2
- ✓ Playstation 3
- ✓ Playstation Portable
- ✓ Xbox 360

GAME FACTS *

PUBLISHER
Electronic Arts

DEVELOPER
EA Games

FIRST RELEASED
2007-06-26

GAME GENRE	**TIME PERIOD**
Action	Present
THEME	**COMPLEXITY**
Fantasy	Medium

SIMILAR GAMES

Arthur and the Invisibles
Avatar: The Last Airbender
The Polar Express

RATING & MULTIPLAYER

USA	Europe	Network	Offline
	7+ www.pegi.info	🖥️ 🖥️ 🖥️ No	🖥️ No

Harry Potter
AND THE ORDER OF THE PHOENIX

SETTING
After Harry Potter returns to Hogwarts, he discovers that the faculty, including the ministry of magic, doubts Harry's encounter with Lord Voldemort. Without any support from the faculty, Harry is forced to deal with the situation himself with help from his friends Hermione and Ron.

GAME SUMMARY
In this next installment of the Harry Potter franchise, Hogwarts's 85 different locations can be fully explored with many secret chambers, brand new spells, and more people to meet. In order to protect the school from the Dark Arts, Harry needs to find and recruit students to form a defensive alliance called Dumbledore's Army. During the game you will be able to control other important characters, including Dumbledore and Sirius Black, and you have the opportunity to fight against Lucius Malfang, Bellatrix, and the Dark Lord himself. In battle you need to perform different spells strategically in order to defeat your enemies. Harry can also use magic to repair and clean objects in the environment to gain discovery points and earn new spells.

CHALLENGES & HINTS
Aiming your wand can be quite difficult, and it's important to avoid wild waving and button bashing. Be prepared for a lot of backtracking when navigating through Hogwarts, and keep an eye out for secret passages and side missions.

KEY GAMEPLAY ELEMENTS

Steer/Maneuver
Attack/Fight
Explore

		AVERAGE SCORE
GAME WORLD SIZE	Medium	
YOUR ROLE	Wizard	**6.9**
REPLAY VALUE	Once or Twice	out of 10

*Data and images may vary on the various platforms

Haze

SETTING

The year is 2048, and military organizations like NATO no longer exist. You play the role of Sergeant Shane Carpenter who works for the private military corporation, Mantel Global Industries, fighting rebels in South America.

GAME SUMMARY

Mantel Global Industries are experts in the field of biomedical supplements. One of their supplements is called NECTAR, and it is given to their soldiers to enable them to fight harder. However, throughout the course of the game you discover that there is more to NECTAR than meets the eye. This causes you to think twice about the corporation you are fighting for. Haze plays like most first-person shooter games, but the NECTAR power adds a unique gameplay element. Using it increases your strength, accuracy, and speed, as well as gives you the ability to see through enemy cover and detect dangers such as bombs and grenades. Haze features an online multiplayer mode, and you can also invite other players to join you in cooperative play.

CHALLENGES & HINTS

The use of NECTAR is all well and good when you encounter tough times, but if used excessively, it can cause your vision to go blurry and make it difficult to tell friend from foe. Keep in mind that this can happen to your teammates as well, so watch out, as you can't always trust the person next to you!

AVAILABLE ON

Nintendo DS
Nintendo Wii
PC Windows
PC Mac
Playstation 2
✓ Playstation 3
Playstation Portable
Xbox 360

GAME FACTS

PUBLISHER
Ubisoft

DEVELOPER
Free Radical Design

FIRST RELEASED
2007-11-19

GAME GENRE	TIME PERIOD
Shooter	Future
THEME	**COMPLEXITY**
War	Medium

SIMILAR GAMES

TimeShift
Army of Two
F.E.A.R

RATING & MULTIPLAYER

USA	Europe	Network	Offline
	18+ www.pegi.info		
		4 Players	4 Players

KEY GAMEPLAY ELEMENTS

Attack/Fight
Steer/Maneuver
Gather

GAME WORLD SIZE	Large
YOUR ROLE	Solider
REPLAY VALUE	Once or Twice

AVERAGE SCORE

NA

out of 10

4-PLAYER COOP MODE

4-PLAYER COOP MODE

Heavenly Sword

SETTING

Follow the red-haired beauty Nariko on her quest of vengeance. She belongs to a clan that protects the Heavenly Sword, which provides whomever wields it with immense power. Your aim is to defeat King Bohan, who has set out to destroy the clan and gain possession of the sword.

GAME SUMMARY

Heavenly Sword blends beautiful martial arts with hack and slash blade fights similar to Genji: Days of the Blade and God of War. The game features a context-sensitive action control system that works by pressing buttons that correspond to symbols on the screen to perform certain moves and attacks. The Heavenly Sword has the ability to change into three different weapons, all with different abilities: a chain blade, two smaller blades, and one big, heavy blade. The game features a total of six different chapters all set in stunningly beautiful locations.

CHALLENGES & HINTS

Slashing frantically with your blade may seem like an easy way to defeat an enemy, but soon you'll encounter 20 enemies at once, some of whom are heavily armed. They will attack you from behind while you're fighting someone else, so watch out and be precise.

AVAILABLE ON

Nintendo DS
Nintendo Wii
PC Windows
PC Mac
Playstation 2
✓ Playstation 3
Playstation Portable
Xbox 360

GAME FACTS

PUBLISHER
SCEA, SCEE

DEVELOPER
Ninja Theory

FIRST RELEASED
2007-09-25

GAME GENRE	**TIME PERIOD**
Fighting	Fantasy/Timeless
THEME	**COMPLEXITY**
Fantasy	Medium

SIMILAR GAMES

God of War II
Genji: Days of the Blade
Bladestorm: The Hundred Years' War

RATING & MULTIPLAYER

USA	Europe	Network	Offline
		No	No

KEY GAMEPLAY ELEMENTS

Attack/Fight
Steer/Maneuver
Gather

GAME WORLD SIZE	Large
YOUR ROLE	Female Warrior
REPLAY VALUE	Once or Twice

AVERAGE SCORE

8.0

out of 10

Kane & Lynch
DEAD MEN

SETTING
As Kane, you embark on a violent death tour all around the world with your psychopath partner Lynch, whom you strongly dislike. The game is taken to disturbingly brutal levels as you are given missions by the Seven.

GAME SUMMARY
Kane and Lynch were forced to team up when they were kidnapped by a band of soldiers called the Seven and made an offer they couldn't refuse. Completing missions for the Seven, you work alongside Lynch and your squad, directing them with simple commands that initiate enemy attacks and provide supplies and weapons. As the game progresses, you find out more about Kane and Lynch's dark histories, and if you are wounded and dying, your life flashes before your eyes, giving you more insight into Kane's past. Death can be avoided if one of your squad members has an adrenaline shot, but whether or not he or she will administer this shot depends on your relationship with that person. A third-person view adds a cinematic feel to the action-filled game, in particular when you are fighting on crowded streets. Be careful, as thousands of civilians will slow you down and make it hard to escape!

CHALLENGES & HINTS
The action can be overwhelming, so don't be afraid to take cover and buy time to collect your thoughts. If you find it difficult to aim at targets in the third-person perspective, you can bring the camera closer to Kane's shoulder for more accuracy. Remember to stay focused on the mission that you are working on. The Seven will take care of the rest.

AVAILABLE ON

Nintendo DS
Nintendo Wii
✓ PC Windows
PC Mac
Playstation 2
✓ Playstation 3
Playstation Portable
✓ Xbox 360

GAME FACTS *

PUBLISHER
Eidos Interactive

DEVELOPER
IO interactive

FIRST RELEASED
2007-11-20

GAME GENRE
Shooter

TIME PERIOD
Present

THEME
Crime

COMPLEXITY
Medium

SIMILAR GAMES

Gears of War
Stranglehold
Crackdown

RATING & MULTIPLAYER

USA	Europe	Network	Offline
		8 Players	2 Players

KEY GAMEPLAY ELEMENTS
Attack/Fight
Steer/Maneuver
Tactics/Plan

GAME WORLD SIZE	Large
YOUR ROLE	Protagonist
REPLAY VALUE	Once or Twice

AVERAGE SCORE

NA

out of 10

*Data and images may vary on the various platforms

AVAILABLE ON

Nintendo DS
Nintendo Wii
✓ PC Windows
PC Mac
Playstation 2
Playstation 3
Playstation Portable
✓ Xbox 360

GAME FACTS *

PUBLISHER
Capcom

DEVELOPER
Capcom

FIRST RELEASED
2007-01-12

GAME GENRE	TIME PERIOD
Shooter	Future
THEME	**COMPLEXITY**
Sci-Fi	Medium

SIMILAR GAMES

Enemy Territory: Quake Wars
Earth Defense Force 2017
Rogue Trooper

RATING & MULTIPLAYER

USA	Europe	Network	Offline
		16 Players	No

Lost Planet
EXTREME CONDITION

SETTING
You play Wayne Holden, who is suffering from amnesia and finds himself under attack by enormous bugs called Akrids. He is in the frozen wasteland of planet E.D.N III, and the only thing he remembers is the killing of his father...and the bug that is responsible for it.

GAME SUMMARY
In this visually dazzling game, there are eleven missions to complete as you take on a variety of hostile bugs ranging from overhead swarms to huge ground-dwellers. You also have to manage the extreme conditions of the frozen tundra, often trudging through snow that is up to your waist. As you shoot and destroy the gigantic bugs, one of your main objectives is to collect their thermal energy, which is necessary for maintaining your health and, hence, for your survival. The bigger the Akrid, the more thermal energy it has. You have a variety of weapons at your disposal, including a Vital Suit that is useful for taking down bigger forms of Akrids. You also encounter the Snow Pirates, a group of human soldiers that are dangerous, although more passive than Akrids.

CHALLENGES & HINTS
Although you are stuck in a frozen desert, there is a surprising amount of equipment and gear available to you. Don't hesitate to use the Vital Suit to obtain thermal energy. Enjoy the amazing animation and breathtaking landscapes!

KEY GAMEPLAY ELEMENTS
Attack/Fight
Steer/Maneuver
Gather

		AVERAGE SCORE
GAME WORLD SIZE	Medium	
YOUR ROLE	Hero	**8.0**
REPLAY VALUE	Once or Twice	out of 10

*Data and images may vary on the various platforms

AVAILABLE ON

Nintendo DS
Nintendo Wii
✓ PC Windows
PC Mac
Playstation 2
✓ Playstation 3
Playstation Portable
✓ Xbox 360

GAME FACTS*

PUBLISHER
Electronic Arts

DEVELOPER
EA Games

FIRST RELEASED
2007-09-04

GAME GENRE
Shooter

TIME PERIOD
Recent History

THEME
War

COMPLEXITY
Medium

SIMILAR GAMES

Call of Duty 3
Hour of Victory
Battlefield 1942

RATING & MULTIPLAYER

USA	Europe	Network	Offline
		4 Players	No

Medal of Honor
AIRBORNE

SETTING

Follow Private Boyd Travers, a U.S. paratrooper in the 82nd Airborne Division, as he takes on the enemy at famous airborne operations during World War II, such as Operation Market Garden and Operation Overlord.

GAME SUMMARY

Medal of Honor: Airborne features an innovative way of interacting with the game's missions. In each mission, you drop out of a C-47 with the ability to control where on the field you would like to land. Therefore, you can land wherever you like, giving you a nonlinear experience from the beginning. The game also features a wide range of customizable weapons from Thomson machine guns to pistols. The game is free roaming and field modifications remain persistent throughout the game. If an enemy throws a grenade in your direction, you can kick it back to him. The game progresses when you complete a series of objectives. Airborne also features an online multiplayer mode, where you can play as either the allied or Axis forces.

CHALLENGES & HINTS

You have to think strategically about where you want to land. If you land on a rooftop, you can do the mission in stealth with a sniper rifle. If you land near an enemy stronghold, however, you might have a hard time finding cover and getting the upper hand.

KEY GAMEPLAY ELEMENTS

Attack/Fight
Steer/Maneuver
Tactics/Plan

GAME WORLD SIZE	Large
YOUR ROLE	Paratrooper
REPLAY VALUE	Once or Twice

AVERAGE SCORE

7.2

out of 10

Data and images may vary on the various platforms

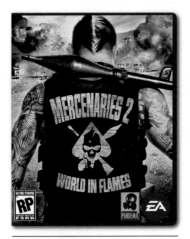

AVAILABLE ON

Nintendo DS
Nintendo Wii
✓ PC Windows
PC Mac
✓ Playstation 2
✓ Playstation 3
Playstation Portable
✓ Xbox 360

GAME FACTS *

PUBLISHER
Electronic Arts

DEVELOPER
Pandemic Studios

FIRST RELEASED
2007-11-27

GAME GENRE	**TIME PERIOD**
Action	Present
THEME	**COMPLEXITY**
Crime	Medium

SIMILAR GAMES

Army of Two
Tom Clancy's Splinter Cell Double Agent
Hitman: Blood Money

RATING & MULTIPLAYER

USA	Europe	Network	Offline
		Yes	No

Mercenaries 2
WORLD IN FLAMES

SETTING
After taking a mission from Ramon Solano, who has connections with the Venezuelan drug trade as well as the military, you have helped him come to power. But when he refuses to reward you for your efforts, you set out on a mission of payback.

GAME SUMMARY
The tyrant Solano has caused chaos in Venezuela's oil supply, thereby transforming the entire country into a war zone. To complete your primary mission of getting back at Solano, you will have to work through 40 lower targets, mainly fighting the Venezuelan army. This is done with the help of other politically powerful employers such as the Chinese, the Allied Nations, and the Peoples Liberation Army of Venezuela. How you complete your tasks is totally up to you. You have a wide array of weapons and all the freedom you want to move around and set fire to buildings, vehicles, and people. Everything is meant to be blown up, and it's up to you to choose between using a weapon to do it or to spill some oil and "casually" light a match. The game features a transit system that doesn't require direct transportation, although you may find it fun to latch on to flying vehicles or travel under water.

CHALLENGES & HINTS
If you run out of ammunition, weapons, or cash, there will always be opportunities for you to steal in the field. Remember that you are a mercenary. You play by nobody's rules but your own.

KEY GAMEPLAY ELEMENTS
Attack/Fight
Steer/Maneuver
Tactics/Plan

		AVERAGE SCORE
GAME WORLD SIZE	Medium	**NA**
YOUR ROLE	Mercenary	
REPLAY VALUE	Several Times	out of 10

Data and images may vary on the various platforms

Metroid Prime 3
CORRUPTION

SETTING

Six months have passed since the events on Aether. The Galactic Federation's Base Sector Zero is under attack and bounty hunters are called in to help. As Samus investigates, she and the others will be corrupted by the presumed dead Dark Samus.

GAME SUMMARY

As the Metroid Prime trilogy comes to an end, Samus has to fight alongside other bounty hunters to save the corrupted planets and, ultimately, herself. You set out to explore distant planets, search for information and upgrades, and destroy the Phazon seeds planted by Dark Samus and the Space Pirates. With the Wii remote, you can use the controller to open doors by pulling the locks out and twisting and sliding them back into place, which opens up new puzzle possibilities. You can even use the remote to manipulate Samus's grappling beam to pull doors and enemy shields out of the way. The Phazon corruption has a lot of power, power that can be harvested with the help of a PED unit, giving Samus new abilities to finish Dark Samus once and for all.

CHALLENGES & HINTS

Like the two previous games in the Metroid Prime series, puzzles are the key to advancing in this game. This edition gives you new puzzles that are both challenging and fun to solve. However, your main challenge will be to not abuse hypermode (the phazon power). Although hypermode gives you a lot of power, it also takes a large toll on your health.

AVAILABLE ON

Nintendo DS
✓ Nintendo Wii
PC Windows
PC Mac
Playstation 2
Playstation 3
Playstation Portable
Xbox 360

GAME FACTS

PUBLISHER
Nintendo

DEVELOPER
Retro Studios

FIRST RELEASED
2007-08-20

GAME GENRE	**TIME PERIOD**
Action	Future
THEME	**COMPLEXITY**
Sci-Fi	Medium

SIMILAR GAMES

Halo 3
Quake 4
Half Life 2

RATING & MULTIPLAYER

USA	Europe	Network	Offline
		No	No

KEY GAMEPLAY ELEMENTS

Steer/Maneuver
Attack/Fight
Gather

GAME WORLD SIZE	Large
YOUR ROLE	Heroine
REPLAY VALUE	Once or Twice

AVERAGE SCORE

9.0

out of 10

The area beyond this door is overrun with spent Phazon from the initial pirate invasion.

Ninja Gaiden Sigma

SETTING
Take the role of Ryu Hayabusa as he embarks on a path of vengeance on those who massacred his clan in this updated version of the classic Ninja Gaiden game.

GAME SUMMARY
Although the game is basically a remake of the original Ninja Gaiden game, the graphics have been vastly improved and new content has been added, including new combat moves, new weapons, and a new playable character, Rachel the Fiend Hunter. With the added possibility to play as her, you can play the game from her perspective and use new attacks made just for her. Throughout the game you have to fight against countless enemies and ultimately hard bosses. There are also certain objects that have to be collected in order to reach your goal. While fighting against ninjas, you can jump on them and attack surrounding ninjas from the air. Or you could do backflips off the wall and slice and dice them with your big katana.

CHALLENGES & HINTS
Don't think that you can get away with normal hack and slashing in this game. The bosses are hard to conquer and several enemies will attack you simultaneously. So use the environment to your advantage and hit from behind.

AVAILABLE ON
Nintendo DS
Nintendo Wii
PC Windows
PC Mac
Playstation 2
✓ Playstation 3
Playstation Portable
Xbox 360

GAME FACTS

PUBLISHER
Tecmo

DEVELOPER
Team Ninja

FIRST RELEASED
2007-07-03

GAME GENRE
Fighting

TIME PERIOD
Fantasy/Timeless

THEME
Fantasy

COMPLEXITY
Medium

SIMILAR GAMES
Genji: Days of the Blade
Heavenly Sword
Folklore

RATING & MULTIPLAYER

USA	Europe	Network	Offline
	18+ www.pegi.info	Yes	No

KEY GAMEPLAY ELEMENTS
Attack/Fight
Steer/Maneuver
Gather

GAME WORLD SIZE	Large
YOUR ROLE	Ninja
REPLAY VALUE	Once or Twice

AVERAGE SCORE

8.8

out of 10

so your father is still in the sacred wilderness,

Master Ryu...

AVAILABLE ON

Nintendo DS
Nintendo Wii
✓ PC Windows
PC Mac
Playstation 2
Playstation 3
Playstation Portable
✓ Xbox 360

GAME FACTS *

PUBLISHER
Codemasters

DEVELOPER
Triumph Studios

FIRST RELEASED
2007-06-26

GAME GENRE	**TIME PERIOD**
Action	Medieval
THEME	**COMPLEXITY**
War	High

SIMILAR GAMES

Two Worlds
Prince of Persia: The Sands of Time
Beyond Good & Evil

RATING & MULTIPLAYER

USA	Europe	Network	Offline
		2 Players	Yes

Overlord

SETTING

Take control of a resurrected mysterious figure that has inherited the legacy of the Overlord and wants to rebuild his evil empire. This Tolkien-inspired game engrosses players in its story of fantasy and mystery.

GAME SUMMARY

Your kingdom is in ruins and so is your dark tower, but after being brought back to life by your minions, your hunger for power and evil is growing. The main strategy in Overlord is to use your minions to do your dirty work. Although you are capable of performing magic and managing attacks alone, you can control your minion's actions, which saves you precious energy. They follow you around attentively, and as soon as you point in one direction, they perform the appropriate action such as attacking an enemy, collecting weapons and armor, or retrieving valuable items. Depending on their color, your minions have special abilities to perform various tasks. Every time you eliminate an enemy, they leave behind a piece of life essence that you use to bring yourself back to life and summon more minions to your command. The story is linear but the quests are entertaining.

CHALLENGES & HINTS

The different environments you encounter on your quest are very specific, so be sure to use the right minion for each task. And keep a cool head during fights against halflings, elves, and dwarves.

KEY GAMEPLAY ELEMENTS
Attack/Fight
Steer/Maneuver
Build & Design

GAME WORLD SIZE	Large
YOUR ROLE	Evil War Lord
REPLAY VALUE	Once or Twice

AVERAGE SCORE

7.7

out of 10

Data and images may vary on the various platforms

AVAILABLE ON

Nintendo DS
Nintendo Wii
PC Windows
PC Mac
Playstation 2
✓ Playstation 3
Playstation Portable
Xbox 360

GAME FACTS

PUBLISHER
SCEA, SCEE

DEVELOPER
Insomniac Games

FIRST RELEASED
2007-10-30

GAME GENRE
Action

TIME PERIOD
Future

THEME
Fantasy

COMPLEXITY
Medium

SIMILAR GAMES

Ratchet and Clank: Size Matters
Gradius Collection
Daxter

RATING & MULTIPLAYER

USA	Europe	Network	Offline
EVERYONE 10+ E CONTENT RATED BY ESRB	NOT RATED www.pegi.info	No	No

Ratchet & Clank Future
TOOLS OF DESTRUCTION

SETTING

Ratchet and Clank once again find themselves facing galactic danger. This time around, they have to track down the evil Emperor Percival Tachyon to stop him from annihilating the Lombaxes, which happen to be Ratchet's own family.

GAME SUMMARY

To find out just why the Emperor is so bent on destroying the Lombaxes, Ratchet and Clank set out on a journey that leads to a great deal of self-discovery while they explore vast worlds throughout the galaxy. On their way, our heroes come across enemies that range from local wildlife to enemies on missions for the evil Emperor. However, these enemies should be no problem to defeat considering the wide arsenal of entertaining weapons available. These include multitargeting homing rockets, death springs that hone in on your enemies, and even a combat device called the Groovitron that forces the enemy to dance to 70s disco hits. All your armor can be upgraded. Ratchet even has a spaceship that can travel through millions of asteroids while it annihilates the enemy.

CHALLENGES & HINTS

To get the most out of this game, it is recommended that you use all of the gadgets at your disposal so that Ratchet can bounce, fly, and redefine gravity. The light atmosphere of old-school comedy makes overcoming the enemy thoroughly enjoyable.

KEY GAMEPLAY ELEMENTS

Attack/Fight
Steer/Maneuver
Gather

GAME WORLD SIZE	Large
YOUR ROLE	Hero
REPLAY VALUE	Once or Twice

AVERAGE SCORE

9.3

out of 10

Lombax Ruins

AVAILABLE ON

Nintendo DS
Nintendo Wii
PC Windows
PC Mac
Playstation 2
✓ Playstation 3
Playstation Portable
Xbox 360

GAME FACTS

PUBLISHER
SCEA, SCEE

DEVELOPER
Insomniac Games

FIRST RELEASED
2006-11-13

GAME GENRE	**TIME PERIOD**
Action	Recent History
THEME	**COMPLEXITY**
Sci-Fi	Medium

SIMILAR GAMES

The Darkness
BlackSite: Area 51
F.E.A.R.

RATING & MULTIPLAYER

USA	Europe	Network	Offline
		40 Players	4 Players

Resistance
FALL OF MAN

SETTING

It's the year 1951 and the Chimera race has attacked without warning, moving like a tidal wave from Russia across Europe. They infect everything and anything that comes in their way, transforming humans into monsters. Humanity's only hope is Lieutenant Nathan Hale and the American army.

GAME SUMMARY

Instead of World War II, this world faces a much larger threat—the Chimera virus that transforms humans into monsters. In a short period of time, the Chimera race has occupied Russia and most of Europe. Great Britain is next. You play Lieutenant Nathan Hale from the U.S. who has been assigned to fight alongside the British against the Chimera. In an intense fight between man and virus, you battle your way through multiple cities. Gradually, you acquire more information on this unknown threat and get access to more effective weapons. However, while fighting off the Chimera virus, you become infected, too. Will you be able to save yourself and your allies before it's too late? The game allows you to complete the missions with the help of friends or to fight against others.

CHALLENGES & HINTS

With such a wide selection of weapons, you would assume you are safe, but when the monsters are intelligent and appear from out of nowhere, you are anything but!

KEY GAMEPLAY ELEMENTS

Attack/Fight
Steer/Maneuver
Gather

		AVERAGE SCORE
GAME WORLD SIZE	Large	
YOUR ROLE	Hero	**8.7**
REPLAY VALUE	Once or Twice	out of 10

Full health

Rossmore 236 Ammo Full

Picked up 2 40mm grenades
M5A2 Carbine Ammo Full

Defend the bus depot.

S.T.A.L.K.E.R.
SHADOW OF CHERNOBYL

SETTING

The game takes place in a quarantined area surrounding the nuclear power plant at Chernobyl, Ukraine, which exploded a couple decades ago. Referred to as the Zone, the area has a strange anomalous energy that causes Stalkers like you to enter the area in search of artifacts, technology, and information.

GAME SUMMARY

As a first-person shooter suffering from amnesia, you venture through the bleak atmosphere of the Zone and follow an impressively nonlinear storyline. The military knows you as the Marked One. To other characters, you are simply a threat, and most will not hesitate to lunge at you from out of nowhere. Your main concerns are your rifle skills and collecting enough weapons, ammunition, and medical kits from fallen enemies. You need these to fight off the various human and nonhuman creatures that you encounter. You have a wide arsenal of weapons at your disposal, but you are also restricted to what you can carry by weight. While exploring the vast 30-square-kilometer Zone, you encounter a wide array of potential allies and enemies and an authentic and constantly evolving world. The postapocalyptic setting makes for the dark atmosphere of S.T.A.L.K.E.R.

CHALLENGES & HINTS

Keep in mind that your ultimate task is to figure out who you are, and that it is your thirst for knowledge that leads you through the Zone. Also remember that a Stalker is a thief and that people are out to get you. Be judicious when selecting weapons, use the surrounding terrain as cover, but don't hesitate to engage in combat in order to gain supplies and ammo.

AVAILABLE ON

Nintendo DS
Nintendo Wii
✓ PC Windows
PC Mac
Playstation 2
Playstation 3
Playstation Portable
Xbox 360

GAME FACTS

PUBLISHER
THQ

DEVELOPER
GSC

FIRST RELEASED
2007-03-20

GAME GENRE	**TIME PERIOD**
Shooter	Present
THEME	**COMPLEXITY**
War	Medium

SIMILAR GAMES

Enemy Territory: Quake Wars
BioShock
Gears of War

RATING & MULTIPLAYER

USA	Europe	Network	Offline
	16+ www.pegi.info	16 Players	No

KEY GAMEPLAY ELEMENTS
Attack/Fight
Steer/Maneuver
Gather

GAME WORLD SIZE	Medium
YOUR ROLE	Protagonist
REPLAY VALUE	Once or Twice

AVERAGE SCORE

8.1
out of 10

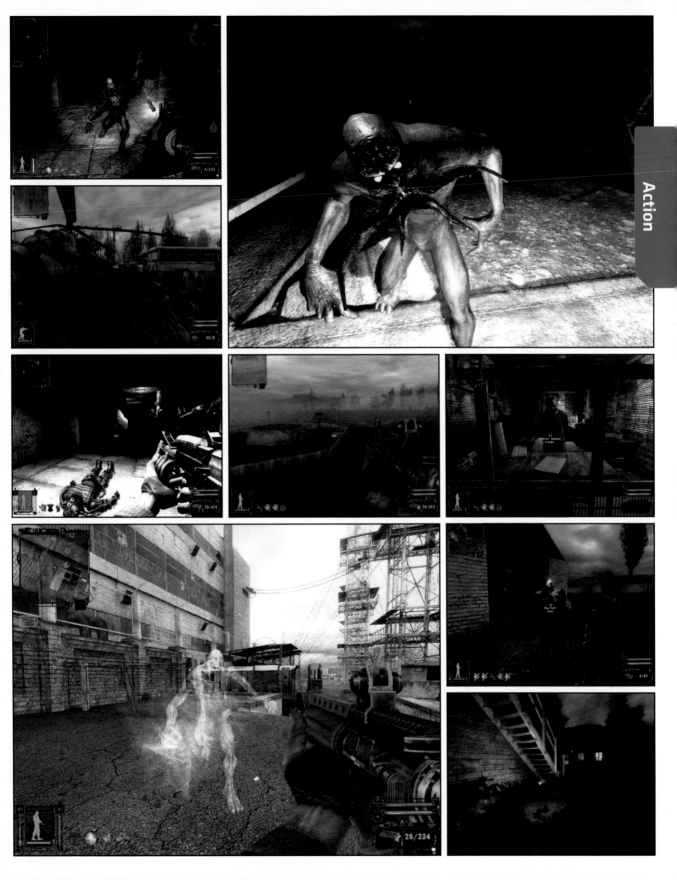

AVAILABLE ON

Nintendo DS
Nintendo Wii
✓ PC Windows
PC Mac
Playstation 2
✓ Playstation 3
Playstation Portable
✓ Xbox 360

GAME FACTS *

PUBLISHER
Midway

DEVELOPER
Midway

FIRST RELEASED
2007-09-07

GAME GENRE	**TIME PERIOD**
Shooter	Present
THEME	**COMPLEXITY**
Crime	Medium

SIMILAR GAMES

Max Payne 2: The Fall of Max Payne
Dead to Rights
The Club

RATING & MULTIPLAYER

USA	Europe	Network	Offline
		6 Players	No

Stranglehold

SETTING

Your name is Chow Yun-Fat, but you go by the name of Inspector Tequila. Working for the Hong Kong police in a constant battle against the crime gangs of the city, your personal life is all of a sudden pulled into the action.

GAME SUMMARY

One of the many criminal gangs of Hong Kong has kidnapped your former girlfriend and your daughter, which heavily interferes with your police work. You are faced with moral and ethical questions regarding how you intend to deal with the dramatic situation, but the storyline is just the backdrop for the incredible amount of fighting and shooting you engage in. Toward the end of the game, the body count is through the roof. On your mission to save your family, enemies attack you from every corner, and shots are fired quite casually. One of the best features of the game is Tequila's ability to interact with everything around him whether it's a building, table, or rail. This provides for open gameplay as the physics adapts to the way in which each gamer chooses to play. Tequila can dive and jump, ultimately filling up a Tequila bomb that allows you to do everything from recharge your health to pulling off stylish yet lethal moves on the enemy.

CHALLENGES & HINTS

What's great about Stranglehold is that the guns are so unrealistic that anything is possible. You can kill a guy from a hundred feet away with one bullet from a shotgun. This game is perfect for those who enjoy a flexible game where destructibility reigns supreme.

KEY GAMEPLAY ELEMENTS

Attack/Fight
Steer/Maneuver
Tactics/Plan

		AVERAGE SCORE
GAME WORLD SIZE	Medium	
YOUR ROLE	Hero	**7.5**
REPLAY VALUE	Once or Twice	out of 10

Data and images may vary on the various platforms

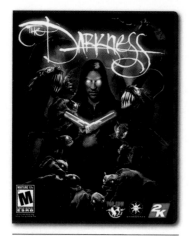

AVAILABLE ON

Nintendo DS
Nintendo Wii
PC Windows
PC Mac
Playstation 2
✓ Playstation 3
Playstation Portable
✓ Xbox 360

GAME FACTS *

PUBLISHER
2K Games

DEVELOPER
Starbreeze Studios

FIRST RELEASED
2007-06-25

GAME GENRE
Action

TIME PERIOD
Present

THEME
Horror/Thriller

COMPLEXITY
Medium

SIMILAR GAMES

F.E.A.R.
Gears of War
Far Cry Instincts Predator

RATING & MULTIPLAYER

USA	Europe	Network	Offline
		8 Players	No

The Darkness

SETTING

In this first-person shooter you play the fearless hit man Jackie Estacado, who is betrayed by his mafia family's head Paulie. Jackie seeks to overthrow his boss but is suddenly possessed by a terrifying and evil force called the Darkness.

GAME SUMMARY

Along Jackie's path of revenge, the Darkness grants him with different helpful but horrific abilities, like razor-sharp tentacles and wicked minions. These can be upgraded as you devour the hearts of fallen enemies. Even though these powers almost make Jackie unbeatable in combat, they wither in the light. For that reason, it's necessary to get rid of light bulbs and hide in the dark. When the Darkness is at its peak, the surrounding tentacles glow, which indicates that you are capable of unleashing its full power. By using the city's subways, Jackie can freely explore the gritty streets of New York, including Chinatown, the harbor, and Little Italy. The Darkness offers atmospheric and dark, gory visuals, which balance the slightly slow pace of the gameplay.

CHALLENGES & HINTS

It's often unclear when your Darkness powers are fading, so make sure to stay in the shade while in combat. The horrifically charming minions, called the Darklings, are often necessary to get by certain obstacles. Just keep in mind that they, too, are useless in lit environments.

KEY GAMEPLAY ELEMENTS

Attack/Fight
Steer/Maneuver
Gather

		AVERAGE SCORE
GAME WORLD SIZE	Medium	**8.2**
YOUR ROLE	Hitman	
REPLAY VALUE	Once or Twice	out of 10

Data and images may vary on the various platforms

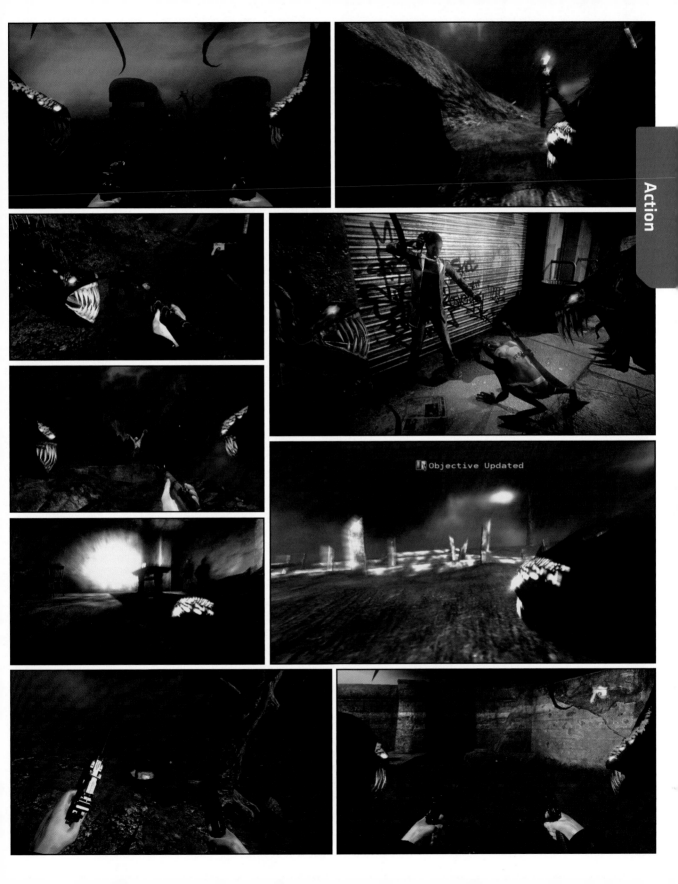

Objective Updated

TimeShift

SETTING

Set in a future ruled by a madman, the story follows Michael Swift, a scientist who was sent back in time and has come back to the present only to discover that the world he knew has become unrecognizable. The atmosphere of this engrossing storyline is very grim, putting the very existence of human life into question as it posits that the future we know may never occur.

GAME SUMMARY

As Swift returns to the lost futuristic world, he must figure out who is behind this dramatic change and try to set things straight. Your task soon develops into a fierce mechanical war. Although you are equipped with weapons such as machine guns and grenade launchers, your main weapon will be your Quantum Suit, which allows you to defy time itself. Join the secret police in the rebellion against the wicked ruler. Your AI suit automatically adapts according to the situation by slowing, stopping, or reversing time. Grenades can be used to freeze the enemy in four or five seconds as you fire shots in his or her direction. These grenades are manufactured by your suit according to how much time energy you've acquired, which also determines how fast the grenades react and how well they work. You'll be able to play your way through death matches, capture the flag, and a countdown mode.

CHALLENGES & HINTS

To fully experience this game, take on the 35 different combat missions. Take time to get used to the grenades and how they function with regard to radius and distance, as they will be your primary weapon against the deadly war machines of the enemy.

AVAILABLE ON

Nintendo DS
Nintendo Wii
✓ PC Windows
PC Mac
Playstation 2
✓ Playstation 3
Playstation Portable
✓ Xbox 360

GAME FACTS *

PUBLISHER
Sierra Entertainment

DEVELOPER
Saber Interactive

FIRST RELEASED
2007-10-30

GAME GENRE	**TIME PERIOD**
Shooter	Multiple/Timetravel
THEME	**COMPLEXITY**
Sci-Fi	Medium

SIMILAR GAMES

Gears of War
The Orange Box
BioShock

RATING & MULTIPLAYER

USA	Europe	Network	Offline
	18+ www.pegi.info	16 Players	No

KEY GAMEPLAY ELEMENTS

Attack/Fight
Steer/Maneuver
Gather

GAME WORLD SIZE	Large
YOUR ROLE	Hero
REPLAY VALUE	Once or Twice

AVERAGE SCORE

NA

out of 10

Data and images may vary on the various platforms

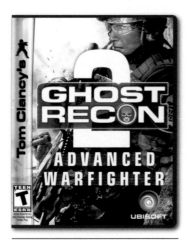

Tom Clancy's Ghost Recon
ADVANCED WARFIGHTER 2

SETTING

The year is 2014 and 48 hours have past since the events in Tom Clancy's Ghost Recon Advanced Warfighter. The civil war taking place in Mexico has escalated to such a level that there is now a threat to the U.S. The game takes place at the U.S.-Mexico border, where a Mexican rebel group has caused a lot of unrest.

GAME SUMMARY

This game has many of the same gameplay elements of the original, but there are a variety of new and improved features, such as the cross-com system that gives you a full screen view of what your team is looking at. There are a range of weapons to choose from, such as the MP5A3 and SCAR-H. The game's AI has been improved, which helps your team seek cover when needed and call out accurate enemy positions like "enemy spotted behind red truck ahead." The game also has more support abilities so that you can call in air strikes and gun support from the Apache helicopters and more. You can now also heal your teammates during battle with new medics.

CHALLENGES & HINTS

This is the perfect time for you to show your tactical abilities on the battlefield. But be careful because even though your teammates have become smarter, so has the enemy. And when bombs start to fall, keeping track of where your friends and foes are can become a serious challenge.

AVAILABLE ON

Nintendo DS
Nintendo Wii
✓ PC Windows
PC Mac
Playstation 2
✓ Playstation 3
✓ Playstation Portable
✓ Xbox 360

GAME FACTS *

PUBLISHER
Ubisoft

DEVELOPER
Grin, Ubisoft

FIRST RELEASED
2007-03-06

GAME GENRE	**TIME PERIOD**
Shooter	Present
THEME	**COMPLEXITY**
War	Medium

SIMILAR GAMES

Battlefield 2
Tom Clancy's Rainbow Six: Vegas
America's Army

RATING & MULTIPLAYER

USA	Europe	Network	Offline
		Yes	Yes

KEY GAMEPLAY ELEMENTS

Attack/Fight
Steer/Maneuver
Tactics/Plan

		AVERAGE SCORE
GAME WORLD SIZE	Large	**8.8**
YOUR ROLE	Ghost Recon Soldier	
REPLAY VALUE	Once or Twice	out of 10

Data and images may vary on the various platforms

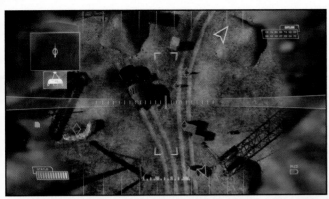

Tom Clancy's Rainbow Six
VEGAS

SETTING
Who do you call when one of the world's most famous cities is under hostage by terrorists? Rainbow Six, of course! The famous counterterrorist group is back, this time to win back control of Las Vegas. At your disposal are more than 40 real-life weapons including assault rifles, tactical explosives, and handguns, all of which give you a wide and varied experience.

GAME SUMMARY
Las Vegas is under attack by terrorists and you are called in to hunt them down. Rainbow Six: Vegas comes with a variety of new features such as the ability to regenerate health when you are not under fire. It doesn't work quickly, though, so you have to be speedy in seeking cover as one or two shots can send you to an early grave. With a new command system, you can order your men to do specific things, such as scale a wall and drop explosives. And with added help from the snake-cam, you can pinpoint targets so that your team can neutralize the enemy with ease. Your teammates will now come with intelligent real-time tactical suggestions, such as hacking computers and bringing down doors.

CHALLENGES & HINTS
This game is very realistic, so you will not be able to withstand a barrage of bullets before you're actually "hurt." If you are hit once or twice in the right spots, you will be dead. So be sure to get those terrorists before they get you!

AVAILABLE ON

Nintendo DS
Nintendo Wii
✓ PC Windows
PC Mac
Playstation 2
✓ Playstation 3
✓ Playstation Portable
✓ Xbox 360

GAME FACTS *

PUBLISHER
Ubisoft

DEVELOPER
Ubisoft

FIRST RELEASED
2006-11-20

GAME GENRE	**TIME PERIOD**
Action	Present
THEME	**COMPLEXITY**
Crime	Medium

SIMILAR GAMES

Call of Duty 4: Modern Warfare
Battlefield 2: Modern Combat
Tom Clancy's Ghost Recon A.W 2

RATING & MULTIPLAYER

USA	Europe	Network	Offline
		16 Players	Yes

KEY GAMEPLAY ELEMENTS

Tactics/Plan
Attack/Fight
Steer/Maneuver

GAME WORLD SIZE	Large
YOUR ROLE	Rainbow Team Leader
REPLAY VALUE	Once or Twice

AVERAGE SCORE

8.9
out of 10

Data and images may vary on the various platforms

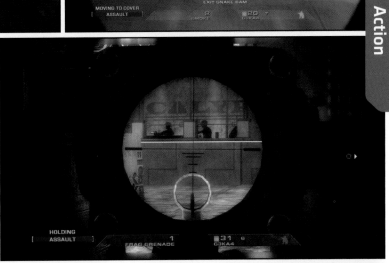

AVAILABLE ON

Nintendo DS
✓ Nintendo Wii
✓ PC Windows
PC Mac
✓ Playstation 2
Playstation 3
✓ Playstation Portable
✓ Xbox 360

GAME FACTS *

PUBLISHER
Eidos Interactive

DEVELOPER
Crystal Dynamics

FIRST RELEASED
2007-06-01

GAME GENRE	TIME PERIOD
Action	Present
THEME	**COMPLEXITY**
Adventure	Low

SIMILAR GAMES

Prince of Persia: The Two Thrones
Tom Clancy's Splinter Cell
Tomb Raider: Legends

RATING & MULTIPLAYER

USA	Europe	Network	Offline
		No	Yes

Tomb Raider
ANNIVERSARY

SETTING

Celebrate the 10th anniversary of Lara and the original Tomb Raider game, which brought the 3D action-adventure genre to a new level. Take on the role of Lara Croft, the world's sexiest female action hero, on a mission to find the secret of the mysterious Scion of Atlantis.

GAME SUMMARY

Using an updated version of the famous Tomb Raider Legend game engine, this edition brings improved graphics and new features to the classic game. Go back to the roots of Tomb Raider, but take on new and exciting missions. Explore the ancient tombs and cities of Egypt, Greece, and Peru with new moves and equipment to fight off your enemies. Packed with secrets and puzzles, you must use your brains to progress through the game. A lot of the puzzles force you to maneuver acrobatically across obstacles in order to proceed to the next stage. Although parts of the game might give you déjà vu, the maps and puzzles have been elaborated upon greatly, so it's like playing a totally new game. Lara is in better shape than ever, and you can make her perform almost any move you want. Bring on the bloodthirsty bears and wolves created with improved AI—Lara is prepared! But more importantly, are you?

CHALLENGES & HINTS

Even though Lara is fit for a fight, her faith lies in your hands. Precision and timing is essential when you jump from one ledge to another. Otherwise, Lara may cease to exist, and what a shame that would be!

KEY GAMEPLAY ELEMENTS

Steer/Maneuver
Tactics/Plan
Attack/Fight

GAME WORLD SIZE	Large
YOUR ROLE	Heroine
REPLAY VALUE	Once or Twice

AVERAGE SCORE

8.4

out of 10

Data and images may vary on the various platforms

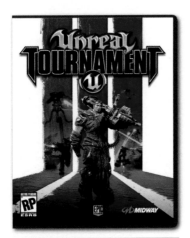

AVAILABLE ON

Nintendo DS
Nintendo Wii
✓ PC Windows
PC Mac
Playstation 2
✓ Playstation 3
Playstation Portable
✓ Xbox 360

GAME FACTS *

PUBLISHER
Midway

DEVELOPER
Epic Games

FIRST RELEASED
TBA

GAME GENRE	**TIME PERIOD**
Shooter	Future
THEME	**COMPLEXITY**
Sci-Fi	Medium

SIMILAR GAMES

Gears of War
BioShock
Halo 3

RATING & MULTIPLAYER

USA	Europe	Network	Offline
		Yes	Yes

Unreal Tournament III

SETTING

Prepare for intense action and fierce battles in this first-person sci-fi shooter where you play a futuristic warrior. Fight alongside the remainder of your clan that was slaughtered by the invading Necris in an epic battle that takes place on an immense ice-blasted coastland.

GAME SUMMARY

The game features an expanded single-player campaign as well as online multiplayer battles. Through various game modes including Deathmatch, Team Deathmatch, Capture the Flag, and a new Warfare mode, you engage in contests of intense shooting against your enemy that are controlled either by other players online of by AI. You have more than two dozen weapons that are upgraded for maximum destruction potential. Use the Link Gun to blow up the enemy at a distance or the Bio Rifle to destroy something at close range. You can even open your guns to see how they are built. There is also a possibility of battling in vehicles. The Dark Walker is loaded with weapons that can blast anything even if it doesn't hit the target directly. Move across the 40 maps via hoverboard—an antigravity transportation vehicle that moves three times faster than a human can. UT3 even has features catering to the mod community, including a Tool Kit for a mod system.

CHALLENGES & HINTS

Use your massive Leviathan vehicle to destroy areas on the map and remember to create obstacles for your enemy as you go. You can also use your hoverboard, but the enemy can easily stun your board, making you vulnerable to attack. The Walker can be effective, but remember that it can be a huge target as it releases a large power up if destroyed.

KEY GAMEPLAY ELEMENTS

Attack/Fight
Steer/Maneuver
Tactics/Plan

GAME WORLD SIZE	Large	
YOUR ROLE	Hero	
REPLAY VALUE	Several Times	

AVERAGE SCORE

NA

out of 10

Data and images may vary on the various platforms

WarHawk

SETTING

Warhawk is the biggest and most intense aerial combat game this season with an enormous arsenal of weapons and armor. Your task is to defend your territory from the invading Chernovan armada.

GAME SUMMARY

Fight a war both on the ground and in the skies using the deadliest modern weapons. Attacks come from everywhere in this fight to defend your homeland—and there is nowhere to hide. Warhawk gameplay is based on capturing enemy bases and, from there, spawning to gain points. Death matches, capture the flag, and zone modes are all thrilling ways to experience the destruction of futuristic warfare. As a player, you can take control fighter pilots and ground troop commanders, while high-tech vehicles equipped with maps provide you with the exact locations of target bases. The aircraft circling overhead are of tactical use when launching attacks alongside ground troops. And you can take a step back to follow your own progress. As you accomplish tasks, you are rewarded with badges and medals based on your overall counts.

CHALLENGES & HINTS

Turrets can be found and used in defense against attacking aircraft overhead but are not very useful in defense against vehicles. Ground troops will benefit more from using weapons such as the rocket launcher to destroy tanks.

AVAILABLE ON

Nintendo DS
Nintendo Wii
PC Windows
PC Mac
Playstation 2
✓ Playstation 3
Playstation Portable
Xbox 360

GAME FACTS

PUBLISHER
SCEA, SCEE

DEVELOPER
Incognito Entertainment

FIRST RELEASED
2007-08-28

GAME GENRE	**TIME PERIOD**
Shooter	Recent History
THEME	**COMPLEXITY**
War	Medium

SIMILAR GAMES

Blazing Angels 2: Secret Missions of WWII
Armored Core 4
Chromehounds

RATING & MULTIPLAYER

USA	Europe	Network	Offline
TEEN T ESRB	16+ www.pegi.info	32 Players	4 Players

KEY GAMEPLAY ELEMENTS

Steer/Maneuver
Attack/Fight
Tactics/Plan

GAME WORLD SIZE	Large
YOUR ROLE	Various
REPLAY VALUE	Several Times

AVERAGE SCORE

8.7

out of 10

Adventure GAMES

An interview with Al Lowe

What defines adventure games, back in the early days, now and in the future?

The early days were defined by a strict set of rules that had to do with finding and manipu-lating objects, discovering their owners, who were interested in them, and swapping them for something else -- working puzzles like that. That to me defined adventure games. There was a lot of conversation; RPG's quickly picked up on that, but object manipulation was a big part of adventure games.

In the middle period, adventure games became a storytelling device. They were the games that had the plot, which had character definition and character development, because they had the time to do so. Adventure games took time to cover a limited environment. Unlike racing games and action games where you have replayability, adventure games had to milk their gameplay out of an environment the first time through because, as we discovered, very few people went back to replay them. In the heydays, around 1990, there were so many adventure games coming out that it was a rare person who went back

"..how it would be wonderful if 10% of American homes had a computer..."

-Al Lowe

and said, "Oh, I think I can better my score. I'll go back and play the game again."

Now many people play the games again because they want a deeper experience and frankly because there is such a dearth of new games available now.

The future is more difficult. My feeling hasn't really changed in the 10 years since I retired. I believe the adventure game was the perfect game for the 80s. It required typing, as did DOS. It required puzzle solving, as did all programs then. But primarily, just to get your computer up and running in the early 80s, you had to be a puzzle solver, you had to enjoy logic problems, because that's what it took to get it running. I remember clearly one conversation that I had with Ken Williams at Sierra. We were talking about how it would be wonderful if 10% of American homes had a computer which of course is laughable today, but we thought this would be great because our sales would soar. We never even dreamed to say

DEVELOPER: AL LOWE

Al Lowe (61), also known as "the world's oldest computer games designer," has been a vital member of the Sierra On-line design team. As the first retired game designer we know of, he is most famous for creating the popular Leisure Suit Larry adventure-series. Lowe is a self-taught programmer with a background in teaching high school music. In 1982 he developed his first three games for Apple II that was eventually bought by Sierra On-Line in 1982. From there, he helped create Disney-based games such as Winnie the Pooh in the 100 Acre Woods, Donald Duck's Playground and The Black Cauldron. He was given the role of lead programmer on King's Quest III and Police Quest I in 1987 and, after the hugely successful Leisure Suit Larry series, he also managed to design Torin's Passage and Freddy Pharkas Frontier Pharmacist. In his long career of game design, Lowe has influenced over two dozen Sierra game titles. Over the many years that Lowe dedicated to gaming, his contribution to the world of game design has been and continues to be very prominent and humorous.

LEISURE SUIT LARRY IN THE LAND OF THE LOUNGE LIZARDS

Land of the Lounge Lizards was the first ever game where you played as Larry Laffer, a 40-year old virgin who basically was looking for a good time with the woman of his dreams. Based on the title "Softporn Adventure", released years earlier by Sierra, Al Lowe started to add his own sense of style and humour to the title. Most famous however, the on-screen protagonist, Larry. Throughout the game Larry has to keep track on money spent and solve puzzles in order to get what he wants... sex.

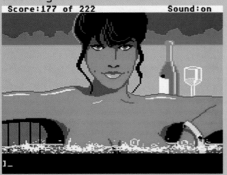

half of the homes. And yet we are well beyond that now. But what we found was that, as the number of computer owners went up, their IQ level went down. I don't mean that as an insult, just that an average person with an average intelligence just

"..But what we found was that, as the number of computer owners went up, their IQ level went down...."

-Al Lowe

could not possibly use a computer back in those days. Or, if you had average intelligence you would need to have extreme perseverance (out the arse). The history comes from the fact that as the computer user became much more "normal," I think they wanted a more normal game experience. Most people don't subscribe to Games Magazine, or solve puzzles, or belong to MENSA, or play competitive chess. Therefore the kinds of games that appeal to a broad base of people became more prominent. I think there remains a niche market, more so in Europe than in America.

Yes, the last adventure game I played was Dreamfall by Funcom, but they recently announced that they would stop making single player games due to piracy.

Piracy is an interesting issue. For years I would copy software and give it to friends with the condition that, if you use the software, you have to buy a copy. That is only fair. I did so myself. But I don't think everybody has that same attitude. I know I was one of the first victims of piracy. I talked to a Russian software engineer in the late 80s, before the fall of the Soviet Union, and he said he had never seen a hard drive in Russia that didn't have a Larry subdirectory. [laughs] He said it was like it was a part of the operating system, like DOS. And of course we got no money for this.

Days after Larry 7 shipped, one of Sierra's sales representatives was in Moscow and saw it on the street for two dollars. They had completely over-dubbed all the voiceovers with Russian language; they had reverse engineered the text system, and changed it to Russian text. It was fantastic! I still have a copy here. When I saw it, I said "we should hire these guys! They should be working for us!".

Which of your games is your favorite and why?

My favorite is Leisure Suit 7: Love for Sail!, frankly because, by that time I felt that I had finally fig-ured out how to properly design a game. All the earlier games I'd done, I always felt "I hope no-body figures out that I don't know what I am doing." But by the time I got to Larry 7, I thought "I now know how this works." That is one reason. I also think it was the best design of the bunch. It has the best music and, as a musician and former music teacher, that was important to me. By that time, we could have real live musicians digitized and play that back while you were playing the game. I was also very pleased with the voiceovers. I was fortunate enough to go to Germany and France to record the French and German version as well, and I think our translators and voiceover directors did a good job with those – although since I don't speak the languages, I can't be sure.

Plus there were some subtleties to the game de-sign that people didn't realize until well along in the game such as the PA announcer on the ship, who you thought was just doing jokes and silly announce-ments but who eventually became a help giver, a

LEISURE SUIT LARRY GOES LOOKING FOR LOVE (IN SEVERAL WRONG PLACES)

After getting the girl of his dreams in the first Larry title, his girl, Eve gets cold feet and decides to leave him. Seeing the pos-sibility of more fish in the sea, Larry sets of to find a new woman. Almost by chance, he wins a cruise trip and a blind date; before Larry gets to go he discovers that the KGB is perusing him, as well as Dr. Nonookee. However, once Larry comes to the tropical island of Nontoonyt, he takes a shine to the daughter of the native leader.

LEISURE SUIT LARRY LOVE FOR SAIL

Like most of the Larry games, the game picks up where the previous one ended, with him being dumped. In Love for Sail Larry is a passenger on a cruise ship, where you will find loads of famous people. The plot is to compete in a weekly contest where you win another week stay on the ship, with Captain Thygh, a very attractive woman. Larry has to compete in many different mini-games ranging from bowling to checking his sexual expertise. Ultimately spending time with the Captain in her cabin... or bed.

subtle sort of help structure that watched where you were in the game and, if you weren't making progress, gave announcements that gave you clues you wouldn't hear otherwise. And eventually, at the end of the game, he played a key role in the plot. I was just most pleased with that game.

Did you have anything to do with Leisure Suit Larry Magna cum Laude?

I'm proud to say I had nothing to do with that game.

When that project first started I heard rumors from people who still worked at Sierra that the company was doing another Larry game. Frankly, I was surprised and hurt, because I had talked with them about doing another game myself. I said, "I would love to do it. I am 10 minutes away from your office – anytime you would like to talk, I can be there in 10 minutes." But I never heard from

"..I'm proud to say I had nothing to do with that game. ..."

-Al Lowe

anyone. When the game was first shown to Sierra at an in-house meeting, I got several phone calls from people who said: "Oh, Al you are going to be so disappointed with this game. It is terrible!" The game got such a bad reception in-house that the company went back to the developer and told them to throw out a year's worth of work and start all over. And they did; they threw out everything. At various times during that next year, I got phone calls from people who worked at Sierra, not anyone who was in charge, but people who said, "Can you help? This game sucks." I would respond "Sure, anytime. I'd be glad to." I finally got hold of somebody who had some authority and he tried to get me involved, but the more he dealt with management the more it was obvious that they didn't want to deal with me. They put restrictions on my involvement to the point where what they really wanted was to put my name on the box without me having any involvement.

In a way, it was flattering that the game was so bad. It proved that my games were more about funny than sexy. The line I used on my website was:

Playing the game was like receiving a video from your son's kidnappers, on one hand you are glad to see that he is still alive, but on the other O' my God look at what they have done to him!

You helped define this game genre almost from the start. What do you think is the main difference in development cycle from the first games until e.g. Torin's Passage and beyond that?

For the first Larry game I signed my contract in December and had written, programmed and created the music for the entire game by March, a three month cycle of development . Mark Crowe, the artist who worked with me on the game, was also working fulltime on Space Quest. They didn't have any other artist trained to use the software. So they told Mark if you do this game on weekends and evenings, we can't pay you, but we will give you a big piece of the action. He was a young kid, just out of high school, he said, "Yeah, Sure!" He worked one month of weekends and evenings, because he was working 40 hours a week on Space Quest. So our development cycles was 4 man-months total. Contrast that with Larry 7: over fifty people working on it for over a year.

We thank Al Lowe for this interview.

GAMES CREDITED AL LOWE

Publisher/Developer: Sierra On-Line, Inc.

1998: Leisure Suit Larry's Casino

1996: Leisure Suit Larry 7: Love for Sail!

1995: Torin's Passage

1994: Leisure Suit Larry 6: Shape Up or Slip Out!

1993: Freddy Pharkas: Frontier Pharmacist

1993: Leisure Suit Larry 6: Shape Up or Slip Out!

1991: Leisure Suit Larry 1: In the Land of the Lounge Lizards (VGA remake)

1991: Leisure Suit Larry 5: Passionate Patti Does a Little Undercover Work

1990: The Laffer Utilities

1989: Leisure Suit Larry 3: Passionate Patti in Pursuit of the Pulsating Pectorals

1988: Leisure Suit Larry Goes Looking for Love (In Several Wrong Places)

1988: King's Quest IV: The Perils of Rosella

1987: Space Quest II: Vohaul's Revenge

1987: Police Quest: In Pursuit of the Death Angel

1987: Leisure Suit Larry in the Land of the Lounge Lizards

1986: Donald Duck's Playground

1985: King's Quest III: To Heir is Human

1984: The Black Cauldron

1983: Mickey's Space Adventure

1983: King's Quest II: Romancing the Throne

1983: Winnie the Pooh in the Hundred Acre Wood

1983: A Gelfling Adventure

1982: Troll's Tale

1982: Bop-A-Bet

1982: Dragon's Keep

Castlevania
PORTRAIT OF RUIN

SETTING

In the second installment of Castlevania for the Nintendo DS, vampire hunters Jonathan Morris and Charlotte Orlean set out on a dangerous mission to stop vampire artist Brauner from executing his evil plans.

GAME SUMMARY

The evil vampire artist Brauner plans to exterminate all humans by using the powers of magical portraits from Dracula's castle, but Jonathan and Charlotte are determined to stop him. As the game begins, our two heroes are poorly equipped, but you will soon gain access to more powerful tools and develop new skills to fight the castle's monsters. Jonathan and Charlotte have their own sets of abilities which you can combine for more effective attacks. You can also freely switch between characters to maximize damage to certain enemies. Players have to explore many environments via the many paintings in the large castle, such as the City of Haze and the Forest of Doom. A map helps you keep track of the areas you have visited. The main campaign is single-player, but you can invite a friend to join in a separate boss-fighting mode or trade items with other players in shop mode.

CHALLENGES & HINTS

Taking out the various monsters requires that you make use of the best skills of both characters. Portrait of Ruin has alternate endings, depending on the actions you take throughout the game, so be sure to make the right decisions!

AVAILABLE ON

✓ Nintendo DS
  Nintendo Wii
  PC Windows
  PC Mac
  Playstation 2
  Playstation 3
  Playstation Portable
  Xbox 360

GAME FACTS

PUBLISHER
Konami Digital Entertainment

DEVELOPER
Konami

FIRST RELEASED
2006-12-05

GAME GENRE
Adventure

TIME PERIOD
Recent History

THEME
Horror/Thriller

COMPLEXITY
Medium

SIMILAR GAMES

New Super Mario Bros.
Sonic Rush Adventure
Yoshi's Island DS

RATING & MULTIPLAYER

USA	Europe	Network	Offline
		Yes	No

KEY GAMEPLAY ELEMENTS

Steer/Maneuver
Attack/Fight
Gather

GAME WORLD SIZE	Medium
YOUR ROLE	Vampire Killer
REPLAY VALUE	Once or Twice

AVERAGE SCORE

8.5

out of 10

Loretta

This wasn't the only one
of my father's paintings.

Medusa Head

2P   1P

Merman

Merman

Hotel Dusk
ROOM 215

SETTING
The place is Los Angeles, and the year is 1979. You take on the role of former police officer Kyle Hyde, who is now a salesman with an assignment to pick up a package at the Hotel Dusk. What happens next is much more than he bargained for!

GAME SUMMARY
Kyle Hyde's partner from his police days is missing and all the clues, coincidentally, point to the Hotel Dusk. Delve into this interactive thriller by holding the DS like a book and using the touch screen to search for clues, talk to hotel guests and staff, and solve puzzles that range from picking locks to removing a toilet's back lid. The game is visually atmospheric with its film noir feel, mature plot and dialog, and black-and-white hand-drawn characters. Except for the characters and the movement screen, the hotel is three-dimensional, making this game a visual tour de force.

CHALLENGES & HINTS
You can easily spend an hour trying to solve a puzzle or find the object needed to fix it. It's amazing how the smallest things, like a pen or a piece of wire, can become your biggest leads in your search for the truth.

AVAILABLE ON
✓ Nintendo DS
Nintendo Wii
PC Windows
PC Mac
Playstation 2
Playstation 3
Playstation Portable
Xbox 360

GAME FACTS
PUBLISHER
Nintendo

DEVELOPER
Cing

FIRST RELEASED
2007-01-22

GAME GENRE
Adventure

TIME PERIOD
Recent History

THEME
Crime

COMPLEXITY
Medium

SIMILAR GAMES
Trace Memory
Lost In Blue 2
Phoenix Wright: Trials and Tribulation

RATING & MULTIPLAYER

USA	Europe	Network	Offline
	12+ www.pegi.info	No	No

KEY GAMEPLAY ELEMENTS
Steer/Maneuver
Solve Puzzles
Gather

GAME WORLD SIZE	Medium
YOUR ROLE	Detective
REPLAY VALUE	Once or Twice

AVERAGE SCORE

7.8
out of 10

89th Precinct,
this is Hyde.

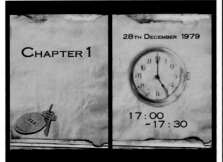

CHAPTER 1

28TH DECEMBER 1979

17:00
~17:30

Kyle
Huh. Cute sign, pal. Guess
that's where I check in.

Room 215

? I'm waiting for a pa...

? You had a guest wi...

? My room grants wis...

Kyle
I saw you standing alone by
the side of the road.

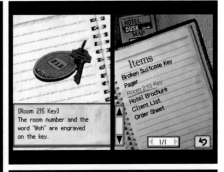

[Room 215 Key]
The room number and the
word "Wish" are engraved
on the key.

Items
Broken Suitcase Key
Pager
Room 215 Key
Hotel Brochure
Client List
Order Sheet

1/1

Rachel
Well, I wouldn't dream of
speaking for the boss, but I
trust you.

Adventure

Okami

SETTING

Based on a Japanese legend, in this game you control the sun god, Amaterasu, who appears in the shape of a white wolf. Your job is to bring color back into a darkened world with the power of a paintbrush.

GAME SUMMARY

As Amaterasu, your mission is to rid Japan of a curse cast by an eight-headed serpent that has been reborn. A conventional battle of good versus evil, the subplots of the story unfold through beautiful cut scenes. Apart from fighting the demonic creatures that are sucking the life out of Japan, you help villagers, prevent plagues, and rejuvenate the land to earn points that are spent improving Amaterasu's powers. Although not frequent, the combat is fast-paced and initiated by touching a floating talisman. You become more powerful as you develop your brushing techniques, which Amaterasu uses to defeat enemies. She can change night into day simply by painting a circle in the sky. Different techniques help you through the many puzzles and battles as you progress.

CHALLENGES & HINTS

Remember that Amaterasu's divine powers are what earn her experience points. Use them to bring color and therefore life back into Japan by helping people. With the faith of the people, Amaterasu become stronger, making it possible to defeat the evil serpent.

AVAILABLE ON

Nintendo DS
Nintendo Wii
PC Windows
PC Mac
✓ Playstation 2
Playstation 3
Playstation Portable
Xbox 360

GAME FACTS

PUBLISHER
Capcom

DEVELOPER
Clover Studio

FIRST RELEASED
2006-09-19

GAME GENRE
Adventure

TIME PERIOD
Fantasy/Timeless

THEME
Fantasy

COMPLEXITY
Medium

SIMILAR GAMES

Prince of Persia: The Sands of Time
Shadow of the Colossus
Onimusha: Dawn of Dreams

RATING & MULTIPLAYER

USA	Europe	Network	Offline
TEEN T CONTENT RATED BY ESRB	12+ www.pegi.info		
		No	No

KEY GAMEPLAY ELEMENTS

Attack/Fight
Explore
Steer/Maneuver

GAME WORLD SIZE	Medium
YOUR ROLE	Wolf
REPLAY VALUE	Several Times

AVERAGE SCORE

9.1

out of 10

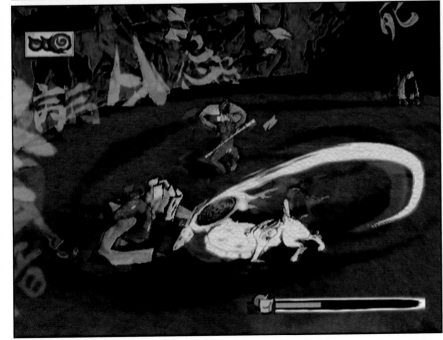

Sonic Rush Adventure

SETTING

Sonic and Tails are investigating a mysterious energy signal. As they set off in Tails's plane, a storm appears, and they lose control and crash into a remote island. There they encounter some pirates before Blaze, the cat, shows up! Why did she come back from her time plane? And who is behind all of these strange events?

GAME SUMMARY

Sonic is back for another 2D adventure on the DS, but like Sonic Rush, there are also 3D elements, such as during boss battles and sea travel. To get to the different islands, you have to plot out a course on the map for where you want to sail. This is also a great opportunity to collect rings and boost your gauge meter. There are seven different worlds to play, ranging from jungles to coral-themed worlds. And, like in most Sonic games, speed is the name of the game. In order to progress, you have to get to the end of the course as fast as possible with the most enemy kills and rings collected. The game also features network play where you can play with a friend and engage in racing and mission-based battles.

CHALLENGES & HINTS

Sonic is fast—really fast—so when you are shooting along the stage and going through loops, you have to make sure you stay focused because you might run into the enemy and get hurt. On top of that, you always have the challenge of beating yourself at your own game, like with speed records.

AVAILABLE ON

✓ Nintendo DS
Nintendo Wii
PC Windows
PC Mac
Playstation 2
Playstation 3
Playstation Portable
Xbox 360

GAME FACTS

PUBLISHER
Sega Europe, Sega of America

DEVELOPER
Dimps, Sonic Team

FIRST RELEASED
2007-09-14

GAME GENRE
Adventure

TIME PERIOD
Fantasy/Timeless

THEME
Fantasy

COMPLEXITY
Low

SIMILAR GAMES

Sonic Rush
New Super Mario Bros.
Yoshi's Island DS

RATING & MULTIPLAYER

USA	Europe	Network	Offline
		2 Players	No

KEY GAMEPLAY ELEMENTS

Steer/Maneuver
Gather
Attack/Fight

GAME WORLD SIZE	Medium
YOUR ROLE	Blue Hedgehog
REPLAY VALUE	Once or Twice

AVERAGE SCORE

8.0

out of 10

Super Mario Galaxy

AVAILABLE ON

Nintendo DS
✓ Nintendo Wii
PC Windows
PC Mac
Playstation 2
Playstation 3
Playstation Portable
Xbox 360

GAME FACTS

PUBLISHER
Nintendo

DEVELOPER
Nintendo

FIRST RELEASED
2007-11-12

GAME GENRE
Adventure

TIME PERIOD
Fantasy/Timeless

THEME
Fantasy

COMPLEXITY
Low

SIMILAR GAMES

NiGHTS: Journey of Dream
Super Mario 64 DS
Dewy's Adventure

RATING & MULTIPLAYER

USA	Europe	Network	Offline
		No	2 Players

SETTING
Princess Peach has been kidnapped by a strange creature and taken out to space, and Mario, being the hero that he is, goes after her while exploring the deepest corners of the galaxy.

GAME SUMMARY
Super Mario Galaxy features a gameplay style never seen before in a Mario game. As Mario travels through space he experiences many different gravitational shifts that have Mario running upside down, on the wall, or in the air. Like the previous 3D Mario games, you have to collect stars in order to progress through the six different areas. You control Mario with the Nunchuk controller and perform moves like spin attack by swinging the Wii remote. The game also features a multiplayer co-op mode, where the second player can pick up a controller and help Mario by stopping rolling boulders or collecting colored stars to shoot down enemies.

CHALLENGES & HINTS
This game is pretty big and has you traveling through almost 40 galaxies in six different areas to collect your 120 stars. On top of that, the new vivid gravities might set your head spinning.

KEY GAMEPLAY ELEMENTS

Steer/Maneuver
Attack/Fight
Explore

GAME WORLD SIZE Gigantic
YOUR ROLE Overweight Plumber
REPLAY VALUE Once or Twice

AVERAGE SCORE

NA

out of 10

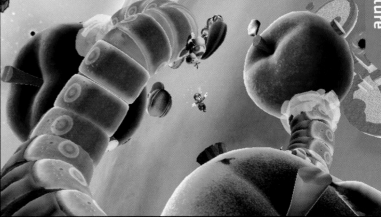

AVAILABLE ON

Nintendo DS
✓ Nintendo Wii
PC Windows
PC Mac
Playstation 2
Playstation 3
Playstation Portable
Xbox 360

GAME FACTS

PUBLISHER
Nintendo

DEVELOPER
Intelligent Systems

FIRST RELEASED
2007-04-09

GAME GENRE	**TIME PERIOD**
Adventure	Fantasy/Timeless
THEME	**COMPLEXITY**
Fantasy	Medium

SIMILAR GAMES

New Super mario bros.
Dewy's Adventure
Anubis II

RATING & MULTIPLAYER

USA	Europe	Network	Offline
		No	No

Super Paper Mario

SETTING

Paper Mario is back for a brand new role-playing adventure. Although he is in 2D, Mario has to leap across 3D worlds, solving puzzles and doing what Mario does best: saving princesses.

GAME SUMMARY

Princess Peach has been kidnapped (again!), and when Mario sets out to investigate, he finds out that the usual suspect, Bowser, has nothing to do with it. Instead, it's the evil Count Bleck. You can control the four main characters Mario, Luigi, Peach, and Bowser by turning the Wii remote on its side. Unlike the previous Paper Mario titles, this game does not feature a turn-based battle system but has kept the normal role-playing features such as experience points and shops from which you can buy improvements. There are a total of eight chapters to play in four different sections. After every defeated boss you collect Pure Hearts, which you use to unlock the door to the next level.

CHALLENGES & HINTS

As you progress though the game you will eventually get the possibility to transform 2D Mario into 3D Mario. However, in 3D form you will take more damage, so figuring out the right places to use it is key to your survival.

KEY GAMEPLAY ELEMENTS

Steer/Maneuver
Attack/Fight
Role Play

GAME WORLD SIZE	Medium
YOUR ROLE	Pixilated Plumber
REPLAY VALUE	Once or Twice

AVERAGE SCORE

8.4

out of 10

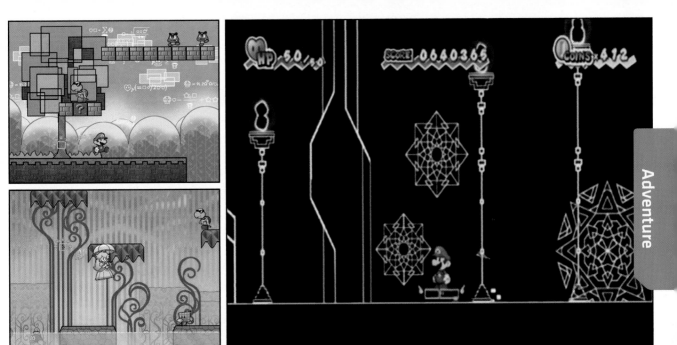

This room... There's something about this room...

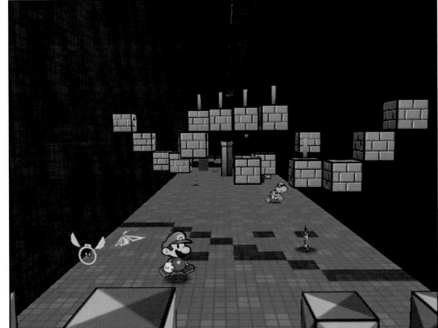

AVAILABLE ON

✓ Nintendo DS
Nintendo Wii
PC Windows
PC Mac
Playstation 2
Playstation 3
Playstation Portable
Xbox 360

GAME FACTS

PUBLISHER
Nintendo

DEVELOPER
Nintendo

FIRST RELEASED
2007-10-01

GAME GENRE	**TIME PERIOD**
Adventure	Fantasy/Timeless
THEME	**COMPLEXITY**
Fantasy	Medium

SIMILAR GAMES

The Legend of Zelda: Wind Waker
Chibi-Robo: Park Patrol
Dragon Quest Heroes: Rocket Slime

RATING & MULTIPLAYER

USA	Europe	Network	Offline
	7+ www.pegi.info	Yes	No

The Legend Of Zelda
PHANTOM HOURGLASS

SETTING
Several months have passed since the epic adventure in The Legend of Zelda: The Wind Waker. Now follow Link, Tetra, and her band of pirates on a new search for unexplored lands in their first Nintendo DS adventure.

GAME SUMMARY
On their new adventure, Link and Tetra discover an abundant ghost ship drifting through the fog. While exploring the ship, Tetra falls into trouble and Link falls into the ocean trying to rescue her. As time runs out for Link, he has to find a way to buy more time and save his pirate friend. The game is played with the touch screen and stylus, where you slash across the touch screen in order for Link to swing his sword. You can even draw notes on your maps and plot out the course your ship will take across the ocean. Throughout Link's adventure, you encounter menacing beasts and giant bosses that will do anything to stop you. As in most Zelda games, you have to crawl through dungeons in order to complete the game. There is also a multiplayer function where you can play against a friend to collect force gems before the enemy closes in.

CHALLENGES & HINTS
As in most Zelda games, this game offers you an array of different puzzles and challenges, but before you can progress in the game, you have to fight countless enemies and defeat bosses. However, the twist with this game is that the dungeons have a time limit, so one of your challenges is to find more time so that you can delve more deeply into the dungeon.

KEY GAMEPLAY ELEMENTS
Steer/Maneuver
Attack/Fight
Solve Puzzles

		AVERAGE SCORE
GAME WORLD SIZE	Medium	
YOUR ROLE	Hero	**9.2**
REPLAY VALUE	Once or Twice	out of 10

Uncharted
DRAKE'S FORTUNE

AVAILABLE ON

Nintendo DS
Nintendo Wii
PC Windows
PC Mac
Playstation 2
✓ Playstation 3
Playstation Portable
Xbox 360

GAME FACTS

PUBLISHER
SCEA, SCEE

DEVELOPER
Naughty Dog

FIRST RELEASED
2007-11-20

GAME GENRE
Adventure

TIME PERIOD
Present

THEME
Crime

COMPLEXITY
Medium

SIMILAR GAMES

Tomb Raider: Anniversary
Tom Clancy's Splinter Cell Double Agent
Metal Gear Solid 4: Guns of the Patriots

RATING & MULTIPLAYER

USA	Europe	Network	Offline
		No	Yes

SETTING

You take on the role of a treasure hunter who believes he is the descendant of the renowned explorer Sir Francis as he sets out on a journey to find the lost treasure of El Dorado.

GAME SUMMARY

On his expedition to find a valuable treasure that, according to legend, can be found in El Dorado, Drake's plane is stranded on a forgotten island in the middle of the Pacific Ocean. He finds himself hunted by mercenaries who are very unhappy with his presence. Only his will to survive and a pistol can save Drake as he uncovers the gruesome secrets of the island. The gameplay consists of navigating through heavy terrain while shooting and combating the enemy. Be sure to use the jungle environment to your advantage by climbing up trees and walking across fallen logs as you try to stay one step ahead of your enemy. Your weapons consist of the handgun you start off with in addition to a handful of grenades and a shotgun. In hand-to-hand combat, action pauses for a brief second and a zoom allows you to perform a one-hit kill move—if you are precise.

CHALLENGES & HINTS

On this exotic island, you have to expect the unexpected. Use maps and clues to complete your journey. Remember that you are limited to carrying only one large weapon at a time, so be certain that you have the right weapon when you need it!

KEY GAMEPLAY ELEMENTS

Attack/Fight
Explore
Tactics/Plan

GAME WORLD SIZE	Large
YOUR ROLE	Hero
REPLAY VALUE	Several Times

AVERAGE SCORE

NA

out of 10

01166

And I love what you do
Don't you know that you're tox - ic - -

P1
P1
TIME   01:14

SING STAR

Entertainment
Games

☐ JOHN TAYLOR

☐ ANDY TAYLOR

☐ ROGER TAYLOR

☐ PETER TAYLOR

650	1100	1000	700	405	325	55
ER 1	PLAYER 2	PLAYER 3	PLAYER 4	PLAYER 5	PLAYER 6	PLAYER 7

BUZZ: THE MEGA QUIZ

Sometimes you don't want to level up, learn confusing button combinations, or die a hundred times just to play a game. It's times like this when games in the entertainment genre truly shine. While you'd win the Worst Host of the Year award for loading up *World of Warcraft* at a party, picking up an axe and challenging your friends to a shredfest in *Guitar Hero III: Legends of Rock* could make your party an event to remember. Why is it that *Tetris*, a game made more than two decades ago, is still being reincarnated now, in next-generation consoles? Because it's still fun. Entertainment games are titles that get back to the grassroots of gaming, proving you don't need to have the best graphics, longest playtime, or biggest explosions just to have a good time.

Innovations in videogame technology are providing more physical ways for players to interact with their games. Gamers can give their joystick thumbs a break by writing answers freehand in the Nintendo DS's *Brain Age*, singing into a microphone in *SingStar*, or stomping their feet onto a *Dance Dance Revolution* dance mat. Whether it's a natural progress toward virtual reality, or simply a way to get off the couch and be involved, the way people are interacting with games is

RED OCTANE: BRYAN LAM

Bryan Lam has been playing videogames ever since he can remember and has been fortunate enough to translate his passion into a career. He came on board RedOctane to help launch Guitar Hero II for the PlayStation2 and Xbox 360, along with Guitar Hero Encore: Rocks the 80s.

GUITAR HERO III

inarguably changing. The entertainment genre relies on intuitive and easy-to-grasp controls and can benefit the most from interactive accessories like guitar controllers or Nintendo's Wii remote.

> **"It's truly amazing to think that any videogame could possibly make this much of a difference..."**
>
> *-Bryan Lam*

With *Guitar Hero* releasing a third installment of what is essentially the same proven formula, at least one company is banking on the idea that an entertainment game can have both immediate appeal *and* longer-lasting depth. EA's *Rock Band* will combine microphone, drum, and guitar controllers in what they hope will become the next groundbreaking hit. However, with so many accessories, some fear the price tag will scare away casual gamers, and the shelf-space required to stock the game have some retailers cringing.

Even though some titles are attempting to revolutionize the genre, there are plenty of developers who've realized you simply can't have enough of a good thing. 2007 saw many sequels being released for already successful entertainment franchises, like *Brain Age, WarioWare, Dance Dance Revolution, Fuzion Frenzy, BUZZ!, SingStar and Big Brain Academy.*

GUITAR HERO III

Appealing to the masses, entertainment games are on the front lines of the entire gaming industry's potential for growth. While the industry expands its audience from its core of young males to include more women and older adults, these games provide quick satisfaction, with friendly controls, and require little previous gaming experience. That's not to say this genre is exclusive to newbies, however. Even hardcore gamers are known to take a break from questing and leveling up to play a round of *Super Monkey Ball*.

INTERVIEW WITH BRYAN LAM

What do you think has been the greatest achievement of the Guitar Hero franchise?

Hmm...that's a good question. There's definitely a lot to be proud of, though, being able to effectively promote musicianship around the world and to genuinely touch the lives of people in a passionate and wholly positive way. [That] definitely has to be some of our greatest achievements. I've heard countless stories of everything from Guitar Hero being used in school music classes to helping bring families closer together to even treating individuals with multiple sclerosis. It's truly amazing to think that any videogame could possibly make this much of a difference, but Guitar Hero has for many, and I'm proud to be a part of that.

We are seeing a new trend in gaming; girls and older people are picking up games as entertainment. In what ways do you feel the Guitar Hero games have contributed to this?

Guitar Hero is extremely easy to pick up and play, and everyone immediately gets the concept. They don't have to worry about remembering tons of different button combinations like pressing triangle to jump, square to punch, or whatever, it's all about having fun and unleashing that inner rock star. Further, music is one of the most common threads of interest amongst all people, and it's not nearly as intimidating or complicated as a lot of other games like, say, a first-person shooter, MMORPG, or fighting game. It's a game that everyone, including parents, girls, and grown-ups can all feel good about playing, and we're excited to be part of the movement in helping change the perception of videogames in the mass market.

How will future technological developments, like the expansion of online capabilities for consoles, affect the way people play games? Do you think a game like Guitar Hero could have been made 10 years ago?

All of the advancements are really helping push the gaming experience to a whole new level, as developers are getting exponentially creative in their design, and just with online capabilities alone, the experience of gaming has already changed with different achievements, downloadable content, real-time updates, and the ability to play against players around the world. In regards to Guitar Hero, it really wouldn't be what it is today 10 years ago because the wide audience just wasn't there. It's different now, though, it's no longer side-scrolling shooters and 2-D nonlinear jumping games that only nerdy kids play. Rather, everyone is into gaming now because the genres of games have expanded to parallel the growing set of casual gamers and target demographic.

What does the future hold for Guitar Hero after the third installment, Guitar Hero III: Legends of Rock, is released?

Our tentative plan is to have at least one major release every year and release various other titles intermittently. Beyond that, we have a number of ideas as to where we want to take the franchise, and we're currently exploring our options.

What is your favorite song to play in Guitar Hero III?

If I can only pick one song, it'd have to be Muse's Knights of Cydonia...it's an absolute shredfest that'll demoralize your ego and kill your forearms. I've never had to warm up prior to playing a videogame before, but trust me, you'll definitely need to for this track.

Thank you for your time Bryan Lam!

ROCK BAND

BOOGIE

Boogie

SETTING

Get into the groove with Boogie, a music- and rhythm-based game that will get you singing and swinging with the Wii controls. Create your own music videos or follow a storyline with your own customized character.

GAME SUMMARY

Boogie offers five characters, and its storyline follows five hilarious chapters. Move your character around with the analog stick on the Wii Nunchuk and unlock songs along the way. You can choose to either sing or dance to the various songs. The music video feature allows you to be creative while cutting your video and adding special effects. The editing tools are very simple, guaranteeing you good results. To dance, simply move the Wii Remote rhythmically in the appropriate direction. String together dance combos by making the right moves in quick succession. This will increase your score and thus your "boost meter," earning you big points. There's lots of fun to be had in this game, and it does not require much skill to master. In karaoke mode you are tested mainly on pitch. Most of the singalong options are catchy '70s hits.

CHALLENGES & HINTS

In dance mode, you should avoid repeating your dance moves no matter how much fun they are - in the end, it will cost you scores of points. Boogie is definitely more fun if you get off the couch and dance to the disco grooves!

AVAILABLE ON

- ✓ Nintendo DS
- ✓ Nintendo Wii
- PC Windows
- PC Mac
- ✓ Playstation 2
- Playstation 3
- Playstation Portable
- Xbox 360

GAME FACTS

PUBLISHER
Electronic Arts

DEVELOPER
Electronic Arts

FIRST RELEASED
2007-08-07

GAME GENRE
Music & Dance

TIME PERIOD
Present

THEME
Comedy

COMPLEXITY
Low

SIMILAR GAMES

SingStar
Dance Dance Revolution
Guitar Hero III

RATING & MULTIPLAYER

	USA	Europe	Network	Offline
	E 10+	3+	No	Yes

KEY GAMEPLAY ELEMENTS

Steer/Maneuver
Build & Design
Tactics/Plan

GAME WORLD SIZE	Small
YOUR ROLE	Dancer/Singer
REPLAY VALUE	Several Times

AVERAGE SCORE

5.6

out of 10

★275,109

546
1,568

1:22

SHAKE IT DOWN SHAKE IT DOWN NOW
SHAKE IT DOWN SHAKE IT DOWN NOW

★100,390

11,6?2

2:19

SHE'S MIGHTY MIGHTY A-JUST LETTIN' IT ALL HANG OUT
AW SHE'S A BRICK HOUSE

39
★374,180

4,208

1:03

ME AND YOU DANCING IN THE STREETS
DON'T YOU KNOW THERE'LL BE DANCIN'

★181,249

743
743

1:58

MM THE CLOTHES SHE WEAR HER SEXY WAYS
MAKE A OLD MAN WISH

Brain Age 2
MORE TRAINING IN MINUTES A DAY

SETTING

This sequel to the highly acclaimed Dr. Kawashima's Brain Age comes with a set of new exercises to challenge your brain and keep you up to speed.

GAME SUMMARY

Like the first game in the series, this game puts your brain to the test and helps you improve brain activity. Although very similar to its predecessor, this edition features new training exercises based on cutting-edge neurological research, including solving word puzzles, playing simple songs on the piano, memorizing numbers, computing simple mathematics, calculating days and dates, giving back the right amount of change, and more. You can practice all the unlocked exercises as often as you like, but only the first attempt of the day will be stored in your profile. You can also check your brain age once a day with a test that consists of three randomly chosen exercises. This test determines how old you brain is, and how active it is compared to your real age. The game also features a minigame, somewhat similar to Tetris, which is meant to relax your brain.

CHALLENGES & HINTS

If you thought the first game kept your brain in tip-top shape, then you might experience déjà vu playing this version. There are many tests here to keep your brain thinking hard and fast. Trying to remember 25 numbers in two minutes or tell the time upside down is harder than you think. Some of the exercises are made to trick you. Are you smart enough not to be fooled?

AVAILABLE ON

✓ Nintendo DS
   Nintendo Wii
   PC Windows
   PC Mac
   Playstation 2
   Playstation 3
   Playstation Portable
   Xbox 360

GAME FACTS

PUBLISHER
Nintendo

DEVELOPER
Nintendo

FIRST RELEASED
2007-06-29

GAME GENRE
Puzzle

TIME PERIOD
Present

THEME
Various

COMPLEXITY
Medium

SIMILAR GAMES

Big Brain Academy
My Word Coach
Flash Focus

RATING & MULTIPLAYER

USA	Europe	Network	Offline
EVERYONE E	3+	Yes	No

KEY GAMEPLAY ELEMENTS

Solve Puzzles
Tactics/Plan
Build & Design

GAME WORLD SIZE Small
YOUR ROLE Your Brain
REPLAY VALUE Infinite

AVERAGE SCORE

7.6

out of 10

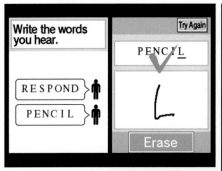

Write the words you hear.

RESPOND

PENCIL

Try Again

PENCIL

Erase

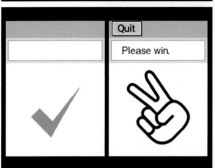

Keep track of the runner.

Erase

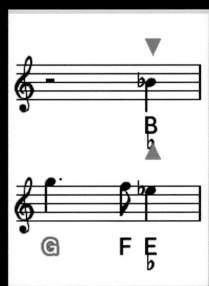

A B D E G

GABCDEFG

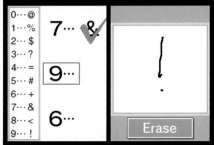

Quit

Please win.

0···@
1···%
2···$
3···?
4···=
5···#
6···+
7···&
8···<
9···!

7··· &
9···
6···

Erase

Touch the highest number.

¹6   14
   1   10
9 3 0 7
       8

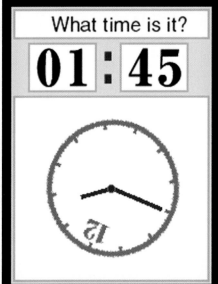

What time is it?

$01:45$

Erase

Hours

Erase

Minutes

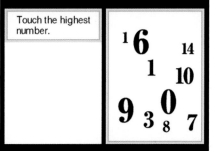

1 Min. 54 Sec.
Memorize all.

15 18 16 20 25
4 9 5 21 11
10 3 19 8 14
13 7 12 17 24
1 22 6 23 2

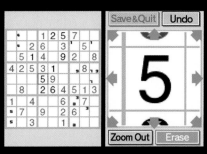

Save&Quit Undo

5

Zoom Out Erase

AVAILABLE ON

Nintendo DS
Nintendo Wii
PC Windows
PC Mac
✓ Playstation 2
Playstation 3
Playstation Portable
Xbox 360

GAME FACTS

PUBLISHER
SCEE

DEVELOPER
SCEE

FIRST RELEASED
2007-05-30

GAME GENRE	**TIME PERIOD**
Quiz	Future
THEME	**COMPLEXITY**
Comedy	Low

SIMILAR GAMES

Ape Escape 3
Family Feud (2006)
WarioWare: Smooth Moves

RATING & MULTIPLAYER

Europe	Network	Offline
	No	4 Players

Buzz! Junior: RoboJam
(EUROPE ONLY)

SETTING

It's time for another round of fun and challenge for the juniors. Similar to Buzz! Junior Jungle Party, players use simple buzz controllers with color buttons to maneuver their robot characters through a series of minicompetitions.

GAME SUMMARY

The main objective of Buzz! Junior RoboJam is to control tiny but fearless robots through various dangerous challenges. Create your own robot and use the color buttons to perform different moves that push your reaction and coordination skills to the limit! The minigames are particularly childish, to great enjoyment for both young and old. Your skills will be put to the test through bizarre challenges, such as eating beans and farting without the chef noticing. Or try to compete with the other robots to see who has what it takes to be the last one to open the parachute. As you might imagine, timing is of great importance here! The difficulty level is mixed, and you can choose between challenging your friends or playing against the machine.

CHALLENGES & HINTS

Even though the game may look like a piece of cake to you, your reaction time will be put to the test, and one wrong move can be fatal! Hurry up, don't lose focus, and you might just become robot of the month!

KEY GAMEPLAY ELEMENTS

Steer/Maneuver
Solve Puzzles
Explore

GAME WORLD SIZE	Small
YOUR ROLE	Crazy Robot
REPLAY VALUE	Several Times

AVERAGE SCORE

6.5

out of 10

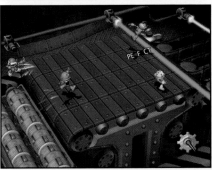

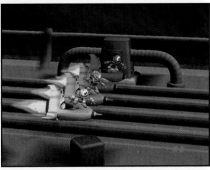

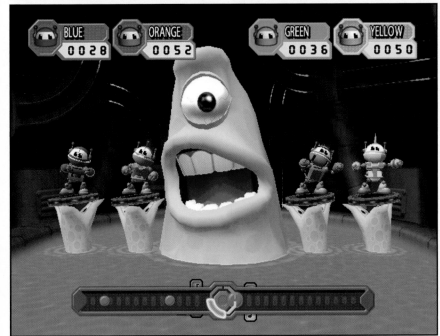

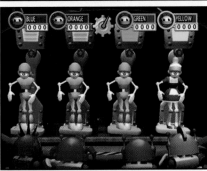

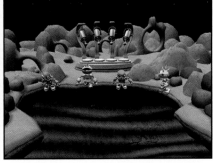

AVAILABLE ON

Nintendo DS
Nintendo Wii
PC Windows
PC Mac
✓ Playstation 2
Playstation 3
Playstation Portable
Xbox 360

GAME FACTS

PUBLISHER
SCEA, SCEE

DEVELOPER
Relentless Software

FIRST RELEASED
2007-04-27

GAME GENRE	**TIME PERIOD**
Quiz	Present
THEME	**COMPLEXITY**
Various	Medium

SIMILAR GAMES

Buzz! The Hollywood Quiz
Buzz: The Big Quiz
Family Feud (2006)

RATING & MULTIPLAYER

USA	Europe	Network	Offline
EVERYONE 10+ E	12+ www.pegi.info	No	8 Players

Buzz! The Mega Quiz

SETTING

Have you ever dreamt of being on a TV show and becoming the next millionaire? In Buzz! The Mega Quiz you will most certainly not become rich, but at least you will be on an interactive TV show and get the chance to prove what a genius you are!

GAME SUMMARY

Buzz! The Mega Quiz continues where Buzz! The BIG Quiz left off. With more than 5,000 questions, this game, based on the structure of a TV game show, challenges every part of your brain. Your skills are tested on almost every imaginable topic, ranging from music and movies to nature, sports, and science. This time around, the showman Buzz gives you even more video clips, music videos, and photos, along with several new question modes to challenge your memory. Take the Pie Fight, for example, which lets you throw a pie in your competitor's face! With the possibility of playing with up to eight players, fighting for the highest score can be a tough job. But in return, it will be hard to wipe that big smile off your face once you win! Where did that pie fly?

CHALLENGES & HINTS

With the extraordinary amount of questions Buzz has lined up for you this time, knowing all the answers is simply impossible. And even if you do, you must be quicker than the rest. Stay concentrated, apply a bit of tactics, push the right buttons, and you will gather points faster than your brain ever imagined!

KEY GAMEPLAY ELEMENTS

Solve Puzzles
Tactics/Plan
Steer/Maneuver

GAME WORLD SIZE	Small	
YOUR ROLE	TV-Show Contestant	
REPLAY VALUE	Several Times	

AVERAGE SCORE

8.0

out of 10

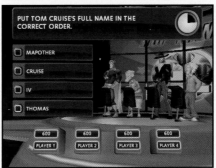

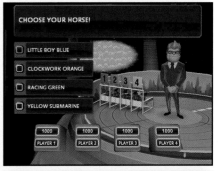

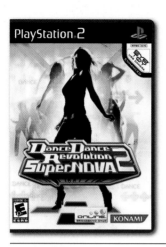

AVAILABLE ON

Nintendo DS
Nintendo Wii
PC Windows
PC Mac
✓ Playstation 2
Playstation 3
Playstation Portable
Xbox 360

GAME FACTS

PUBLISHER
Konami Digital Entertainment

DEVELOPER
Konami

FIRST RELEASED
2007-09-25

GAME GENRE	**TIME PERIOD**
Music & Dance	Present
THEME	**COMPLEXITY**
Music & Dance	Low

SIMILAR GAMES

Dance Dance Revolution Universe
Dance Dance Revolution Hottest Party
Boogie

RATING & MULTIPLAYER

USA	Europe	Network	Offline
E10+	3+	4 Players	2 Players

Dance Dance Revolution
SuperNOVA 2

SETTING
The popular arcade dancer is back for its 10th installment. The fast-paced dance game will really make you sweat and dance 'till your feet are sore!

GAME SUMMARY
Like the other Dance Dance Revolution titles, the game is played by stepping on the icons on the dance mat that correspond with those on the screen. The key is to step on the correct squares on your dance mat the moment the icon passes through the trigger point. SuperNOVA 2 introduces a new feature called e-amusement that tracks your weight and calories burned after each session. It's also able to track other statistics, such as your dancing skills. The game features loads of songs from both unknown and known artists like Fatboy Slim, A-ha, Natasha Bedingfield, Paul Oakenfold, and many more. The online multiplayer mode lets up to four players compete against each other.

CHALLENGES & HINTS
If you play at a slow pace, this game will be easy. But once you jump into higher skill levels, you will quickly learn that becoming a master takes more than just good practice—it takes talent.

KEY GAMEPLAY ELEMENTS
Steer/Maneuver

GAME WORLD SIZE	Small
YOUR ROLE	Dancer
REPLAY VALUE	Infinite

AVERAGE SCORE
NA
out of 10

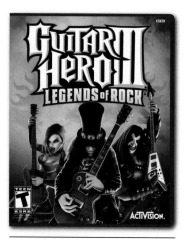

Guitar Hero III
LEGENDS OF ROCK

SETTING
The third version of the popular Guitar Hero series is bigger and better than before. The game's simple nature of just picking up a guitar, selecting a song, and pushing fret buttons in time with the music's corresponding colors on the screen makes this game another Guitar Hero classic.

GAME SUMMARY
Similar to its prequels, Guitar Hero III offers a career mode where you choose between popular guitar models such as the Gibson and the Kramer, as well as a selection of extreme rock heroes. Unlock all of the 45 legendary rock anthems at different difficulty levels, or choose to enter head-to-head guitar battles against a friend or rock legend in a boss battle. As you crank up the volume and your fret skills develop, you travel to destinations around the world and play for cheering crowds backed up by a magnificent light show. Sponsors line up to pay you for gigs and big concerts. Songs made famous by artists such as the Rolling Stones, Beastie Boys, Muse, Kiss, and Heart appear in this version of the game. You can also download songs to expand your repertoire.

CHALLENGES & HINTS
As you choose higher difficulty levels, your fingers will have to move a whole lot faster! If you are having trouble shredding to a hard song, use the practice mode to slow the song down so that you can master the fret button sequence before returning to the high-paced version.

AVAILABLE ON

Nintendo DS
✓ Nintendo Wii
✓ PC Windows
✓ PC Mac
✓ Playstation 2
✓ Playstation 3
Playstation Portable
✓ Xbox 360

GAME FACTS *

PUBLISHER
Activision

DEVELOPER
Neversoft, Aspyr

FIRST RELEASED
2007-10-01

GAME GENRE	TIME PERIOD
Music & Dance	Present
THEME	**COMPLEXITY**
Music & Dance	Low

SIMILAR GAMES

Guitar Hero II
Guitar Hero I
Guitar Hero Encore: Rocks the 80s

RATING & MULTIPLAYER

USA	Europe	Network	Offline
		No	Yes

KEY GAMEPLAY ELEMENTS
Steer/Maneuver

		AVERAGE SCORE
GAME WORLD SIZE	Small	**NA**
YOUR ROLE	Guitar Player	
REPLAY VALUE	Several Times	out of 10

Data and images may vary on the various platforms

Jam Sessions

SETTING

Jam Sessions is not a game but software that turns your DS into an ultraportable musical instrument. A rhythm-guitar simulator lets you create, record, and play back guitar grooves whenever and wherever.

GAME SUMMARY

Play your DS like a guitar. Use one hand on the directional pad to switch instantly between chords displayed on the upper screen and the other hand to strum a groove with your finger or stylus on the touch-sensitive virtual strings on the lower screen. A total of 16 prestored chords can be accessed by toggling between two active palettes. More than 100 real chord samples from various guitars enable you create everything from blues and rock songs to heavy metal grooves. A variety of adjustable effects like distortion, chorus, tremolo, etc. let you to create your own personal sound. With tutorials and play-alongs, Jam Sessions is easy to pick up for beginners, but it is also a great tool for professional musicians who want to capture spur-of-the-moment ideas, whether on the bus, at a café, or at work.

CHALLENGES & HINTS

Even though Jam Sessions makes it easier than ever to lay down guitar grooves, it is still up to you as a creative genius to create catchy riffs. This takes a bit of practice combined with rhythmic and harmonic skill.

AVAILABLE ON

✓ Nintendo DS
Nintendo Wii
PC Windows
PC Mac
Playstation 2
Playstation 3
Playstation Portable
Xbox 360

GAME FACTS

PUBLISHER
Ubisoft

DEVELOPER
Plato

FIRST RELEASED
2007-09-11

GAME GENRE
Music & Dance

TIME PERIOD
Present

THEME
Music & Dance

COMPLEXITY
Low

SIMILAR GAMES

Elite Beat Agents
Rhythm n'Notes
Rock Band

RATING & MULTIPLAYER

USA	Europe	Network	Offline
		No	No

KEY GAMEPLAY ELEMENTS

Steer/Maneuver
Build & Design
Explore

GAME WORLD SIZE	Small
YOUR ROLE	Musician
REPLAY VALUE	Infinite

AVERAGE SCORE

7.4

out of 10

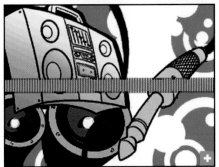

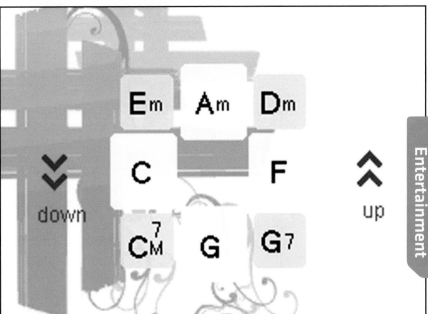

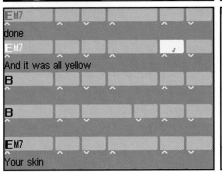

EM7
done
EM7
And it was all yellow
B

B

EM7
Your skin

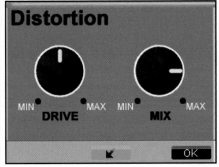

Distortion

MIN • **DRIVE** • MAX   MIN • **MIX** • MAX

OK

EM7
turn into
G#m7   F#
something   beautiful
EM7
And you know
G#m7   F#
you know I   love you so
EM7

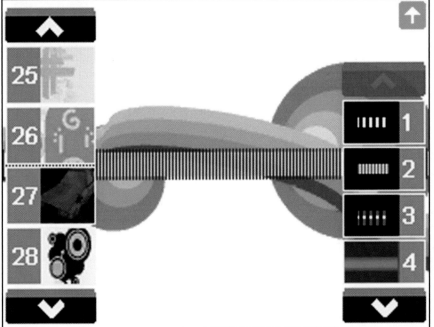

25

26

27

28

1

2

3

4

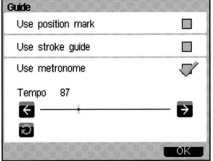

Guide

Use position mark	☐
Use stroke guide	☐
Use metronome	✓

Tempo   87
←ーーーー|ーーーー→

OK

Theme

Live mode Live

Chord Palette Editor

Settings

Effects

Recordings

Tuning

AVAILABLE ON

Nintendo DS
Nintendo Wii
PC Windows
PC Mac
Playstation 2
✓ Playstation 3
Playstation Portable
Xbox 360

GAME FACTS

PUBLISHER
SCEA, SCEE

DEVELOPER
SCEE

FIRST RELEASED
TBA

GAME GENRE	TIME PERIOD
Music & Dance	Present
THEME	COMPLEXITY
Music & Dance	Low

SIMILAR GAMES

Boogie
Dance Dance Revolution SuperNOVA 2
Guitar Hero III: Legends of Rock

RATING & MULTIPLAYER

USA	Europe	Network	Offline
	12+ www.pegi.info	Yes	2 Players

SingStar

SETTING

SingStar is back, once again letting you take center stage to impress the crowd with your vocal skills. With more than 300 songs available for download, there is nothing to stop you from moving to the top of the charts...except perhaps your own voice?

GAME SUMMARY

SingStar for PlayStation 3 comes with a variety of features and modes. Play SingStar measures your pitch and timing to a music video or a live performance. You can sing solo or as a duet with a friend, and it's even possible to challenge another player to a singing battle. After a song is completed, you have the option to save your vocal performance to My SingStar Online and upload footage from the EyeToy. In the SingStore you can browse through the more than 300 songs and music videos to purchase, download, and add to your personalized playlist, including artists like Gorillaz, Coldplay, and OutKast. The visuals and graphics can be updated by downloading different skins from the SingStore, and the game comes with authentic microphones.

CHALLENGES & HINTS

SingStar is all about pitch and timing. It doesn't matter if you know the lyrics by heart. You can still hum the tune and get a perfect score. But in all honesty, singing along to the lyrics of your favorite artists is what makes SingStar such a great game to play.

KEY GAMEPLAY ELEMENTS

Steer/Maneuver

		AVERAGE SCORE
GAME WORLD SIZE	Small	**8.4**
YOUR ROLE	Singer	
REPLAY VALUE	Infinite	out of 10

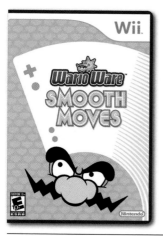

Wario Ware
SMOOTH MOVES

SETTING
Wario stumbles upon a strange device called a form baton (a Wii remote). He and his friends use it to learn smooth, strange, and funny moves to complete many minigames before time runs out.

GAME SUMMARY
The hectic and bizarre Wario Ware game series has arrived on the Wii, and Wario and his friends have just made it even stranger. Like previous games in the series, Wario Ware: Smooth Moves is comprised of hundreds of minigames strung together in a continuous sequence. Play until you fail, with each challenge lasting no longer than a few seconds. The game uses the Wii remote to perform different actions to complete each stage, such as smacking flies, pumping iron, balancing items, eating, etc. Each "chapter" has a series of many minigames, and before each game you are shown a hint of what kind of action you are about to perform. If you fail to complete four of the minigames during a single chapter, it will be "game over!" After you complete the single-player mode, you can unlock the multiplayer mode, where you can play against up to 12 people on the same machine.

CHALLENGES & HINTS
Only receiving a small hint before each minigame makes it harder to fully grasp what to do, but that is also part of the challenge—to test how quickly you understand the concept. Not only that, but these games are fast! Doing a new move every five seconds can be really hectic, but also really fun—especially for those watching you.

AVAILABLE ON

Nintendo DS
✓ Nintendo Wii
PC Windows
PC Mac
Playstation 2
Playstation 3
Playstation Portable
Xbox 360

GAME FACTS

PUBLISHER
Nintendo

DEVELOPER
Intelligent Systems

FIRST RELEASED
2007-01-12

GAME GENRE	TIME PERIOD
Entertainment	Fantasy/Timeless
THEME	**COMPLEXITY**
Comedy	Low

SIMILAR GAMES

Mario Party 8
Rayman Raving Rabbids
Super Monkey Ball: Banan

RATING & MULTIPLAYER

USA	Europe	Network	Offline
		No	Yes

KEY GAMEPLAY ELEMENTS

Steer/Maneuver
Solve Puzzles
Tactics/Plan

GAME WORLD SIZE	Small
YOUR ROLE	None
REPLAY VALUE	Several Times

AVERAGE SCORE

8.2
out of 10

MMORPG
GAMES

An MMO, or massive multiplayer online game, is a genre defined by the ability for thousands of gamers to play simultaneously over the Internet in the same world. Emerging from text-based multiplayer games called multi-user dungeons, or MUDS, graphical MMOs have been around since the 1980s, yet only recently have they achieved mainstream success.

MMOs allow players to work cooperatively as teams or compete against each other in a vast and enormous virtual world. MMOs come in almost every gameplay type, from racing games (MMORG) to first-person shooters (MMOFPS), but the most popular are role-playing games, or MMORPGs. In this subgenre, players create and customize their own heroes and navigate them through the game's interactive world. Role-playing elements like classes, quests, and leveling up are all blended into a community of thousands of other players. Unlike some turn-based role-playing games, the multiplayer nature of MMOs necessitates real-time combat and action.

Only recently has the MMO genre branched off from hardcore gamers to attract a mainstream audience. In December of 2003, the *Financial Times* published research conducted on the most popular MMO at the time, *EverQuest*. Economist and videogame scholar Edward Castronova, noticing that people were selling their platinum—the game's online currency—on auction websites like eBay, col-

EVE ONLINE

lected financial data on the game's virtual currency. If the *EverQuest* universe of *Norrath* were an actual country, Dr. Castronova concluded, its per-capita gross national product would have been $2,266, making it the 77th richest country on Earth and ranking it between Russia and Bulgaria.

While Dr. Castronova's research was revolutionary at the time, the numbers have changed dramatically since his study. The incredibly successful MMORPG *World of Warcraft*, or WoW, has since dethroned *EverQuest* to quickly become the MMO with the largest subscriber base. The 2003 *Financial Times* article reported that there were a total of 6 million people playing all MMOs combined; now there are more than 9 million playing

WoW alone. Some MMOs, like *Lineage 2*, are successful in Asian countries but relatively unheard of in the West. While *Lineage 2* may not be recognized in Western culture, the game boasts almost one million subscribers.

Although some MMOs have become incredibly popular, simply building one isn't a recipe for success. Unlike any other game genre, MMOs require a large staff that can play and monitor the world 24 hours a day, 7 days a week. And although an MMO must constantly be staffed, the player base has no obligation to be as consistent. Unable to sustain this level of commitment, MMOs like *Matrix Online* and *Asheron's Call* have been discontinued, leaving the players who invested so much time in their

WARHAMMER ONLINE: AGE OF RECKONING

characters stranded.

These failures haven't scared off developers from continuing to create new MMOs in both familiar and new universes. Some MMO developers are hoping the worlds of *Star Wars, Lord of the Rings,* or *Conan the Barbarian* will entice players to branch off from the dominant *World of Warcraft*. Other developers are creating entirely new and different MMO universes with the same goal: to dethrone the one MMO King. The sci-fi MMO *Eve Online* focuses on customizable spaceships that players can control, and unlike most MMOs, players gain skills through training, rather than experience points.

An MMO can provide players with an entire so-cial community that is living, breathing, and never sleeping. Some speculate that the addictive and never-ending nature of MMOs is causing gamers to neglect their real life. One MMO doesn't even try to hide this fact: the aptly named virtual world called *Second Life*. For players who want to experience an entirely different life from their own, *Second Life* offers a user-defined world in which players can interact, play, do business, communicate, and even create their own virtual property.

Being such a new phenomenon to mainstream gaming, the lifetime of MMOs and their ability to sustain audiences is something that only time can tell. For now, players have to subscribe, roll the dice, and see for themselves.

Rob Pardo, 37, is currently the senior vice president of game design for Blizzard Entertainment. Together with a large team of very skilled game developers, he led the design of *World of Warcraft*, the largest massively multiplayer online game ever made, as well as its first expansion, *The Burning Crusade*.

Rob began his career in game development back in 1994, when he began working for Interplay Entertainment Corp. He started his career at Interplay as a game tester before working his way up to a producer role.

In 1997, Rob joined Blizzard Entertainment as a designer, working on *StarCraft* (1998). He eventually moved up to become lead designer on the expansion, *StarCraft: Brood War*. After this success, Rob was the lead designer on *Warcraft III: Reign of Chaos* (2002) and its expansion, *Warcraft III: The Frozen Throne*. He is now working on the second expansion for *World of Warcraft, Wrath of the Lich King*, and also on *StarCraft II*.

AN INTERVIEW WITH ROB PARDO

What do you think have been the greatest achievements in MMOGs so far?

I will limit this to the *Ultima Online* (UO) period and beyond. UO was a huge achievement in terms of scale—before it came out, things were very different. Here you had the ability to have 1,000 other players in one place—it was just a whole different concept.

I was in the beta before the game was released, and I remember the first time I played it: I saw someone killing birds, collecting feathers, and then making arrows. It looked boring, but once I tried it I went: "Hey! I can make things!" And that was pretty cool.

UO was the start of the graphical MMO genre. It was kind of like the Wild West of MMOs, but I don't think we will see a game like that again. People have gotten used to a more user-friendly environment.

I would say the milestone games that drove the genre were *Ultima Online, EverQuest* (EQ), and *World of Warcraft*.

UO was picking out the genesis of the concept. EQ really added more "game" to the experience—you could accomplish bigger goals in it. The biggest step forward of *World of Warcraft* was that it provided mass-market, highly accessible gameplay mechanics and a user-friendly interface. It also seamlessly combined PvP and PvE gameplay, as well as offering a dynamic quest-driven experience.

How do you think people benefit from playing games like this?

The purpose of any game is to entertain its players. One thing that MMOs do well in comparison to other game styles is to reward achievements graphically. People can actually see what you have done. I mean, when I play *Half-Life 2*, which is a game I enjoy very much, no one can see how well I have played. But in MMOs, the results of your accomplishments are visible to other players, increasing the sense of achievement. Another element is the socialization, and the fact that one learns to communicate and work together with others. As another benefit, I learned to type really quickly playing MMOs.

"...in MMOs the results of your accomplishments are visible to other players, increasing the sense of achievement."

-Rob Pardo

Most importantly, you meet people. As an example, the current lead designer of World of Warcraft came from my *EverQuest* guild. Back then I was a guild leader, but the production of *Warcraft III* was demanding all my time so I had to step down, and the officer, Jeffrey Kaplan, took over. It turned out that he was local. So we'd meet for lunch nearby, and when there was a job opening at Blizzard I knew that he had the right skills so I contacted him. His wife was also in the guild—they met in the game, and then in real life, and now they are married.

GAMES CREDITED ROB PARDO

Publisher/Developer: Blizzard

2007: World of Warcraft: The Burning Crusade

2004: World of Warcraft

2003: Warcraft III: The Frozen Throne

2002: Warcraft III: Reign of Chaos

2000: Diablo II

2000: StarCraft 64

1999: Warcraft II: Battle.net Edition

1998: StarCraft: Brood War

1998: StarCraft

STARCRAFT

WARCRAFT III: THE FROZEN THRONE

ART: WORLD OF WARCRAFT

We are seeing a new trend in gaming: more girls and older people are picking up games as entertainment. How do you think this game genre will develop from here?

We are seeing an incredible growth and increasing diversity right now. There is an explosion in MMOs, with games going in a hundred different directions. We will probably also see a whole bunch of cross-genre mergers in the future.

I think what *World of Warcraft* has done for the industry is to put a spotlight on the genre. People are investing huge amounts of money and resources into developing new MMOs now, in part due to the attention drawn by the success of *World of Warcraft*.

As for the business part of it, we'll probably also see a whole bunch of different business models, new and different ways of making money on games: ad-driven games that are free to use, micro-payments, traditional subscription models, etc.

What is your favorite game? (One that you didn't make yourself?)

Warcraft II. I was a great fan. It was released at the time I was at Interplay Productions. *Warcraft II* hit the office like a hurricane. We would play all the time; we could come in the morning at six and play an hour before work, and then again at five after work. *Warcraft II* was, in a way, what got me into Blizzard and to where I am now.

Gaming is increasing its share of the media landscape. How do you think the different games will interact (if at all) in the future?

We are seeing games interacting with other media in Sony's PlayStation 3 Home feature. It's like your own virtual apartment where you can see and download trailers. Steam and iTunes are also doing it. I think we are starting to see media trying to leverage themselves with the games industry. This sort of convergence will just continue in the future, and virtual worlds like *Second Life* are on the right track.

What can you tell us about the next expansion for World of Warcraft? There has been mention that there will be siege weapons. Will this mean that there will also be player-built constructions?

Players can expect to see unique, challenging encounters in *Wrath of the Lich King*. The game's first hero class, the death knight, will add new gameplay mechanics to grouping and raiding. All the new spells, abilities, and talents players will gain access to as they advance to level 80 will also bring new elements to raiding, and we'll definitely be designing encounters to take advantage of these new features. There will also be a host of new instances, including several 10-person instances and the continued functionality of Heroic difficulty for 5-person dungeons.

As for siege weapons, they are intended to be a fun and interactive new element to PvP battles. The goal is to spice things up and add some more variety, not to drastically change the mechanics of our PvP system. Players will be able to construct, aim (at enemy buildings or players), and drive siege weapons. It should also be mentioned that every class will be able to use the siege weapons.

Thank you for your time Rob Pardo!

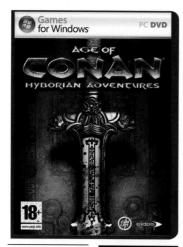

AVAILABLE ON

AVERAGE SCORE
NA out of 10

Nintendo DS
Nintendo Wii
✓ PC Windows
PC Mac
Playstation 2
Playstation 3
Playstation Portable
✓ Xbox 360

GAME FACTS

PUBLISHER
Eidos

DEVELOPER
Funcom

FIRST RELEASED DATE
Mars 25, 2008

GAME GENRE
MMORPG

TIME PERIOD
Medieval

THEME
Fantasy War

COMPLEXITY
Medium

SIMILAR GAMES

World of Warcraft
Lord of the Rings Online
Lineage 2

Age of Conan
HYBORIAN ADVENTURE

Age of Conan: Hyborian Adventures (AoC) is a more mature game than most other MMOs, but so are the original stories written by Robert E. Howard. Set in the ancient pseudohistoric world of Hyboria, the game continues the storyline from the Conan novel, The Hour of the Dragon, written in 1934. Conan the Barbarian has become King Conan who rules the fragile empire of Aquilonia, which is filled with mythological creatures, vicious gods, and a beleaguered human race.

As you enter your adventure in Hyboria, you are a slave on a trireme. Your ship wrecks and you drift ashore to a brutal world where most women exist solely to please men and men who can't defend themselves don't last long. Whether you choose to play as a male or female, you have to fight your way to the nearest city leaving a trail of dead thugs and slave masters behind you.

The first quests introduce you to the storyline and teach you how to use the interface in a single-player environment. AoC has a more interactive approach to fighting called Real Combat, where you actually wield the sword in real time, creating a heightened feeling of immersion similar to single-player action games. As you gain experience, you learn special combos that greatly improve your fighting capabilities, such as the ability to decapitate your enemies with a single blow of your sword.

Once you get to the nearest town, Tortage, you meet other players who also survived the shipwreck. You can team up with them and complete quests together.

CHARACTER CREATION, RACES AND CLASSES

In AoC, you can spend a lot of time creating a unique character appearance. You can change almost every physical aspect of your character, including your nose, cheekbones, hairstyle, eye width, scars, tattoos, and much more.

For the first five levels you play as a "commoner" without a class, but of one of three racial origins. The three races are Aquilonian, a race similar to the Romans; the Stygians, a race inspired by the ancient Egyptians; and Cimmerians, who resemble northern cultures such as the Celts. Once you have reached level five you may choose from three of four main classes called archetypes. Each class has several subclasses. Depending on the race you chose to play, you can choose to play as a Rogue, Priest, Soldier, or Mage..

GUILDS

As part of a guild, you are able to build a keep. Keeps are only possible at special designated locations in the border kingdom where player vs. player (PVP) combat occurs. Each server supports up to nine battle keeps for the largest guilds, 15 forts for medium guilds, as well as resource nodes for smaller guilds.

Similar to SimCity, there is a given set of places to build structures. Restricted by space, you cannot build all the possible buildings, so you have to make some tactical decisions. Start by erecting a trade post and collecting basic resources such as gold, iron, wood, etc. Your guild must cooperate to build various structures, and some are more expensive than others. Even though you have bank access and auction house access in the guild village, the actual goods are not physically in the village and

will not be lost if the village is captured. Each guild can only have one village.

COMBAT

Real combat is being touted by Funcom as a revolutionary approach to combat in online RPGs because the player is in direct control of his or her character's weapon strikes in real time. This multipoint melee and ranged combat

system is purportedly easy to learn and one of the prime attractions of this game. The real combat system takes the ritualized combat experience previously found in online RPGs in a new direction. For this system, Funcom has also added formation combat, mounted combat, siege combat, and hive combat.

MOUNTED COMBAT

In AoC, player-owned mounts have an additional role. Most MMOs allow a player to choose a mount at a certain point in the game. This mount is used for faster transportation inside the game world. In AoC, a mount is not only a way of moving from one point to

another but can also be used to fight your opponents. When mounted you inflict more damage, but it is harder to hit targets. You hold your weapon over your side and swing it as you approach your enemy. At level 40, you can even have mounts like a horse or camel.

PVP AND SIEGE BATTLES

PVP combat is important in AoC, even though you can easily play without fighting other players. PVP combat also includes real-time combat.

Each guild that owns a city has a window of opportunity where other guilds can attack it in siege battles. This window is limited in the number of possible attacks since it is closed at night and in the morning so that the guild has a chance to defend itself. When first building a keep, you have seven days before any other guild can attack. For larger keeps, finishing the keep in time can be quite a challenge, as it requires a great effort to build these keeps within such a short timeframe.

The attacking guild has to break through the keep's defenses, first through its walls and then by killing the guild's inhabitants and taking down buildings before the window of opportunity closes. Mammoths and Rhinos are effective beasts to attack a city. Objectives such as taking control points and killing enemies add points to the guild's score. The guild with the most points at the end of the battle wins.

The city is used actively during sieges by placing archers on the battlements and melee soldiers by the city gate. It is even possible to hire mercenaries to help your battle keep. Mercenaries are other players on the same server that, if they accept the job, are instantly teleported into battle. There is a cap on how many you can hire, though, so a guild cannot rely solely on mercenaries. Each city gives buffs

and bonuses, so there is always a reason for conflict between the guilds. You choose how to pay your mercenaries.

At level 20, you can choose from among four prestige classes: Crafter, Commander, Lord, and Master. Each of these has special abilities that give them great advantage over other classes.

For example, the Crafter has access to all forms of crafting that are learned by completing quests. There are five main crafting skills: Weaponsmith, Armorsmith, Alchemy, Architect, and Gemcutter. Weaponsmiths specialize in making weapons and Armorsmiths in making armor. Weapons and armor also have gem sockets that allow you to customize extra properties with the help of a Gemcutter. Alchemists create compounds with various beneficial effects. Architects design buildings and siege engines. When choosing one of these skills you gradually become better at practicing it until you master it and can offer your services or products to other players.

SINGLE PLAYER

Most MMOs focus largely on the social interaction between players and have adapted their game to this aspect of the game. However, AoC has also put a lot of effort into its single-player mode, allowing players to enjoy themselves in the game without necessarily having much social interaction. Just like with other MMOs, quests are an important aspect of the game. First you engage in a conversation with non-player characters who give you tasks that vary greatly in length, difficulty, and style. You still need to play online on the servers, though. For instance, in the first levels in AoC, you can play

Laetio (1)

a large number of quests in single-player mode where you learn how to play and act in Hyboria. Once you reach level 20, though, you are thrown out in the open multiplayer universe. You can also switch between the single-player and multiplayer environments when you are below level 20 in order to adventure with your friends. But beware: there aren't many peaceful areas in Hyboria.

MMIV Clayton Bunce

SCALE IN MILES

300   600   1200

Games for Windows — PC DVD

AVAILABLE ON

Nintendo DS
Nintendo Wii
✓ PC Windows
PC Mac
Playstation 2
Playstation 3
Playstation Portable
Xbox 360

AVERAGE SCORE

9.4
out of 10

GAME FACTS

PUBLISHER
US: Midway   EU:Codemasters

DEVELOPER
Turbine

FIRST RELEASED DATE
Mars 24, 2007

GAME GENRE	TIME PERIOD
MMORPG	Medieval

THEME	COMPLEXITY
Fantasy War	Medium

SIMILAR GAMES

World of Warcraft
GuildWars
Lineage 2

Lord of the Rings Online
SHADOW OF ANGMAR

If you love J.R.R. Tolkien and The Lord of the Rings trilogy, you will enjoy exploring The Lord of the Rings Online (LOTRO). The game is set in the same world as The Fellowship of the Ring. As you start your adventure, you follow a parallel storyline to that of the books.

Like in most MMORPGs, you find yourself exploring the vast world of LOTRO for many, many hours. This representation of Middle Earth is very similar to that of the films, so you will recognize many familiar places like Bagends in the Shire and the Prancing Pony in Bree. Enter into the Old forest and talk to Tom Bombadil or ride to the north to see the great Thorin's Hall home of many Dwarves.

When the game was first released, only a few parts of Middle Earth were accessible: the land spanning from north–west of Hobbiton, through Bree, and all the way past Rivendell. The Mines of Moria had not been opened, and so the way to the Mirkwood and Gondor was blocked. The game is, however, regularly updated with new territories. Eventually, all of Middle Earth will be made accessible.

In order to progress both as a character and to unveil the story within the game, you need to complete a long list of quests. Some quests are quite humorous, for example, running errands for lovers and helping them get back together after a silly dispute. However, most quests require that you slay a certain amount of monsters or animals, which makes the game exciting and scary. There are also a fair amount of grinding quests, where you have to go out and slay, for example, 25 monsters of one kind and 25 monsters of another. Grinding quests are a great way to level-up, as is common in most MMORPGs.

If you travel the land and discover all the points of interest in a certain area, you will gain experience and a new trait. You can also gain traits by completing a series of quests or killing a whole bunch of monsters. Traits increase your statistics or skills and must be activated by a Bard, typically found in a Tavern. Each time you gain enough experience to advance to a new level, you learn new skills at the class trainer. Activating a trait or buying a new skill costs money—a lot of money as you reach higher levels.

There are special kinds of epic quests in the game where you meet heroes from the books and are enlisted to help them. If you play a human, you will meet Strider early on in the Prancing Pony. Many quests and levels later, you will meet him again as Aragon in Rivendell. If you play a Dwarf, you get to meet Gandalf at the beginning of the game. The epic quests follow a parallel storyline to that of the books, making you feel like you are part of the story of the Fellowship.

While wandering in the wilderness, you will stumble over resources that you can gather if you have the required skills. Fallen branches from great trees can be used to make bows and clubs, and there is metal ore to mine if you brought your pick axe. A slain bear or dragon can yield useful leather. With crafting skills like weapon or armor building, jewel crafting, and more, you can create lots of useful equipment, which can also be sold at the nearest auction house or traded with friends or family. More importantly, much of what you create yourself is better than what you can find as loot on fallen foes.

If you enjoy role playing, you can buy yourself a surname and get married. You can even have children and eventually have your own family history. LOTRO also has an interesting approach to getting beaten in battle.

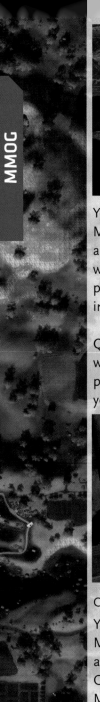

You don't die like you would in many other MMORPGs, but rather you lose your morale and succumb. Where a priest in another game would resurrect you, a Minstrel in LOTRO plays a melody that brings back your fighting spirit.

Questing is also a great way to obtain good weapons, armor, and equipment. Many non-player characters (NPCs) will have quests for you at one point or another.

CHARACTERS

You can choose between being a Hobbit, Man, Elf, or Dwarf, and create your character from among seven classes: Burglar, Captain, Champion, Guardian, Hunter, Lore-Master, and Minstrel. In all the races but the Dwarves, you can also choose to be a man or woman (the Dwarves lock their women up

so no one will ever see them, so only male dwarves actively play the game).

Each class has particular powers. The Burglar exposes hidden enemies and weakens the group's foes. With a sneaky approach to combat, the burglar uses stealth to surprise unsuspecting targets.

The burglar also pickpockets humanoid NPC enemies. The Captain's main job is to increase group morale, but he or she is also a reasonably good fighter and solo player. With a Captain in the group, beaten members can be revived during battle. The Champion is the main offensive strength of the group. Wielding dual swords and some good multiple-target blows, the Champion is the spear point of the group. The Guardian, who is typically

referred to as the Tank and hidden behind a massive shield and heavy armor, can take a serious beating—hence the name. With an ability to draw aggression from enemies, the Guardian saves weaker members of the group should they be unlucky enough to attract the attention of strong enemies. The Hunter—often referred to as the Nuker—is the master of ranged attacks and can deal large amounts of damage to one or multiple foes. To inflict maximum damage, the Hunter must concentrate in one place for a long while. Because ranged attacks are easily disturbed, he is almost useless in close combat, but with traps, the Hunter can make a pin cushion out of the enemy at a safe distance. The Lore-Master is the group's main motivator or buffer. He has the best crowd control of all the classes, so he can share his power with other group members, and he has reasonable healing skills. The Lore-Master can befriend animals that help in battle. The Minstrel is the group's main healer and can effectively get fallen group members fit for fighting again. With songs and music, the Minstrel raises the morale of the group and lowers the enemies' spirits. Minstrels do not solo well at higher levels because they can only inflict very low attack damage.

MONSTER PLAY

If you like player-vs.-player combat, you can, once you have reached level 10, join the hordes of Mordor. You will be working for the Lich lord Angmar. You can choose to be an Urukai, an Orc, a Wolf, or a Spider. As your skills increase, you will also be allowed to play as a Troll. The classes in the ranks of Mordor are very similar to those that fight for good, so it is easy to get familiar with your role as a Minion of Sauron. The Spiders work much like Burglars, the War-Chief works like a Captain, the Orc is like a Champion,

and the Urukhai is like a Hunter. Character progression in Monster Play is somewhat limited compared to that of normal play. Luckily, for the merry hobbits of the Shire, the monsters are restricted to a specific area of the world where only the most experienced players can enter.

MUSIC

One unusual aspect of LOTRO is that players

can actually play the instruments in the game in real time. Once a character has gained the necessary skills to play a given instrument, you can activate the instrument and use the keyboard to play over three octaves. The music is then broadcasted to nearby players. Sometimes while wandering about in the wilderness of Middle Earth, you can hear someone sitting alone, practicing their melody.

FELLOWSHIPS AND KINSHIP

There are two types of groups in the game. Short-term groups are called Fellowships. They are easily created and easily abandoned but are very useful for taking down multiple enemies and large foes. Some quests require that you be in a Fellowship to complete them.

Kinships require more commitment and are similar to guilds in other MMORPGS. Being part of a kinship is an excellent way to enjoy the social experience of an MMORPG. See the feature on Hardcore Territory (p. 86) for more on guilds.

The first LOTRO update, Book 9: Shores of Evendim, was released on June 14, 2007. It added the area of Evendim and more than 100 new quests, more monsters, collectible armor sets, and an updated music system.

The second update, Book 10: The City of Kings, was released at the end of August 2007 and added new storyline quests, Critter Play, and Legendary Play. Critter play allows you to play smaller animals to explore the world, and Legendary play enables you to play Trolls and Rangers from the North.

The third update, Book 11, released in November 2007 and opened up the game for player housing. It also introduced the first Balrog to the game.

The Lord of the Rings Online is an amazing representation of Middle Earth and a terrific game in and of itself, providing both fans of the books and MMORPGs with countless hours of exploration and challenges.

AVAILABLE ON

Nintendo DS
Nintendo Wii
✓ PC Windows
PC Mac
Playstation 2
Playstation 3
Playstation Portable
Xbox 360

AVERAGE SCORE

NA
out of 10

GAME FACTS

PUBLISHER
NCsoft

DEVELOPER
Destination Games

FIRST RELEASED DATE
Nov 2, 2007

GAME GENRE
MMORPG

TIME PERIOD
Future

THEME
Sci-Fi War

COMPLEXITY
Medium

SIMILAR GAMES

Anarchy Online
Lord of the Rings Online
World of Warcraft

RICHARD GARRIOTT'S
Tabula Rasa

Richard Garriot's Tabula Rasa is a massive multiplayer on-line role playing game published by Destination Games and NCsoft. Breaking away from the usual fantasy storyline, Tabula Rasa immerses the player into an alternate universe of alien wars and human survival. The story is based upon the Eloh, an ancient race of aliens who mastered the use of Logos and thus gained the ability to manipulate matter, energy, and force in unique and powerful ways. The Eloh were a peaceful race and they spread their knowledge throughout the universe.

Another alien race, the Thrax, turned upon the Eloh after learning their secrets. Although the Eloh's survived their initial conflict with the Thrax, a rift was created within their culture that ultimately led to their downfall. Some of the Eloh felt their knowledge should be withheld from others who should instead be given "guidance" by the Eloh. They became known as the Neph. Eventually, the Neph joined forces with the Thrax and the remaining Eloh fled to the far corners of the universe.

Many years later, Earth caught the attention of the Bane, a group that included not only the Thrax but also many other races and genetically engineered creatures that fight for the Neph. The planet was invaded for its resources, both biological and natural, and within five days, the aliens overran the planet. Humans were embroiled in a celestial war of the Bane. A small number of human refugees were able to escape and join the remaining Elohs and other races to fight the Bane on alien planets. They became the Army of the Allied Free Sentients (AFS).

All players are members of the AFS and seek to destroy the Bane and other enemy alien creatures. Character creation is fairly simple and straightforward. The player chooses a first name unique to the character and a last name that

CHARACTER SELECT

will be used for all characters they create on the particular server. The player then chooses the appearance of the character and can select the gender, customize the skin and hair color, choose among a number of faces, and decide on a variety of clothing options.

New characters begin in a tutorial area called Bootcamp. Here characters learn to move, engage in combat, chat with other players, and are taught how to use explosives and other items. They also are given the opportunity to locate and learn to use Logos. Several missions are available in the training area.

Experience is gained by killing creatures and completing missions. After completing all the missions in the training area, characters are told to leave via a transport ship that takes new recruits to another area of the planet.

Character development consists of gaining new abilities and skills as you advance as well as adding new points to your attributes. Tabula Rasa introduces three attributes—Mind, Body, and Spirit—that are different than traditional attributes found in other MMOs. Mind increases your power, similar to Mana in fantasy games; Body involves the number of hit points given to the character; and Spirit affects the regeneration rate of your character.

The skills and abilities a character can gain through advancement depend on the career path the player chooses for their character. Careers are arranged in a pyramid format and the character moves forward by choosing a divergent path at critical points in the character's development. Each path leads to a different specialty and may focus on areas such as ranged combat, stealth, heavy combat, engineering, or biotechnology.

When a player reaches level five, he may choose between two careers: Soldier or Specialist. The Soldier trains in skills and abilities related to weapons and armor, while the Specialist focuses on technical support areas. At level 15, players again

choose from two divergent career paths, depending on their original path. The Soldier can choose either the Commando or Ranger path while the Specialist can select to be a Biotechnician or a Sapper. At level 30, the Career choice is made. Commandos can choose Grenadier or Guardian while Rangers can choose Sniper or Spy. Sappers can choose Demolitionist or Engineer while Biotechnicians can choose Medic or Exobiologist. Acquiring skills along each path allows you to use various weapons, armor, and tools at the various

career levels. Abilities for each career path and level require the acquisition of specific Logos. Logos are a language developed by the Eloh to communicate with other beings they encounter. Mastering this language opens up the ability to manipulate matter and energy with the mind.

Hidden throughout the game, Logos can be found in various areas, and can be uncovered through exploration while on missions. The Logos Tablet can be opened by pressing the "J" key on the keyboard. All Logos found appear in the Tablet. Once you have the correct Logos, the corresponding ability is available for use as long as your character is at the correct level and career path. You can drag often-used abilities to the Ability Tray for quick access during combat. Abilities give the character

special attacks and powers, such as resistance to various attacks or special physical feats.

Missions are found by looking for non-player characters (NPCs) with communicators above their heads. The NPC will give players a short briefing regarding the mission, which can then be

selected or rejected. Not all missions are strictly combat-related, but most players will encounter combat during some portion of the mission. Various missions require players to gather items, kill a specific number or type of creature, or scare off creatures. Once a mission is completed, the character may gain money or a choice of an item. At the end of the mission, the player may be given the option to join another mission, often related to the first.

Crafting is available to all characters along all career paths, although depending on the character's career path or level, they may not be able to use the crafted item. In order to craft, the player must first train the character in at least one of the four crafting skills available. The skills include Thermodynamics, Photonics, Chemistry, and Genetics. Recipes for items can be bought from NPCs, found as loot, or obtained through trade with other players. Specific resources must be gathered for each recipe, and these can also be purchased from an NPC, gathered, or obtained through trade. Once the recipe and resources are in the character's inventory, a Crafting Station must be located at one of the AFS bases. Not all bases have a crafting machine so the player may need to travel to find one. The recipes and raw materials are put into the hopper of the Crafting Station and after a few seconds, the new items will appear.

Many types of items can be found in the game, including assorted guns, missile launchers, melee weapons, med packs, resources, skins, ammunition, DNA, clothing, and armor with abilities. Besides crafting items, players can obtain items through looting defeated foes, as rewards for completing missions, as purchases from NPCs, or through trade with other players. Most items can also be sold to NPCs. Armor and weapons can become damaged and be repaired by some

NPCs. The condition of an item can be discovered by hovering over the item with the mouse.

Players can clone their characters if they have clone points, which are given at tier levels 5, 15, and 30. If the player chooses to spend the point to clone the character, the character creation screen will appear and the player will be asked to change the first name of the cloned character and be given the option to modify the cloned character's appearance. The cloned character will be at the same career level and path as the original character. This allows the player to clone at a lower level and then use the clone to explore other career paths without starting from scratch.

Most of the game's content focuses on combat, which blends some shooter elements into the traditional MMO style of combat. However, it is not strictly a first-person shooter. Bullets will "stick" to the target, even turning corners around buildings. Combat is in real time, so movement and positioning on the battlefield is important, creating an element of strategy. Tactical elements can be implemented, such as crouching while firing to gain better accuracy or taking cover before the enemy shoots. Different types of NPCs and aliens use various methods of attack, creating exciting and unpredictable combat scenarios. If the character takes cover, the enemies may circle to try to get a shot. The majority of combat weapons are ranged, including various rifles, shotguns, and machine guns, although melee does exist as well. The Weapons Tray allows you to drag and drop your most-used weapons so you can quickly cycle through different weapons during combat. An integrated voice chat allows players to coordinate attacks and work together as a team. Soloing is also a valid option in the game and many missions can be done alone. Tabula Rasa does include optional player–vs.–player combat, so players can be challenged by targeting them and choosing the duel option from the Radial Menu.

When a character dies, a map is displayed with locations of various hospitals. The player can choose a known hospital and the character will be teleported there. Once at the hospital, the character will recover after a short period of time. During this time, the character's attributes are lowered. If another death occurs during this recovery period, the length of time is increased significantly.

The game world in Tabula Rasa is unique compared to many current MMOs. You can read more about Tabula Rasa's lore and learn about the game by going to the website at: HTTP://WWW.RGTR.COM

· BLADE HEA FORMED FROM IVORY – LIKELY A LARGE BORGAR-LIKE CREATURE'S TUSKS

FORAN RUNES

RINGS ARE USED WHEN SUSPENDING TRIBAL COLORS OR STANDARDS FROM SPEAR.
✗ ALSO USED BY TROOPS AS A LASH-POINT AND SUPPORT POLE FOR FIELD TENTS.

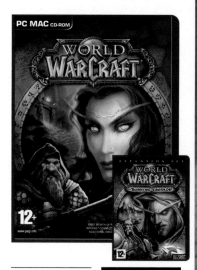

PC MAC CD-ROM

12+
www.pegi.info

AVAILABLE ON

Nintendo DS
Nintendo Wii
✓ PC Windows
✓ PC Mac
Playstation 2
Playstation 3
Playstation Portable
Xbox 360

AVERAGE SCORE

9.1
out of 10

GAME FACTS

PUBLISHER
Vivendi Universal Games

DEVELOPER
Blizzard Entertainment

FIRST RELEASED DATE
Nov 23, 2004

GAME GENRE	**TIME PERIOD**
MMORPG	Medieval
THEME	**COMPLEXITY**
Fantasy War	Medium

SIMILAR GAMES

Lord of the Rings Online
GuildWars
Lineage 2

World of Warcraft
THE BURNING CRUSADE

World of Warcraft (WoW) is a massive multiplayer online role-playing game, where you have the opportunity to discover the world of Azeroth through the eyes of your self-created hero. Its background story revolves around the universe of Blizzard's previous *Warcraft* games, as well as written novels and comics that tell of crucial events that happen all the way back to 10,000 years before the game takes place. *World of Warcraft* is a role-playing game set in a massive multiplayer online environment and as such is different from its predecessors, which were real-time strategy games similar to Command & Conquer and Age of Empire. *World of Warcraft* is set four years after the end of the previous game, *Warcraft III: The Frozen Throne*.

The central conflict in the game is between the Alliance, which mainly consists of the Humans, Elves, Dwarfs, and Gnomes, and the Horde, which are at first Orcs, the Undead, Trolls, and Taurens. After picking your side of the conflict you create a character from one of the races mentioned above as well as your character's class. Classes play a major role in the game, and your choice of class is one of the most important you make. Classes decide what you will be doing most of the game, as well as your role, if you decide to join a group. The classes are Warrior, Priest, Mage, Rogue, Warlock, Hunter, Druid, Paladin, and Shaman. Although not essential, your choice of race also has consequences for your choice of class because some races have special bonuses and abilities that work better with certain classes than with others. If you are unhappy with your class selection, you are free to make another character, but that does require starting over. So that you have the opportunity to get it just right, many gamers recommend experimenting a bit with a variety of characters. The commitment to the character you eventually go with can last months, even years!

After choosing your class and the appearance of your character, you begin playing in one of the start areas of the game. In the firsts levels you are introduced to the basics of the game as well as some of the mechanics. You have all of Azeroth except the northern land Northrend available for exploring, and there are almost no limitations to where you can go. However, the areas are created to fit different levels, so surviving can become quite a challenge if you decide to go to places where opponents are stronger than you are. Azeroth is filled with all kinds of creatures that are not player controlled called NPCs. You can attack these at any time, and defeating them will give you experience points. Experience points take you from one level to the next. Your level indicates how good, strong, and experienced your character is. You need a certain amount of experience points to get to the next level, and the amount increases from level to level. You may also pick up loot from opponents you defeat, loot that may be used or sold. The experience and loot you find varies with the level of your opponent.

As your character develops, you gain access to more parts of the game, for instance professions. Having a profession helps you create items that you can use to help your progress through the game. You can also earn money from trading items you gather and create with other players. There are primary and secondary professions. You can only have two primary jobs at the same time, and if you choose to discard a job to learn a new one, you will have to start from the bottom again if you decide to return to your former job. The primary jobs are Mining, Blacksmithing, Engineering, Skinning, Alchemy, Tailoring, Enchanting, Herbalism, and Leatherworking. There are also two paths to follow inside each profession, i.e. a blacksmith has the choice of specializing in weapon-making or armor -making. Because you are restricted to two primary jobs, keep in mind that there are certain combinations that work better together than others. A blacksmith needs metal ore to create items, so what better combination is there than a miner who can extract metal ore from veins found scattered around Azeroth? Secondary jobs are Cooking, First Aid, and Fishing, and you can learn all three of these if you want to.

With cooking, for example, you can learn new recipes from special trainers as you improve. Recipes can also be found on opponents.

At level 10 you receive your first talent point. There are three talent trees for each class, where you can

spend points to improve different aspects of your character. After you hit level 10 you gain one talent point per level. For instance if you are a Mage, you can choose to work on the fire, frost, or arcane talent trees, while hunters have marksmanship, beast mastery, and survival. These points improve certain skills you already have, and sometimes you can learn new skills from a tree. If you want to reset your trees and retrieve all of your talent points so that you can apply

them differently, you have to pay a trainer. However, this costs money, and each time you reset your talent points the cost increases. The way you spend your

talent points greatly affects your character and its specialization, especially for classes like warriors, priests, paladins, shamans, and druids, where their entire role in the game changes depending on what talent tree they choose to specialize in.

Class abilities are similar to job abilities. To learn new abilities you need to be at a certain level as well as have money to buy new skills from a trainer. As you progress, the cost of abilities increases, and

eventually you will notice how hard this hits your purse! But have no fear: you can get money quite easily from selling things, finding it on opponents, and completing quests. Quests can be found around the world, and they give different rewards upon completion. There are also instances scattered around the world. Instances are special places where you

meet harder opponents as well as bosses. To successfully do these instances, you will need a group, most often of five players. The items dropped inside instances are often better than those found elsewhere, but each instance has a level requirement. The instances are separated from the world, and if you enter as a group, the dungeon will be created only for you.

For some instances, called raid instances, you are required to be in a raid group, which can vary from 6–40 players. Instances have caps depending on how many are intended to do them. Originally WoW had one 10-man raid instance, two 20-man, and five 40-man encounters. In the expansion pack, Burning Crusade, there are two 10-man raids, and seven 25-man raid instances. As you may have guessed, these require a high level of coordination from players, and therefore most often you will enter these instances together with your guild or a raiding com-

munity (people who join up just for raiding). Raid instances include some of the most challenging encounters since they require both a high level of coordination and tactics from all players, but the rewards are also greater than any you will find elsewhere in the game.

Guilds in *World of Warcraft* are for many a central reason for playing the game. A guild is a coalition of players, where one guild master starts out by purchasing a guild charter and then gets 10 signatures to create the guild. A guild can be named pretty much whatever you want, although not many people are going to join a guild named "I pwn noobs." After the guild has been created, the guild master and whoever he appoints as helpers can invite more people to the guild. There are several reasons to join a guild. Some might join because of a common nationality, some out of common interests, and some because they share the same goals in

Possible Dive in 10sec!

the game. A guild is a good way to make friends with other players and join up for group quests and instances.

There are many different items in *World of Warcraft*. They are not only separated by type, but also by quality. The names of the items have different colors indicating its quality. The qualities are Poor, Com-

mon, Uncommon, Rare, Epic, and Legendary. A better quality item isn't necessarily stronger than a lower quality item, although usually it is. Also, there are set items that give small bonuses if you collect all the pieces in the set. However, they are not found everywhere and are more common at the higher levels. Note that after level 20, gray (poor item quality) items can safely be sold to a vendor. Common items (white item names) are often used to make stuff or are part of a quest but should not be worn as armor or weapons after level 30.

The expansion pack the Burning Crusade has a couple of additions to the game. There are two new races: the Blood Elves on the Horde side and the Draenei for the Alliance. There is also a new profession called Jewelcrafting, and a new introduction to the equipment called sockets. The sockets can have gems attached to them, but you won't see any socketable items before Outland because the Jewelcrafters make these gems.

In addition, a new area is accessible through a dark portal. It leads to Outland, a torn world full of new dangers, as well as instances, but you need to be at level 58 in order to do quests there. Some more *Warcraft* lore lies behind this place, and its history can be traced to the previous games. In Outland you also have areas that cannot be reached by foot, so you will have to purchase a flying mount. The level cap is increased to level 70, which gives already maxed-out characters something to work for.

In the second expansion, Wrath of the Lich King, new aspects of the *Warcraft* lore are brought back into the game. Arthas, which fused with the Lich King in the previous game, is now back together with the playable area of Northrend. The level cap is increased to level 80 and the new Inscripting

profession is available. A new special hero class is added, the Death Knight, which will be available through a quest chain.

If you wish to explore the history of the universe of *World of Warcraft*, check out

HTTP://WWW.WORLDOFWARCRAFT.COM/INFO/STORY/INDEX.HTML

TRACKMANIA UNITED

Racing
GAMES

COLIN MCRAE: DIRT.

Racing games are very popular and continue to thrill gamers and casual visitors alike. Whether it's a boys' night in with *Burnout Dominator* or a family event with *Excite Truck*, it's the speed and tight maneuvering that separate the racers from the rest.

Racing games have a natural connection to real-world racing. Just about all types of racing events have their electronic counterparts. It was, therefore, a terrific opportunity to talk with WRC champion and virtual racer Petter Solberg. Since some of the appeal of racing games is the opportunity to pilot vehicles that are beyond most people's physical grasp, we asked him about how close electronic racing is to the real world. "Some games," he explains, "are very close to reality, both with the car's physics and the graphics. The biggest difference is that the feedback from the car is missing—and, of course, that there is no 'restart' button."

PETTER SOLBERG

WORLD RALLY CHAMPION PETTER SOLBERG

Born: November 18, 1974

Petter Solberg grew up in a motor sport home with both parents racing in the Bilcross, a Norwegian form of entry-level Rally Cross with inexpensive cars. Petter was present at almost every event and eagerly assisted the rest of the family in repairing competition cars. He participated in his first Bilcross race the day after he received his license in 1992. In 1995 and 1996, he won the Norwegian Championship in both Rally Cross and Hill Climb, and then moved on to rally racing, winning the Norwegian Rally Championship in 1998. Soon afterwards, he signed a three-year junior contract with Ford Motor Company to participate in the World Rally Championship (WRC). He was expected to take on a low profile as a junior, but he managed to score points for his team even in his first year. In 2003, he won the WRC championship with the Subaru World Rally Team and has since remained among the world's top drivers. After Petter moved on to WRC, his older brother Henning Solberg won the Norwegian Rally Championship for an impressive five years in a row from 1999–2003. Henning is a big videogame enthusiast and plays both for fun and training to learn the courses before a race. Petter is married to Pernilla Walfridsson, considered one of the world's fastest female rally drivers, and together they have a son named Oliver. She also comes from a motor sport family as the daughter of European Rally Cross Champion Per-Inge "Pi" Walfridsson.

MOTO GP 07

But as always, one needs to find a balance. Only a select few get the opportunity to drive a real rally car through one of the WRC circuits, but it's as much work as it is fun. "The toning down of the real-world physics and difficulty does make it easier for beginners and children to get started with their virtual racing," says Solberg. "It might not be what hardcore players want, but I do believe that a combination is important in giving as many players as possible the most fun."

Solberg views racing games as a great recruitment tool for real-world racing. "I believe that many get their first experience of Rally through racing games, and this is important for the interest in the sport. With

the quality of games today, they are even used in the training of drivers. My brother [successful WRC driver Henning Solberg] has been doing this for years." He even thinks this might bring female drivers to the fore. "A lot of girls are rally drivers and co-pilots. I don't think it will be long before we see some

NEED FOR SPEED: PRO STREET

MOTORSTORM

female national drivers making a name for themselves."

This season saw a long string of exciting releases, ranging from the slightly weird (*Crazy Frog Racer 2*) and the polished and true-to-life (*Project Gotham Racing 4*) to titles that took racing online, such as *Trackmania* United's virtual world series. Some games are updates of on-going franchises, while others take their inspiration from other cultural spheres. EA's *NASCAR '08* takes one of the world's toughest racing challenges to the PlayStation 3 with official drivers, teams, and cars, while Data Design's *Earache Extreme Metal Racing* opts for using record company Earache's roster of dark metal artists as the basis for the game's teams

and soundtrack. If your musical tastes lie in another direction, there's always Pimp My Ride, featuring hip-hop icon Xzibit, just as in the MTV show.

Both the gaming and the racing community were hit by a tragedy during 2007. Just days after the release of his latest game, WRC superstar and racing game mogul Colin McCrae died, with his son, in a helicopter accident. *Colin McCrae DIRT* will therefore be the last game with Colin's active participation, but his legacy will undoubtedly live on. His contribution to elevating the rally genre to its current status has been invaluable and has given thousands of electronic racers countless hours of fun.

FORMULA ONE: CHAMPIONSHIP EDITION

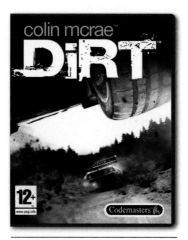

AVAILABLE ON

Nintendo DS
Nintendo Wii
✓ PC Windows
PC Mac
Playstation 2
✓ Playstation 3
Playstation Portable
✓ Xbox 360

GAME FACTS *

PUBLISHER
Codemasters

DEVELOPER
Codemasters

FIRST RELEASED
2007-06-15

GAME GENRE	TIME PERIOD
Racing	Present
THEME	**COMPLEXITY**
Sport	Low

SIMILAR GAMES

WRC: Rally Evolved
Forza Motorsport 2
Motorstorm

RATING & MULTIPLAYER

USA	Europe	Network	Offline
EVERYONE **E** ESRB	12+ www.pegi.info	100 Players	No

Colin McRae: DiRT
(USA: DiRT)

SETTING
This extreme rally game stays true to its name—DiRT. Offering both an arcade experience and more difficult challenges, you can drive close to 50 vehicles and attend more than 60 different racing events on mud and dirt courses all over the world.

GAME SUMMARY
Prepare for a rush of adrenaline as you speed through the woods, around bumpy mud courses, or down steep mountainsides on narrow gravel roads. The cars are without exception beautifully detailed, and one of the game's many impressive features is its damage animation. Whether you find yourself in the rainy countryside of Japan or on dusty Italian backroads, stay focused to avoid critical damage. DiRT offers a great career mode in which you earn both points to unlock new tiers and money to spend on new vehicles. In career mode you can race internationally or participate in beat-the-clock races. If winning becomes too easy you can crank up the difficulty and suddenly the driving settings change and racing becomes risky again. Each car handles differently, and vehicles have their own unique sounds.

CHALLENGES & HINTS
DiRT's realism will surely put your driving skills to the test. As the cars take damage and every mistake has its consequence, climbing to the top of the ranking lists will take hours of intensive training. Altering the difficulty levels quickly changes the pace and feel of the game. Although not recommended in Career mode, a bit of extra fun can be had by crashing your vehicle at high speeds; the game features some pretty amazing feats of physics!

(Rally legend Colin McRae tragically passed away the 15th of September 2007)

KEY GAMEPLAY ELEMENTS
Steer/Maneuver
Tactics/Plan
Build & Design

GAME WORLD SIZE	Large
YOUR ROLE	Race Driver
REPLAY VALUE	Infinite

AVERAGE SCORE

8.3
out of 10

*Data and images may vary on the various platforms

Forza Motorsport 2

AVAILABLE ON

Nintendo DS
Nintendo Wii
PC Windows
PC Mac
Playstation 2
Playstation 3
Playstation Portable
✓ Xbox 360

GAME FACTS

PUBLISHER
Microsoft Game Studio

DEVELOPER
Microsoft Game Studio

FIRST RELEASED
2007-05-29

GAME GENRE	**TIME PERIOD**
Racing	Present
THEME	**COMPLEXITY**
Sport	Low

SIMILAR GAMES

Gran Turismo 4
Need for Speed: Prostreet
Colin McRae: DiRT

RATING & MULTIPLAYER

USA	Europe	Network	Offline
		8 Players	2 Players

SETTING

Forza Motorsport 2 gives you full control of the racing world. Drive almost any car anywhere in the world, including exhibition races, time trials, and online races. You can also build your own career from scratch.

GAME SUMMARY

Career mode is where the heart of this game lies by allowing you to earn money and increase your driver level. Choose at which continent you would like to start and the game goes from there. Forza offers a wide range of vehicles including everything from a Volkswagen Golf and Mini Cooper to Ferraris and Saleens, but the cars you drive are mainly based on the region you select. Cash earned in races can be used to upgrade car parts and unlock new races. You earn discounts with local automakers as you establish various relationships. There is also an option to upgrade your car into new letter classes, which define your driver level. While driving, you can keep track of damage and tire temperature. The cars are designed with individual handling, and the physics and simulations are authentic. Race through real locations like Rio de Janeiro and personalize and tune one of 300 cars.

CHALLENGES & HINTS

To complete races and move up in your career, you must avoid spinning out of control. Likewise, passive driving leads to a decrease in placing. Use your upgrades right, and you will outclass your competition.

KEY GAMEPLAY ELEMENTS
Steer/Maneuver
Tactics/Plan
Build & Design

GAME WORLD SIZE	Medium
YOUR ROLE	Race Driver
REPLAY VALUE	Infinite

AVERAGE SCORE

8.9

out of 10

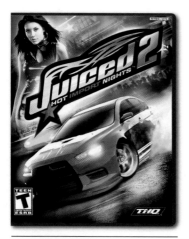

Juiced 2
Hot Import Nights

SETTING

Based on the popular street-racing event, Juiced 2 is all about heavily tuned street cars, hip DJs, and super hot ladies. So boost up your NOS power and drift your way to the top to earn the respect of every racer and hot lady from London to Tokyo.

GAME SUMMARY

Juiced 2: Hot Import Nights features 90 cars that can be fully modified with more than 350 parts from famous companies such as MOMO and BBS. There are several racing modes, with street racing and drifting being the primary modes. Your performance alters during the course of a race depending on how many times you crash and which parts get damaged. The game also has a lot of different online features, where you can buy and sell cars or race other people for cars. If you lose, you lose your car as well. An interesting feature is the driver DNA profiling system, where the game tracks all of your driving habits. Other players can download your DNA and race against it before they challenge you. There is also an online gambling system that lets you bet on other people's races and win extra cash for parts.

CHALLENGES & HINTS

You have to stay sharp in this game. Your opponents are smart and will do whatever it takes to make you lose. Since the game features a lot of betting, don't get too eager. You may end up loosing more than just your money.

AVAILABLE ON

- ✓ Nintendo DS
- Nintendo Wii
- ✓ PC Windows
- PC Mac
- ✓ Playstation 2
- ✓ Playstation 3
- ✓ Playstation Portable
- ✓ Xbox 360

GAME FACTS *

PUBLISHER
THQ

DEVELOPER
Juice Games

FIRST RELEASED
2007-09-09

GAME GENRE	**TIME PERIOD**
Racing	Present
THEME	**COMPLEXITY**
Sport	Low

SIMILAR GAMES

Project Gotham Racing 4
Forza Motorsport 2
Need for Speed Carbon

RATING & MULTIPLAYER

USA	Europe	Network	Offline
TEEN T CONTENT RATED BY ESRB	12+ www.pegi.info	Yes	Yes

KEY GAMEPLAY ELEMENTS

Steer/Maneuver
Build & Design
Trade

GAME WORLD SIZE	Medium
YOUR ROLE	Race Driver
REPLAY VALUE	Several Times

AVERAGE SCORE

6.8
out of 10

Data and images may vary on the various platforms

Motorstorm

SETTING

Join in on the wild races in Monument Valley as you compete with spectacular off-road vehicles through magnificent landscapes that resemble the real thing.

GAME SUMMARY

A bunch of crazy race drivers with custom-built high-performance off-road vehicles have gathered in the desert of Monument Valley for Motorstorm. It's the wildest off-road race ever put together as big trucks, buggies, ATVs, motorbikes, and monster trucks fight side by side for honor and glory. There is only one rule: no rules! So the best way to get ahead is to make sure those in front of you crash. As you fly through sand, smoke, and flames with car parts and the bodies of unlucky drivers swirling around you, you must use tactics and cunning to survive. The nitro boost gives explosive speed, but don't use it too much or your vehicle will explode. The tracks are large and varied with breathtaking jumps and steep cliffs. There is more than one way to the finish line, but only one way is fastest. If you succeed in securing a top three position, you will qualify for the next race that has only more carnage!

CHALLENGES & HINTS

Disaster is never far away when you're flying with full boost power through a brutal rocky landscape on slippery sand and mud. The competitors want to win as much as you do and will do everything they can to kick you off the track. You need to find the smartest routes and optimize the nitro boost to win.

AVAILABLE ON

Nintendo DS
Nintendo Wii
PC Windows
PC Mac
Playstation 2
✓ Playstation 3
Playstation Portable
Xbox 360

GAME FACTS

PUBLISHER
SCEA, SCEE

DEVELOPER
Evolution Studios

FIRST RELEASED
2007-03-06

GAME GENRE
Racing

TIME PERIOD
Present

THEME
Sport

COMPLEXITY
Low

SIMILAR GAMES

DiRT
Sega Rally Revo
ATV: Offroad Fury

RATING & MULTIPLAYER

USA	Europe	Network	Offline
TEEN T ESRB	12+ www.pegi.info	12 Players	No

KEY GAMEPLAY ELEMENTS

Steer/Maneuver
Tactics/Plan
Attack/Fight

GAME WORLD SIZE	Large
YOUR ROLE	Race Driver
REPLAY VALUE	Infinite

AVERAGE SCORE

7.9

out of 10

03:35.72

BOOST

2 LAP /3

7 POS /12

06:38.35

BOOST

3 LAP /3

5 POS /14

01:52.87

BOOST

1 LAP /4

13 POS /15

FINAL LAP

04:44.44

BOOST

3 LAP /3

7 POS /14

01:36.85

BOOST

1 LAP /3

14 POS /15

00:28.03

BOOST

1 LAP /3

7 POS /14

02:30.09

BOOST

2 LAP /3

4 POS /12

AVAILABLE ON

✓ Nintendo DS
✓ Nintendo Wii
✓ PC Windows
   PC Mac
✓ Playstation 2
✓ Playstation 3
✓ Playstation Portable
✓ Xbox 360

GAME FACTS*

PUBLISHER
Electronic Arts

DEVELOPER
EA Games

FIRST RELEASED
2007-11-14

GAME GENRE	TIME PERIOD
Racing	Present

THEME	COMPLEXITY
Sport	Low

SIMILAR GAMES

Ridge Racer 7
Colin McRae: DIRT
Forza Motorsport 2

RATING & MULTIPLAYER

USA	Europe	Network	Offline
		Yes	Yes

Need for Speed
PROSTREET

SETTING

Need for Speed ProStreet takes street racing from an illegal underground activity to sophisticated and legal competitions. Precision handling and upgraded graphics will no doubt put you in a racing mood!

GAME SUMMARY

Enter race events around the world and compete in four different types of races including grip, drift, speed challenge, and drag racing. You will find music blasting and crowds of fans cheering for the cars on the start line. Depending on the event, you are allowed to bring a certain number of cars, but if you destroy a car, you must start that race over. If you manage to total all of your cars, you have to start the event over. This is a game full of consequence, making the game more serious than ever. The damage you inflict on your car is immediately visible. So is the smoke from burning rubber that sometimes clouds your windshield. Customize your cars' appearance and performance to gain an advantage on your rivals. Each racer is also personalized and displays different attitudes and levels of aggression. With the game's advanced AI, your driving skills will be tested to their limits. Take your racing online to show off your skills and attitude.

CHALLENGES & HINTS

Take the time to customize your cars. Adding a new cooling fan to the engine will in fact prevent the car from overheating. You have 10,000 car parts to choose from, all of which can help you beat out the competition and rush up the rankings.

KEY GAMEPLAY ELEMENTS

Steer/Maneuver
Tactics/Plan
Build & Design

GAME WORLD SIZE	Medium
YOUR ROLE	Race Driver
REPLAY VALUE	Infinite

AVERAGE SCORE

NA

out of 10

Data and images may vary on the various platforms

Project Gotham Racing 4

SETTING

The highly anticipated Project Gotham Racing 4 is here to push your driving skills to the limit. Introducing motorcycles and a new dynamic weather system, this game will take you around the world to an array of challenging racing events.

GAME SUMMARY

A new career mode allows you to create a character from among 25 nationalities, design a race jersey, and join or create a team. Although you race as part of a team, Kudos points that you earn for showing off stunts and complicated maneuvers contribute to your single-player total. Your fans also react to everything you do throughout the game, creating a realistic feel. Your bank account only takes Kudos points, which unlock everything from cars to garages. More than 130 vehicles are available, 30 of which are motorcycles. This brand new addition to the series comes with completely new physics and incredible maneuvering. Different camera views allow you to get a clear view of your hands on the wheel or the throttle. Another addition to the previous version is a weather system that affects the way you race. As the weather changes, you have to adjust your driving to compensate. The weather is specific to the city you're in, which includes Quebec, London, Tokyo, Las Vegas, Shanghai, and Nurnburg Ring.

CHALLENGES & HINTS

Whether you are racing in a car or on a bike, race fast and with style. Win over the fans by doing daring tricks or moves to build your racing reputation. Keep in mind the changing weather conditions when selecting your tires!

AVAILABLE ON

Nintendo DS
Nintendo Wii
PC Windows
PC Mac
Playstation 2
Playstation 3
Playstation Portable
✓ Xbox 360

GAME FACTS

PUBLISHER
Microsoft Game Studio

DEVELOPER
Bizzare Creations

FIRST RELEASED
2007-10-02

GAME GENRE	**TIME PERIOD**
Racing	Present
THEME	**COMPLEXITY**
Sport	Low

SIMILAR GAMES

Forza Motorsport 2
Need For Speed: Prostreet
Gran Turismo 4

RATING & MULTIPLAYER

USA	Europe	Network	Offline
E	3+		
	www.pegi.info	8 Players	2 Players

KEY GAMEPLAY ELEMENTS

Steer/Maneuver
Build & Design
Tactics/Plan

GAME WORLD SIZE	Medium
YOUR ROLE	Race Driver
REPLAY VALUE	Infinite

AVERAGE SCORE

8.9

out of 10

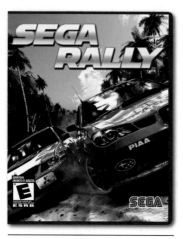

Sega Rally

SETTING

Get ready for more speed and action in this remake of the classic 1995 arcade game Sega Rally. Choose between snow, dirt, or asphalt tracks. This game is all about powersliding, so step on it!

GAME SUMMARY

This is a game for those who like more arcade-style racing, as opposed to serious racing simulators. Realism aside, this game puts speed and drifting in the front seat. Get behind the wheel and drift your way through more than 20 different tracks with great variations (Alpine, Canyon, Arctic, Safari, and Tropical) and a truly arcade feel. Despite the visual improvements, the basics are pretty much the same as in the original arcade game. You can choose between many different 2WD and 4WD rally cars, like the licensed Subaru Impreza. You will also find some of the classic cars from the first game. Worth noting is the brand new terrain deformation feature, which means that your car will leave traces and wounds int he dirt and that no two laps are the same. Watch out so you don't fall behind, 'cause tracks and loose mud will slow you down.

CHALLENGES & HINTS

For those who are used to realistic driving simulators, the drifting and car handling of this game takes some getting used to. But once you do, you'll have hours of drifting perfection and fun ahead of you.

AVAILABLE ON

Nintendo DS
Nintendo Wii
✓ PC Windows
PC Mac
Playstation 2
✓ Playstation 3
✓ Playstation Portable
✓ Xbox 360

GAME FACTS *

PUBLISHER
Sega

DEVELOPER
Sega

FIRST RELEASED
2007-09-25

GAME GENRE	TIME PERIOD
Racing	Present
THEME	**COMPLEXITY**
Sport	Low

SIMILAR GAMES

Ridge Racer 7
Motorstorm
DiRT

RATING & MULTIPLAYER

USA	Europe	Network	Offline
		6 Players	2 Players

KEY GAMEPLAY ELEMENTS

Steer/Maneuver
Tactics/Plan
Attack/Fight

GAME WORLD SIZE	Medium
YOUR ROLE	Race Driver
REPLAY VALUE	Several Times

AVERAGE SCORE

8.1

out of 10

Data and images may vary on the various platforms

AVAILABLE ON

Nintendo DS
Nintendo Wii
PC Windows
PC Mac
✓ Playstation 2
✓ Playstation 3
Playstation Portable
✓ Xbox 360

GAME FACTS *

PUBLISHER
THQ

DEVELOPER
Paradigm

FIRST RELEASED
2007-08-28

GAME GENRE	TIME PERIOD
Racing	Present
THEME	**COMPLEXITY**
Action	Low

SIMILAR GAMES

Stuntman
The Simpsons: Hit & Run
The Fast and the Furious

RATING & MULTIPLAYER

USA	Europe	Network	Offline
	16+ www.pegi.info	8 Players	4 Players

Stuntman
IGNITION

SETTING
Fasten your six-point harness and put the pedal to the metal in the all-new Stuntman: Ignition. Become the envy of all the stunt drivers as you work your way up the Hollywood hierarchy to perform in blockbusters and huge commercial deals.

GAME SUMMARY
In Stuntman: Ignition you perform the most daring stunts captured on film for a total of six fictional Hollywood blockbusters, including Overdrive (a take on the 1970s Starsky & Hutch) and Night Avenger (a take on Batman). Throughout each movie, the director gives you a set of stunt tasks that have to be completed in order to progress in the game. By combining stunts and being especially reckless, you earn points for your Strike Board. A total of 25 vehicles are at your disposal, ranging from motorcycles and sports cars to a hovercraft. Use the Stunt Constructor to design signature stunts and go online to play back-lot battles. Here the goal is to perform as many stunts as possible in a set number of laps. You can also drive back-lot races against up to eight players.

CHALLENGES & HINTS
It can be challenging to stay focused with so many explosions and things going on around you. Just remember to stay alert and keep the action going. Oh, and try not to perform any stunts of your own at home...you might chip the car.

KEY GAMEPLAY ELEMENTS
Steer/Maneuver
Tactics/Plan

		AVERAGE SCORE
GAME WORLD SIZE	Medium	**7.3**
YOUR ROLE	Stuntman	
REPLAY VALUE	Once or Twice	out of 10

Data and images may vary on the various platforms

HELLGATE: LONDON

Role Playing
Games

MASS EFFECT

To older generations, the phrase role-playing might conjure up images of charades, *Dungeons and Dragons*, or even a unique mix of both called live-action role-playing. However, to the wired and wireless generation, role-playing refers only to one thing: RPGs, or role-playing games.

An RPG is a videogame where you take the role of a character and create or follow an elaborate story. Often, you are able to create the hero you play, a process that has traditionally been defined with *Dungeons and Dragons*–themed classifications. For example, in the original *Diablo*, you could create a Warrior, Rogue, or Sorcerer. Nowadays, however, RPGs are pushing the envelope, defying tradition, and exploring new settings.

New RPGs are branching off more and more from the Tolkien-themed world of elves and goblins. In *Eternal Sonata*, for example, you can play as famed composer Frédéric Chopin, discarding the sword and shield for musical-themed combat instead. *Rogue Galaxy*, a futuristic sci-fi RPG, revolves around hero Jaster Rogue's dreams of galaxy, not dungeon, exploration. And games like *Mass Effect* and *Hellgate: London* are blending elements of action games into the genre, like first-person points of views and real-time combat systems.

This revitalization comes at a crucial time for consoles. Now that the dust has settled on the next-gen console launches, the console wars are in full swing, and the role-playing genre will play a significant role in deeming the victor. Microsoft's original Xbox console never captured a large Japanese audience, largely due to its lack of RPG titles. They've gone through great lengths to ensure that won't be the fate of the Xbox 360, even hiring the creator of the *Final Fantasy* series Hironobu Sakaguchi to create an exclusive title for the Xbox 360 called *Blue Dragon*.

While the importance of role-playing

Microsoft's original Xbox console never captured a large Japanese audience, largely due to its lack of RPG titles.

games is inarguable, what does the future hold for the genre? Some speculate that with more than 9 million users now playing the massively multiplayer online role-playing game (MMORPG) *World of Warcraft*, the audience for the typically single-player experience of role-playing games will begin to dwindle.

Much of the thrill of an MMO lies in their enormous, living worlds, and yet this doesn't necessarily interfere with role-playing games. You'd be one in nine million if you played *World of Warcraft*, and unless you devote your whole life to the game, you'll never be the best. That's not the case for role-playing games. Being much more story-oriented, the single-player nature of a role-playing game allows the focus to be placed entirely on the player: you must vanquish the villain, save the village, or in the case of *Rogue Galaxy*, maybe even the universe.

Unlike MMORPGs, role-playing games have a clear finish and ending. There is no monthly subscription, and developers aren't

trying to get you to keep coming back. Instead, they focus on making the finite time you play their games the most fun and enjoyable experience possible. This allows the emphasis to be placed on coloring a lush and detailed world, filled with unique interactions, characters, and experiences.

Still, role-playing game developers are beginning to understand the benefits of requiring online connectivity to play their games. Piracy cuts profits for game developers drastically, and more and more are turning toward an online relationship with their gamers as the answer. Developers at Valve created the distribution software *Steam* to serve as an easy way to have players log on in order to play their games, single player *or* multiplayer. This also benefits the players, who are able to painlessly retrieve updates, find multiplayer matches to play, and even purchase and download entire games online.

Funcom, the developers of the highly successful role-playing games *Longest Journey* and *Dreamfall*, said they stopped making single-player role-playing games because they were such easy targets for piracy. *Age of Conan*, their next feature, is an MMO that will necessitate constant online authentication from their servers, which they hope will stop piracy issues.

Even with MMOs, there will always be an audience for role-playing games. While the genre continues to adapt and change, the core foundation remains the same. Nothing can compete with the satisfaction you get from watching your character, who you worked on for hours, strategically outsmart the enemy's puzzles, outfight the villainous combatants, and succeed in becoming the greatest hero that world has ever seen.

ART: FINAL FANTASY XII

AVAILABLE ON

Nintendo DS
Nintendo Wii
PC Windows
PC Mac
Playstation 2
Playstation 3
Playstation Portable
✓ Xbox 360

GAME FACTS

PUBLISHER
Microsoft Game Studio

DEVELOPER
Mistwalker

FIRST RELEASED
2007-08-24

GAME GENRE	**TIME PERIOD**
RPG	Fantasy/Timeless
THEME	**COMPLEXITY**
Fantasy	Medium

SIMILAR GAMES

Final Fantasy XII
Fire Emblem: Radiant Dawn
Kingdom Hearts II

RATING & MULTIPLAYER

USA	Europe	Network	Offline
		No	No

Blue Dragon

SETTING

The peaceful little village of Talta and its inhabitants are under attack from a ferocious beast known as a "land shark." Three youngsters, Shu, Jiro, and Kluke, set out on an epic adventure to find the source of this evil and rescue their friends and family.

GAME SUMMARY

On their travels through ancient civilizations, Shu and his friends soon discover magical powers that give them the ability to control deadly phantom shadows. Throughout your quest, you can choose who and what to fight, but be aware that the enemy can suddenly launch surprise attacks. Like in a classic RPG, the battles are turn-based. Create your own fighting style by using the Shadow Change system, which includes everything from sword fighting to magical powers. The dynamic class system allows you to apply experience points gained in one combat mode to another—for example, from sword fighting to black magic. Learn to exploit your enemies' weaknesses to light, darkness, water, and fire. Explore the game's magnificent landscapes, and you will come across objects such as treasure chests, rocks, roots, and gold that will help you progress.

CHALLENGES & HINTS

Always remember to identify your enemy's weaknesses. Search everything! Amazing things can be found between dusty pipes and in old drawers. As you increase your experience you will gain new skills and eventually proceed to the next level for your selected class. Oh, and don't forget to stock up on antidote.

KEY GAMEPLAY ELEMENTS

Attack/Fight
Role Play
Gather

GAME WORLD SIZE	Large
YOUR ROLE	Heroes
REPLAY VALUE	Once or Twice

AVERAGE SCORE

7.9

out of 10

It's moving!

Don't you dare mess with Maro!

AVAILABLE ON

Nintendo DS
Nintendo Wii
PC Windows
PC Mac
Playstation 2
Playstation 3
Playstation Portable
✓ Xbox 360

GAME FACTS

PUBLISHER
Namco Bandai

DEVELOPER
Namco Bandai

FIRST RELEASED
2007-09-17

GAME GENRE	**TIME PERIOD**
RPG	Fantasy/Timeless
THEME	**COMPLEXITY**
Fantasy	Medium

SIMILAR GAMES

Final Fantasy III
Blue Dragon
Fire Emblem: Radient Dawn

RATING & MULTIPLAYER

USA	Europe	Network	Offline
	12+ www.pegi.info	No	No

Eternal Sonata

SETTING

The story of Eternal Sonata takes place inside Frederic Chopin's head while he lies on his deathbed. Largely influenced by music, colorful characters venture on a surreal combat-driven journey.

GAME SUMMARY

In his dreams, Chopin follows a girl with an awful destiny and the boy who is fighting to save her. Based largely on the classic battle between good and evil, the game is set during the last three hours of the famous composer Chopin's life. The game features 10 different characters. As you move through the game, your characters' health, attack, defense, and magic levels increase. You will also be able to explore the map and look for items that can help you revive fallen friends and restore your own health. The combat system in Eternal Sonata rewards carefully planned battles and the use of deadly combos. Combat also relies heavily on the powers of light and darkness. The strengths, abilities, and even physical forms of your characters will undergo major changes depending on whether they are venturing through light or dark areas. The same also goes for the enemy: if they spend time in the shadows, their powers increase and they will be stronger in combat.

CHALLENGES & HINTS

Chopin will only learn the secrets of this mysterious world if you use light and darkness in a strategic manner. Beware of your enemies; some can change their entire physical state if they spend time lurking in the shadows.

KEY GAMEPLAY ELEMENTS

Attack/Fight
Role Play
Gather

GAME WORLD SIZE	Large	**AVERAGE SCORE**
YOUR ROLE	Heroes	**8.1**
REPLAY VALUE	Once or Twice	out of 10

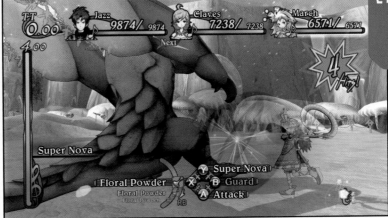

AVAILABLE ON

Nintendo DS
Nintendo Wii
PC Windows
PC Mac
✓ Playstation 2
Playstation 3
Playstation Portable
Xbox 360

GAME FACTS

PUBLISHER
Square Enix

DEVELOPER
Square Enix

FIRST RELEASED
2006-10-31

GAME GENRE
RPG

TIME PERIOD
Fantasy/Timeless

THEME
Fantasy

COMPLEXITY
High

SIMILAR GAMES

Valkyrie Profile 2: Silmeria
Kingdom Hearts 2
Blue Dragon

RATING & MULTIPLAYER

USA	Europe	Network	Offline
		No	No

Final Fantasy XII

SETTING

The game is set in the beautiful Ivalice, where a group of characters from the Kingdom of Dalmasca sets out to secure the freedom of their city from the expanding Archadian Empire. You follow your loyal characters on an epic adventure through this magical country.

GAME SUMMARY

As you explore Invalice by foot, you will have to battle many of the magical creatures that inhabit the country. You will be able to spot your enemy on the battlefield or on the map prior to combat, which enables smooth transitions into fight mode. To manage your characters in battle, you will be dealing with the gambit and license systems. You program a gambit system for each of the characters, which serves as their artificial intelligence in combat. Used properly, you can sit back and watch as your characters engage in battle, but the gambit sequences can be changed at any time during the game. Your characters will gain multiple license points for each defeated enemy, points that can be used to unlock upgrades and add skills and abilities to your characters' repertoires. You will see large aircrafts used for war and trade crowding the skies of Ivalice. Although this game revolves primarily around combat, the cutscenes are also very dramatic and emotionally loaded.

CHALLENGES & HINTS

Faced with tough decisions, you will have to carefully select which weapons, armor, and spells to purchase. The enemy now possesses sophisticated AI which means that you must be more alert than ever. Most importantly, you must stay loyal to your friends and your Kingdom.

KEY GAMEPLAY ELEMENTS

Attack/Fight
Role Play
Explore

GAME WORLD SIZE	Large
YOUR ROLE	Hero/Heroes
REPLAY VALUE	Once or Twice

AVERAGE SCORE

8.5

out of 10

Adds an additional gambit slot.

NOW THEN.
I'LL TAKE THAT.

BHUJERBAN SAINIKAH
YOU MAY SEE IMPERIALS ON OUR STREETS, *BHADRA*,
BUT DO NOT BE ALARMED. BHUJERBA IS NEUTRAL.
OUR PORTS ARE OPEN TO ALL.

YOU ALL RIGHT, VAAN?

AVAILABLE ON

Nintendo DS
✓ Nintendo Wii
PC Windows
PC Mac
Playstation 2
Playstation 3
Playstation Portable
Xbox 360

GAME FACTS

PUBLISHER
Nintendo

DEVELOPER
Intelligent Systems

FIRST RELEASED
2007-11-05

GAME GENRE	TIME PERIOD
RPG	Fantasy/Timeless
THEME	**COMPLEXITY**
Fantasy	Medium

SIMILAR GAMES

Final Fantasy XII
Blue Dragon
Advanced Wars 2

RATING & MULTIPLAYER

USA	Europe	Network	Offline
		No	Yes

Fire Emblem
RADIANT DAWN

SETTING
Three years have passed since the events in Fire Emblem: Path of Radiance. A new war is spreading across the land and Ike and the freedom fighters have to stop the evil powers before all of Tellius lies in ruin.

GAME SUMMARY
Fire Emblem: Radiant Dawn is a turn-based game where you take turns with the computer to move units and strike the enemy with different attacks and magic spells. There are many different kinds of units, all with their own special strengths. The game is pretty long and has a total of 45 chapters, which are divided into four parts. Each part has its own leader, Ike being one of them. The game features a character support relationships system, where the characters form a relationship that allows them to become stronger when fighting together. The game also features a new magic class, Dark Magic, and new weapons and units, which let you customize your team to better suit your strategy.

CHALLENGES & HINTS
It's crucial for you to decide on a tactic early on so that it can evolve and become stronger with time. For all battles, and especially the bigger enemies, you must execute greatly planned attacks in order to win. Keeping an eye on all the units and everyone in your team can become quite challenging!

KEY GAMEPLAY ELEMENTS

Attack/Fight
Role Play
Tactics/Plan

GAME WORLD SIZE	Large
YOUR ROLE	Hero/Heroines
REPLAY VALUE	Once or Twice

AVERAGE SCORE

NA

out of 10

ミカヤ

早くここを離れたほうがいいって
ぼんやり、そう感じるだけで……

†Steel Sword 12   9 Iron Axe

Paving Stones   Move
Victory
Rout enemy
1 Back   2 OK

Steel Axe 27   24 Steel Axe

In a quick half-mark, we'll be in Kisca.
I'd like to stock up there, but...

Begnion will be on the lookout for us.
Let's steer clear of towns for now,
unless we want more trouble.

Sothe

Begnion 20   9 Edward
12

AVAILABLE ON

Nintendo DS
Nintendo Wii
✓ PC Windows
PC Mac
Playstation 2
Playstation 3
Playstation Portable
Xbox 360

GAME FACTS

PUBLISHER
Namco Bandai

DEVELOPER
Flagship Studios

FIRST RELEASED
2007-10-31

GAME GENRE	**TIME PERIOD**
RPG	Future
THEME	**COMPLEXITY**
Horror/Thriller	Medium

SIMILAR GAMES

The Elder Scrolls IV: Oblivion
Gears of War
Arx Fatalis

RATING & MULTIPLAYER

USA	Europe	Network	Offline
		Yes	No

Hellgate
LONDON

SETTING

In a futuristic London, you control the battle against the invading demons alongside the other few survivors, all in a lifeless city burnt to the ground by hellfire. Create your own heroic character from one of seven character classes.

GAME SUMMARY

To save the bloodline of humanity, you work your way through quests, battles, and infinite levels in a ruined, postapocalyptic city. Each character class has a different form of gameplay that is based on his or her history. As a single player, this game absorbs you into the world of fighting demons through sorcery and the conversion of power into ammunition. The demons you come across have their own unique attributes and skills, which make the game, at the very least, unrepetitive. Dynamic levels include large quantities of randomly generated items, events, and quests with a variety of skill and spell systems that allow you to thoroughly personalize your character. While some classes, such as the cabalists, prefer metallic orbs and wands, hunters appreciate true gunfire, for which there is a wide range of weapons and equipment available. The game features a great online multiplayer system in addition to the single-player mode.

CHALLENGES & HINTS

The weapons used in Hellgate: London are designed to destroy demons, a task for which firearms will be of no use. Look for weapons with holy symbols and magic charms, rather than conventional firearms, to save what is left of the human race from this demonic invasion.

KEY GAMEPLAY ELEMENTS

Attack/Fight
Role Play
Tactics/Plan

GAME WORLD SIZE	Medium
YOUR ROLE	Hero of choice
REPLAY VALUE	Once or Twice

AVERAGE SCORE

NA

out of 10

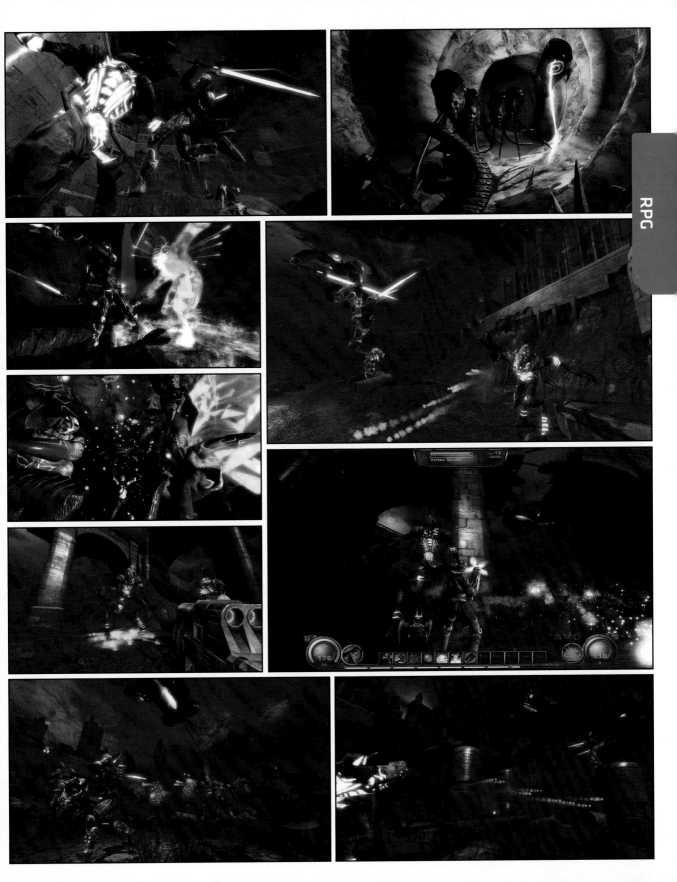

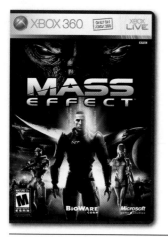

AVAILABLE ON

Nintendo DS
Nintendo Wii
PC Windows
PC Mac
Playstation 2
Playstation 3
Playstation Portable
✓ Xbox 360

GAME FACTS

PUBLISHER
Microsoft Game Studio

DEVELOPER
Bioware

FIRST RELEASED
2007-11-20

GAME GENRE	**TIME PERIOD**
RPG	Future
THEME	**COMPLEXITY**
Sci-Fi	Medium

SIMILAR GAMES

Phantasy Star Universe
Fable 2
Enchanted Arms

RATING & MULTIPLAYER

USA	Europe	Network	Offline
		Yes	No

Mass Effect

SETTING

Mass Effect is set 200 years in the future in a universe where galactic peace is threatened by a renowned agent gone bad. You lead a squad of human freedom fighters known as Specter on a mission through alien territory to stop the fast-moving enemy.

GAME SUMMARY

In this rich and engrossing story, you discover that there is more to defending galactic peace than first meets the eye. An existing conflict between organic life and artificial intelligence means that your decisions and actions become major factors in shaping the destiny of all galactic life. Along with your Specter squad, you explore uncharted planets and discover new alien life, unexploited resources, and advanced technology. You can choose from a variety of realistic characters, and character statistics and talent can be upgraded throughout the game, which will have a positive effect on your performance in battle. Any equipment, weapons, or armor obtained also has a physical effect on the appearance of your character. One thing is certain: the intense and challenging combat action is not for the feint of heart!

CHALLENGES & HINTS

This combat-based action game requires your elite squad to work as a tactical strike force to defeat threatening armies. With unlimited ammunition, you can focus on the most important objective: to complete your mission.

KEY GAMEPLAY ELEMENTS

Attack/Fight
Role Play
Tactics/Plan

GAME WORLD SIZE	Large
YOUR ROLE	Hero
REPLAY VALUE	Once or Twice

AVERAGE SCORE

NA

out of 10

Fai Dan: Looks like a dozen. Maybe more.

Can I help?
What's going on?
Only a dozen?

Note: Games are seperate

Pokémon
DIAMOND/PEARL

SETTING

In Pokémon Diamond/Pearl, you're on a quest to become the greatest pokémon trainer of them all. Search every inch of the region Sinnoh and beat the previous champion of the pokémon league.

GAME SUMMARY

The popular Pokémon series is back, this time with more than 100 new pokémons. Choose to play as a boy or girl and travel though the region of Sinnoh to become champion of the Pokémon League. You have to travel through Sinnoh and catch pokémons, raise them, and fight gym leaders and trainers. Use the DS touch screen to quickly move though the battle menus and deal fatal attacks on your opponents. Go online and battle with your friends from around the world or trade pokémon with other players via the Nintendo WiFi Connection. Both Diamond and Pearl have some variation of pokémons, including the legendary ones. The Diamond version features the legendary Pokémon Dialga and the Pearl version features the legendary Pokémon Palkia.

CHALLENGES & HINTS

To complete the game, you'll have to catch them all, but catching pokémon isn't as easy as it seems. Higher-level pokémons are harder to catch, and you only have one chance with some pokémons. To catch them all, you'll have to trade pokémons with people that have the Pokémon Diamond/Pearl and use the WiFi Connection to become the ultimate pokémon trainer.

AVAILABLE ON

✓ Nintendo DS
  Nintendo Wii
  PC Windows
  PC Mac
  Playstation 2
  Playstation 3
  Playstation Portable
  Xbox 360

GAME FACTS

PUBLISHER
Nintendo

DEVELOPER
Game Freak

FIRST RELEASED
2007-04-22

GAME GENRE
RPG

TIME PERIOD
Fantasy/Timeless

THEME
Fantasy

COMPLEXITY
Medium

SIMILAR GAMES

Final Fantasy XII: Revenant Wings
Digimon World: Dawn
Rune Factory: Fantasy Harvest Moon

RATING & MULTIPLAYER

USA	Europe	Network	Offline
		Yes	No

KEY GAMEPLAY ELEMENTS

Attack/Fight
Role Play
Trade

GAME WORLD SIZE	Large
YOUR ROLE	Pokémon Trainer
REPLAY VALUE	Once or Twice

AVERAGE SCORE

8.3
out of 10

BAG

Dubious Disc	× 1
Lagging Tail	× 1
NeverMeltIce	× 1
Sun Stone	× 11
Damp Rock	× 2
Rare Bone	× 3
Hard Stone	× 6
Heat Rock	× 3

ITEMS POCKET

A bone that is extremely valuable for Pokémon archaeology. It can be sold for a high price to shops.

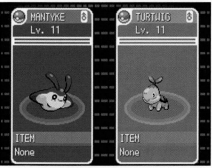

The foe's LUCARIO used Metal Claw!

Angel — Jake

MANTYKE ⇔ TURTWIG

▶YES
NO

Trade MANTYKE in return for TURTWIG?

BUIZEL ♂Lv8

CHATOT ♂Lv18
56/60

What will CHATOT do?

AVAILABLE ON

Nintendo DS
Nintendo Wii
PC Windows
PC Mac
✓ Playstation 2
Playstation 3
Playstation Portable
Xbox 360

GAME FACTS

PUBLISHER
SCEA, SCEE

DEVELOPER
Level-5

FIRST RELEASED
2007-01-30

GAME GENRE	**TIME PERIOD**
RPG	Fantasy/Timeless
THEME	**COMPLEXITY**
Fantasy	Medium

SIMILAR GAMES

Kingdom Hearts II
Odin Sphere
Tales of the Abyss

RATING & MULTIPLAYER

USA	Europe	Network	Offline
		No	No

Rogue Galaxy

SETTING

On the desert planet of Rosa, a young hunter named Jaster ends up with a bunch of space pirates on a galactic treasure hunt. Your goal is to find the ultimate treasure: eternal life. Needless to say, the competition along the way will be fierce and dangerous.

GAME SUMMARY

Explore a fantasy sci-fi world filled with a diverse cast of characters and exotic planets in this Japanese action role-playing game. What makes this game unique is that it features a real-time battle system in an otherwise traditional role-playing adventure. You have two other characters following you in exploration and combat, while Jaster's eight crew members are picked up throughout the galaxy and present different key skills needed to move the story along. Your weapons and outfits can be crafted and upgraded, and as you progress, you obtain exciting magical abilities and special attacks. Rogue Galaxy also features a chess-like game where the player has to capture certain creatures and use them as game pieces. This game offers an extensive single-player experience that features lots of customization as well as item and monster hunting.

CHALLENGES & HINTS

It is "game over" if everyone in your party is wiped out, which they are all the time, so make sure to throw potion their way when needed. It's easy to get lost in the game's detailed ability system, where you place assorted items on a board game-like screen that looks different for each character. But make sure you understand this feature thoroughly as it will help in fully realizing your crew's potential.

KEY GAMEPLAY ELEMENTS

Attack/Fight
Role Play
Tactics/Plan

GAME WORLD SIZE	Large
YOUR ROLE	Hero
REPLAY VALUE	Once or Twice

AVERAGE SCORE

8.0

out of 10

RAIL SIMULATOR

Simulation
Games

BLAZING ANGELS 2: SECRET MISSIONS OF WWII

Sometimes truth is stranger than fiction, and real-life simulation is more challenging than a fantasy world. While some play videogames to battle aliens or conquer dungeons, others choose simulation games to try the extraordinary things that people actually do in the real world, like fly and land a Cessna Skyhawk in *Microsoft Flight Simulator X*, build an intricate system of trains in *Rail Simulator*, or vacation around the world in *The Sims 2: Bon Voyage*.

Simulation games as a genre is difficult to define because there is an element of simulation in almost every game. In *Madden NFL 08* you simulate your favorite football team, in *Guitar Hero 3: Legends of Rock* you simulate a rock star, and in *Medieval II: Total War* you simulate a medieval military commander—yet none of these possess the emphasis on realism and detail needed to make them true simulation games.

In the industrial world, simulators are used as training tools for professions ranging from astronauts and truck drivers to surgeons and even military commanders. These simulators are expensive pieces of equipment that can't be easily purchased for residential tinkering. That's because these simulators aren't made to entertain audiences; as training tools they focus entirely on realism, detail, and practicality.

THE SIMS 2: BON VOYAGE

But what if you wanted to grab the throttle and try your hands at a simulator just for fun? That's where the influence of videogames comes in. If you're interested in trying a simulator in the privacy of your own home, you'd be looking for something with more frills and a cheaper price tag than what the industrial world has to offer. Simulation games do just that by combining the creativity of the entertainment business with the attention to detail necessary in the industrial world. This gives them far more flexibility than their more realistic counterparts: you might bump into Bigfoot in *The Sims 2: Bon Voyage*, or create purple polka dot airplanes in *Flight Simulator X*!

Right out of the box, simulation games let you try your hand at professions that take years of training to do in real life. And as soon as your tanker hits an iceberg in *Ship Simulator 2008* or you derail a train in *Rail Simulator*, you'll understand that these games take patience and studying, too. However, given

TRAUMA CENTER: SECOND OPINION

SIMCITY SOCIETIES

time and dedication, you can experience the thrill of some of the world's most exclusive professions in the comfort and safety of your own home. Best of all, your mess-ups won't appear in tomorrow's headlines.

While games like *Microsoft Flight Simulator X* relish in the complications of simply getting a plane in and out of the air, not all simulation games focus on such minute details. For those who'd rather man the machinegun than monitor the fuel gauge, games like *After Burner: Black Falcon* let you instantly jump into the cockpit for some bogey-fighting action. Or, if you want to experience the excitement of an operating room without spending your time filling out charts, *Trauma Center: Second Opinion* hands over the scalpel for even tutorial missions. And rather than

simulating waiting in line at the airport, *The Sims 2: Bon Voyage* glosses over some of the more boring aspects of travel to give you a real dream vacation.

The depth of simulation games continues to expand as the videogame industry publishes with larger budgets and better technology. It'd be hard to argue that Pong was a realistic depiction of table tennis. Nowadays, though, books are actually being published for pilots-in-training using *Microsoft Flight Simulator*. More than ever before, these games are pushing the boundaries of the geography you explore, the realism you experience, and the expensive equipment you operate (or destroy). Whether you're looking for a career change or simply curious, simulation games provide an escape from the ordinary into the bizarre world of reality.

AVAILABLE ON

Nintendo DS
Nintendo Wii
PC Windows
PC Mac
Playstation 2
Playstation 3
✓ Playstation Portable
Xbox 360

GAME FACTS

PUBLISHER
Sega Europe, Sega of America

DEVELOPER
Planet Moon Studios

FIRST RELEASED
2007-03-20

GAME GENRE	**TIME PERIOD**
Simulation	Present
THEME	**COMPLEXITY**
War	Low

SIMILAR GAMES

Blazing Angels 2: Secret Missions of WWII
Ace Combat X: Skies of Deception
Armored Core: Formula Front

RATING & MULTIPLAYER

USA	Europe	Network	Offline
	7+ www.pegi.info	4 Players	No

After Burner
BLACK FALCON

SETTING

Take to the skies in the PSP's first ever arcade-style combat fighter game. Thirteen top secret prototype planes have been stolen by the Black Falcon terrorist group, and you are ordered to hunt down the enemies and ensure the planes' safe return.

GAME SUMMARY

Prepare for air combat action as After Burner: Black Falcon takes you through a series of arcade-style missions on a variety of courses with unforgiving terrain. You must take out targets at land, at sea, and in the air using high-speed fighters equipped with an array of weapons. Unlock 19 officially licensed fighter planes, ranging from the F-22 Raptor and the A-10 Thunderbolt II to the SR-71 Blackbird. All fighter models can be upgraded with new weapons and engine parts to improve your speed, maneuverability, and deadliness. Shooting down multiple enemies in quick succession will reward you with combo bonuses, and catching parachute drops will give you extra life, ammo, or money to upgrade your crafts. Dogfight against a friend, or cooperate on story missions in multiplayer mode.

CHALLENGES & HINTS

At great speeds it can be difficult to stay on target and spot enemies before they spot you. There can be a dozen of them out there at a time, so be sure to dodge those incoming missiles. And don't get distracted by the beautiful scenery, or you'll be a dead bird!

KEY GAMEPLAY ELEMENTS

Steer/Maneuver
Attack/Fight
Build & Design

		AVERAGE SCORE
GAME WORLD SIZE	Medium	
YOUR ROLE	Fighter Pilot	**7.3**
REPLAY VALUE	Several Times	out of 10

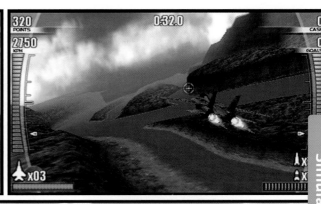

AVAILABLE ON

Nintendo DS
Nintendo Wii
✓ PC Windows
PC Mac
Playstation 2
✓ Playstation 3
Playstation Portable
✓ Xbox 360

GAME FACTS *

PUBLISHER
Ubisoft

DEVELOPER
Ubisoft

FIRST RELEASED
2007-09-07

GAME GENRE
Simulator

TIME PERIOD
Recent History

THEME
War

COMPLEXITY
Medium

SIMILAR GAMES

Attack on Pearl Harbor
Air Battles: Sky Defender
Blazing Angels: Squadrons of WWII

RATING & MULTIPLAYER

USA	Europe	Network	Offline
TEEN T	12+ www.pegi.info	16 Players	No

Blazing Angels 2
SECRET MISSIONS OF WWII

SETTING

During WWII, the American government discovers that the Third Reich is developing a weapon of mass destruction. You are appointed the commanding officer of Operation Wildcard—an elite undercover unit that sets out to disarm the enemy. The assignment sends you overseas to the airspace of Rome, Beijing, Moscow, and even the Himalayas.

GAME SUMMARY

As the commanding officer of Operation Wildcard, your mission is to find and destroy the Third Reich's most lethal weapon. You and your squad will soon learn that the enemy has also deployed an elite unit, and battling these troops makes your task particularly difficult to complete. The game takes you through 18 missions as you gradually work toward disarming the enemy's newly-developed WMD. Air combat allows you to bomb targets and open fire on enemy aircraft. You earn points by taking down the enemy, but also by pulling off risky stunts with your plane. Between levels, you can use your prestige points to upgrade your ammo, weapons, aircraft, and even your squad's training level. Blazing Angels 2 has more than 50 different planes to choose from, many featuring self-guided missiles. Up to 16 players can work together on squad-based missions, deathmatches, or rounds of capture the flag.

CHALLENGES & HINTS

To gain advantage during combat, be on the offensive and take down enemy aircraft before they reach you. Experiment with different weapons like the High Velocity Cannon and the self-guided or TV-guided missiles to see which ones are most effective in defeating different enemy targets.

KEY GAMEPLAY ELEMENTS

Steer/Maneuver
Attack/Fight
Tactics/Plan

GAME WORLD SIZE	Large
YOUR ROLE	Fighter Pilot
REPLAY VALUE	Several Times

AVERAGE SCORE

7.5

out of 10

Data and images may vary on the various platforms

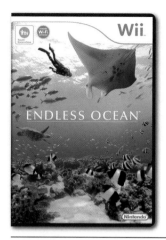

AVAILABLE ON

Nintendo DS
✓ Nintendo Wii
PC Windows
PC Mac
Playstation 2
Playstation 3
Playstation Portable
Xbox 360

GAME FACTS

PUBLISHER
Nintendo

DEVELOPER
Arika

FIRST RELEASED
2007-10-29

GAME GENRE	**TIME PERIOD**
Simulation	Present
THEME	**COMPLEXITY**
Animal	Low

SIMILAR GAMES

Everblue
Everblue 2
Harvest Moon: A Wonderful Life

RATING & MULTIPLAYER

USA	Europe	Network	Offline
	3+ www.pegi.info	Yes	No

Endless Ocean
(AKA. FOREVER BLUE)

SETTING

Here's your chance to go diving without getting wet! Suit up and dive into a deep blue virtual ocean. Swim among all sorts of sea animals in a relaxing game where you can hunt for treasures or simply explore another world you rarely get to see in real life.

GAME SUMMARY

Endless Ocean puts you in the shoes, or rather flippers, of a scuba diver in the Manaurai Sea. You have full freedom to swim wherever you want in the massive ocean, searching for sea creatures and treasures. Several of the songs in the game are sung by the beautiful voice of Hayley Westenra. You can also add your own MP3 files to an SD card and use them as the game's soundtrack. The game's trajectory is as easy as it is relaxing by pointing out areas you may want to explore. There are dolphins in the game that you can play with, and there are also sharks that might scare you, although they don't pose any real threat. You can also connect online with a friend to swim together and explore the hidden depths of the sea.

CHALLENGES & HINTS

The atmosphere, easy gameplay, beautiful music, and stunning surroundings make this game very relaxing. There aren't any challenges, really, it's just a perfect way to kill some time or relax in this overly hectic life.

KEY GAMEPLAY ELEMENTS

Steer/Maneuver
Explore
Gather

GAME WORLD SIZE	Large
YOUR ROLE	Diver
REPLAY VALUE	Several Times

AVERAGE SCORE

NA

out of 10

Flight Simulator X

SETTING

Microsoft Games celebrates the 25th anniversary of the Flight Simulator with the release of Flight Simulator X. The game brings all wannabe pilots one step closer to the sky.

GAME SUMMARY

Be the pilot you always wanted to be and choose among 24 flying beauties, from the Cessna Skyhawk to a Maule M7-260C Orion! Planes and landscape come close to the real thing, and 45 interactive airports and 38 detailed cities with traffic add even more realism to your flight experience. New in this version is the introduction of flight races and mission flights, where you get to try your hand at delivering relief aid materials to countries in need. Fifty-five different missions push your pilot skills to the limit. Learn the controls of each individual aircraft and then you are free to fly! But remember, you're not alone up there, so pay attention to instructions from the tower to avoid disasters: "Cessna cleared to climb to flight level 85, traffic is northbound, Boeing 737 inbound at Kennedy, descending to 4,000 feet, at your 10 o'clock position...." The game offers theoretical and practical lessons for novices and professionals. Ready for takeoff?

CHALLENGES & HINTS

Warning: flying an airplane is not like a walk in the park. If you don't know what you're doing, you might end up crashing into one! Remember, these planes respond like real airplanes, so perhaps it's not such a great idea to pull a loop with that 747...

AVAILABLE ON

Nintendo DS
Nintendo Wii
✓ PC Windows
PC Mac
Playstation 2
Playstation 3
Playstation Portable
Xbox 360

GAME FACTS

PUBLISHER
Microsoft Game Studio

DEVELOPER
Aces Studio

FIRST RELEASED
2006-10-13

GAME GENRE
Simulator

TIME PERIOD
Present

THEME
Technical

COMPLEXITY
High

SIMILAR GAMES

X-Plane 8
Blazing Angels: Squadrons of WWII
Ace Combat Zero: The Belkan War

RATING & MULTIPLAYER

USA	Europe	Network	Offline
	3+ www.pegi.info	Yes	No

KEY GAMEPLAY ELEMENTS

Steer/Maneuver
Explore
Administration

GAME WORLD SIZE	Gigantic
YOUR ROLE	Pilot
REPLAY VALUE	Several Times

AVERAGE SCORE

8.1

out of 10

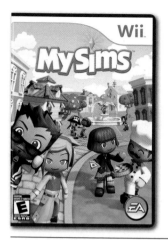

AVAILABLE ON

✓ Nintendo DS
✓ Nintendo Wii
 PC Windows
 PC Mac
 Playstation 2
 Playstation 3
 Playstation Portable
 Xbox 360

GAME FACTS *

PUBLISHER
Electronic Arts

DEVELOPER
EA Games

FIRST RELEASED
2007-09-11

GAME GENRE	TIME PERIOD
Simulation	Fantasy/Timeless
THEME	COMPLEXITY
People	Low

SIMILAR GAMES

The Sims 2
Animal Crossing: Wild Worlds
Harvest Moon: A Wonderful Life

RATING & MULTIPLAYER

USA	Europe	Network	Offline
		No	No

MySims

SETTING

You have just moved into a small, rundown town where only a few residents remain. You have to get your hands dirty to shine things up so that this little town can once again be a happy place to live.

GAME SUMMARY

MySims invites you to be creative. Personalize your own Sim with facial features, clothes, and tattoos. Then start to renovate, customize, and build the town from the ground up. The game has a user friendly, yet rich building editor that allows players to create their own house and furniture. You can even decide how to design the shops and houses. As the town becomes a prettier place, new people will move in, and you can decide who gets to stay and who has to leave. There is a large cast of Sims characters like Cap'n Ginny the pirate, Chef Gino the chef, and many more. You are free to roam around the world as you choose. There are caves to explore, treasure to be found, and even parks in which you can just sit and relax.

CHALLENGES & HINTS

When you have made a pleasant little town, loads of Sims will want to live there. Sadly, though, some will have to leave. It just breaks your heart to see them go now that you've become so close...sniff.

KEY GAMEPLAY ELEMENTS

Build & Design
Explore
Gather

GAME WORLD SIZE	Medium
YOUR ROLE	Sim
REPLAY VALUE	Infinite

AVERAGE SCORE

7.2

out of 10

Data and images may vary on the various platforms

Phoenix Wright
ACE ATTORNEY - TRIALS AND TRIBULATIONS

SETTING
Order in the court! Phoenix Wright: Trials and Tribulations is now in session. Take on the role of defense attorney Phoenix Wright in the third installment of this courtroom simulator.

GAME SUMMARY
The gameplay is similar to the game's predecessors Ace Attorney and Justice for All. For most of the game you play as Phoenix Wright, but for some cases you take on the role of Wright's partner, Mia Fay. In the investigation part of the game, use the touch screen to navigate through the crime scene and look for clues. Weed through court records and evidence to defend your client. You can also study evidence in a three-dimensional view. The game has many new characters and a total of five new cases all packed with the mystery and sarcastic humor that the game is well-known for, which makes the cases all the more fun and interesting to work on.

CHALLENGES & HINTS
While you're in court, you have to listen carefully to witness testimony to find flaws in their statements. Make sure not to make a mistake by claiming something that isn't fully thought through. It will come back to haunt you and can even make you lose the case.

AVAILABLE ON

- ✓ Nintendo DS
- Nintendo Wii
- PC Windows
- PC Mac
- Playstation 2
- Playstation 3
- Playstation Portable
- Xbox 360

GAME FACTS

PUBLISHER
Capcom

DEVELOPER
Capcom

FIRST RELEASED
2007-10-23

GAME GENRE
Simulation

TIME PERIOD
Present

THEME
Crime

COMPLEXITY
Medium

SIMILAR GAMES

Hotel Dusk: Room 215
Trace Memory
Lost in Blue 2

RATING & MULTIPLAYER

USA	Europe	Network	Offline
		No	No

KEY GAMEPLAY ELEMENTS

Tactics/Plan
Gather
Solve Puzzles

		AVERAGE SCORE
GAME WORLD SIZE	Small	
YOUR ROLE	Defence Attorney	**8.0**
REPLAY VALUE	Once or Twice	out of 10

Mia
An unusual death...!?

Phoenix
Kurain Village...
Isn't that...?

Treasure Exhibition
The Sacred Urn
Kurain Village

Phoenix
I, err, I just want to say...
I'll give it all I've got!

Phoenix
Well, your Magatama lets me
see when people are keeping
secrets.

Phoenix
I hardly think you could
forget where you were hit
on the head!

Payne
Students discovered the scene
shortly after the murder. They
found the victim's body...

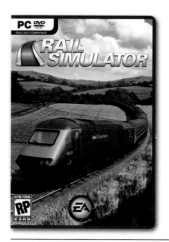

AVAILABLE ON

Nintendo DS
Nintendo Wii
✓ PC Windows
PC Mac
Playstation 2
Playstation 3
Playstation Portable
Xbox 360

GAME FACTS

PUBLISHER
Electronic Arts

DEVELOPER
Kuju Entertainment

FIRST RELEASED
2007-10-04

GAME GENRE
Simulator

TIME PERIOD
Multiple/Timetravel

THEME
Technical

COMPLEXITY
Medium

SIMILAR GAMES

Ship Simulator
Train Simulator 2
Model Train 3D

RATING & MULTIPLAYER

USA	Europe	Network	Offline
		No	No

Rail Simulator

SETTING

Rail Simulator offers the newest and most realistic train experience through a variety of international locations. Build your own old-fashioned train or transform modern diesel and electric rigs.

GAME SUMMARY

Rail Simulator is packaged with five ready-made real-life tracks. Some are in Europe featuring tracks from New Castle to York and Oxford to Paddington. You will get to try your hand at different scenarios throughout history from steam-engine trains of the 19th century to today's modern monorails. In these scenarios, you are given objectives and tasks to complete, including delivering coal and other raw materials or getting from one point to another on time. The difficulty levels of these tasks are adjusted through how much you have to control your train. At easier levels, you only have to control the accelerator and the universal break. At more difficult levels, you control other types of speed and break controls. The physics of Rail Simulator have been are greatly improved, making the trains behave realistically, so you better make sure you give yourself enough time to break!

CHALLENGES & HINTS

To fully experience these magnificent trains, you are encouraged to customize both your trains and your tracks. You can call your terrain editor at any time during the game to alter your surroundings down to the last detail, be it the track itself or the environments you pass through.

KEY GAMEPLAY ELEMENTS

Build & Design
Steer/Maneuver
Tactics/Plan

GAME WORLD SIZE   Medium
YOUR ROLE   Conductor
REPLAY VALUE   Infinite

AVERAGE SCORE

NA

out of 10

Ship Simulator 2008

AVAILABLE ON

Nintendo DS
Nintendo Wii
✓ PC Windows
PC Mac
Playstation 2
Playstation 3
Playstation Portable
Xbox 360

GAME FACTS

PUBLISHER
Lighthouse Interactive

DEVELOPER
VSTEP

FIRST RELEASED
2007-07-13

GAME GENRE	**TIME PERIOD**
Simulator	Present
THEME	**COMPLEXITY**
Technical	High

SIMILAR GAMES

Virtual Skipper 3
Rail Simulator 2008
Microsoft Flight Simulator X

RATING & MULTIPLAYER

USA	Europe	Network	Offline
		No	No

SETTING

Ship Simulator 2008 takes you out on the high seas to experience the life of modern-day crews on large ships ranging from commercial cruise ships to heavy cargo rigs.

GAME SUMMARY

Out on the open ocean, you see what running a ship is like as you take on the mighty role of the captain. Initially, you are assigned simple missions of sailing steadily on a straight course toward ports such as Hamburg, Rotterdam, New York, Portsmouth, San Francisco, and Marseilles. Commanding and steering water taxis, container ships, and even the great Titanic, you will gradually be given more challenging set objectives that include towing oil rigs, rescuing lost ships, and delivering goods. The control system is developed in a very realistic manner. Docking a large cruise ship or repositioning an oil rig is just as difficult in Ship Simulator 08 as in real life. When operating a ship, you also have to deal with an extra element, namely the sea. The aquatic landscapes lack currents and tides, although the open ocean can get aggressive. You will be amazed by the graphics both at sea and while entering busy and dynamic ports.

CHALLENGES & HINTS

Keep in mind that simulators are not meant to be games. They are simply real-life scenarios that you are given the opportunity to enact. To get the most out of this game, it is important that you have an interest in the area of sea transportation.

KEY GAMEPLAY ELEMENTS

Steer/Maneuver
Administration
Tactics/Plan

GAME WORLD SIZE	Large	
YOUR ROLE	Captain	
REPLAY VALUE	Infinite	

AVERAGE SCORE

6.2

out of 10

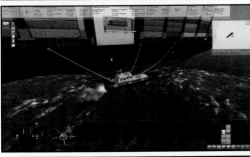

AVAILABLE ON

Nintendo DS
Nintendo Wii
✓ PC Windows
PC Mac
Playstation 2
Playstation 3
Playstation Portable
Xbox 360

GAME FACTS

PUBLISHER
Ubisoft

DEVELOPER
Ubisoft

FIRST RELEASED DATE
2007-03-20

GAME GENRE
Simulation

TIME PERIOD
Recent History

THEME
War

COMPLEXITY
High

SIMILAR GAMES

1914 Shells of Fury
Sub Command
Seawolves: Submarines on Hunt

RATING & MULTIPLAYER

USA	Europe	Network	Offline
	7+		
	www.pegi.info	Yes	No

Silent Hunter 4
WOLVES OF THE PACIFIC

SETTING
The year is 1941, and we are well into World War II when Pearl Harbor is attacked by the Japanese. After the attack, America increases its number of forces and the amount of military activity in the Pacific Ocean. The quiet but deadly U-boats play a vital role as strategic building blocks. This is where you come in—as a captain on one of America's largest submarines.

GAME SUMMARY
Take on the role of commander on one of the submarines stationed at Pearl Harbor. You are given missions across the entire Pacific, often in close proximity to Japan. There are many different missions available, such as torpedoing convoys and spying on the ports of Tokyo. This quickly becomes intense when you quietly move under the ocean surface as the enemy is mass-bombing the waters surrounding you. You are able to stop time and control the camera-angles outside the boat for an amazing visual experience. If you are a retired U-boat captain, the difficulty can be adjusted to match your skills for the ultimate experience.

CHALLENGES & HINTS
Remember to bring a coffee cup for long trips as it takes a long time to cross the Pacific Ocean. Stay under water at all times where you are less likely to be discovered. If you surface, fast destroyers and aircraft will destroy you before you know it. Hitting moving enemy targets can be quite challenging, as you must take into account the distance and angles between you and your target, as well as the speed of your torpedo.

KEY GAMEPLAY ELEMENTS

Tactics/Plan
Attack/Fight
Administration

GAME WORLD SIZE	Gigantic	
YOUR ROLE	Sub Commander	
REPLAY VALUE	Several Times	

AVERAGE SCORE

7.8

out of 10

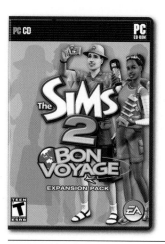

AVAILABLE ON

Nintendo DS
Nintendo Wii
✓ PC Windows
PC Mac
Playstation 2
Playstation 3
Playstation Portable
Xbox 360

GAME FACTS

PUBLISHER
Electronic Arts

DEVELOPER
Maxis

FIRST RELEASED
2007-09-04

GAME GENRE
Simulation

TIME PERIOD
Present

THEME
Travel

COMPLEXITY
Low

SIMILAR GAMES

The Sims 2
The Sims 2 Seasons
The Sims Double Deluxe

RATING & MULTIPLAYER

USA	Europe	Network	Offline
		No	No

The Sims 2
BON VOYAGE

SETTING
This new addition to the popular Sims series expands the world of your animated characters. Give your Sims some rest and relaxation by sending them on luxurious vacations or exciting explorations.

GAME SUMMARY
The Sims have worked hard throughout the many Sims games. Now, they can take some time off and travel to three vacation venues that include sunny beaches, tea gardens, and ancient ruins to relax, learn, and discover. Some start off as classic tourists, checking into luxurious hotels and laying by the pool or on white beaches. However, your Sims quickly turn into savvy vacationers as they learn about their travel destinations that range from the Far East to the beaches of the Caribbean. Your Sims bring back knowledge of international customs from local populations as well as souvenirs with which to decorate their homes. During your vacation, your Sims have the same needs and wants as in previous Sims games. They have to be fed and their hygiene maintained in addition to their social life.

CHALLENGES & HINTS
The Sims 2: Bon Voyage can teach both you and your Sims about the diversity of the world. Although you might enjoy booking your Sims into seven-star hotels and sending them to the spa, take the time to go sight-seeing and enrich your life with another culture.

KEY GAMEPLAY ELEMENTS

Administration
Build & Design
Tactics/Plan

GAME WORLD SIZE Medium
YOUR ROLE Sim
REPLAY VALUE Infinite

AVERAGE SCORE

7.6

out of 10

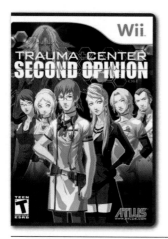

AVAILABLE ON

Nintendo DS
✓ Nintendo Wii
PC Windows
PC Mac
Playstation 2
Playstation 3
Playstation Portable
Xbox 360

GAME FACTS

PUBLISHER
Atlus USA, Nintendo

DEVELOPER
Atlus

FIRST RELEASED
2006-11-14

GAME GENRE	TIME PERIOD
Simulation	Present
THEME	**COMPLEXITY**
Medical	Medium

SIMILAR GAMES

Trauma Center: Under the Knife
Elebits
Bleach: Shattered Blade

RATING & MULTIPLAYER

USA	Europe	Network	Offline
		No	No

Trauma Center
SECOND OPINION

SETTING
You assume the role of a rookie doctor in your job at Hope Hospital. Soon patients line up to receive your care, all of which puts their lives into your hands and makes you feel the pressure of being a doctor.

GAME SUMMARY
As the Wii follow-up and second game in the Trauma Center series, you are now surgeon Dr. Derek Stiles, fresh out of med school. With a dedicated staff, you have to deal with harsh words that they throw out as easily as compliments. Dr. Stiles also has to grow a thick skin to survive the engrossing story told through the cut scenes. Patients come to you with all kinds of diseases, emergencies, and medical mysteries. At first, mentors and nurses guide you, but soon you will be on your own and at a total loss for what to do next. The surgeries become increasingly difficult, and you will have to go to extreme lengths to save a patient's life. Use your Wii remote to control your surgical tools while you make incisions or apply a bandage, and use the Nunchuck to swap tools easily during an operation.

CHALLENGES & HINTS
When in doubt, go with instinct and listen to your gut. Work quickly but accurately. One slip of the hand could be fatal in the life of a professional surgeon!

KEY GAMEPLAY ELEMENTS
Steer/Maneuver
Solve Puzzles
Tactics/Plan

GAME WORLD SIZE	Small
YOUR ROLE	Surgeon
REPLAY VALUE	Several Times

AVERAGE SCORE

8.3

out of 10

: Place the extracted fragments in the tray.

FORCEPS

: The laceration treatment is going
: well. Nice work, Doctor.

HEAL JELLY -ヒールゼリー-

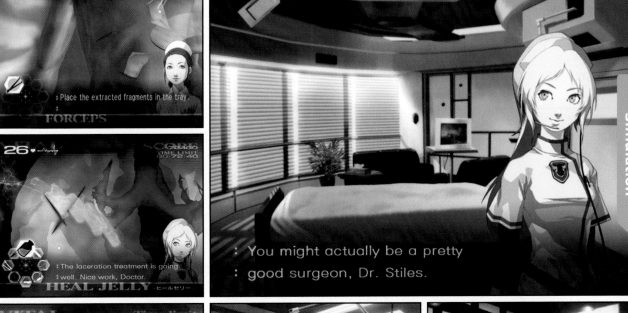

: You might actually be a pretty
: good surgeon, Dr. Stiles.

: Make sure the stitches aren't too
: wide or too narrow.

STITCHES

: Well, it's a difficult operation,
: and we don't have room for mistakes.

Why didn't you just tell him
everything would be fine? ✓

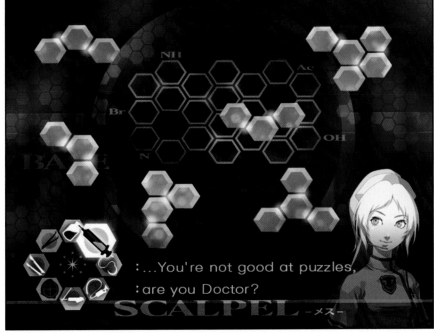

: ...You're not good at puzzles,
: are you Doctor?

SCALPEL -メス-

: The patient's vitals are dropping!
: You have to suture those wounds!

SCALPEL -メス-

: I joined Caduceus so I could
: help people...

Sports
GAMES

An interview with Tony Hawk

Sports games come in a multitude of flavours. From the obvious, such as Madden NFL '08 to the downright strange like Mario Strikers Charged, they continue to introduce new players to the world of videogames. Building on well-known athletic pursuits, the sports game brings the virtual and the physical world together.

Once a sports game title is established, it's quite prone to sequels. All the major sports have their yearly releases, as seen with the FIFA soccer series, the NHL hockey games and the NFL american football franchise. But other, more extreme sports also get their annual refinements and

"...hardcore skaters appreciate that there is a videogame that represents them authentically...."

-Tony Hawk

tune-ups. We talked to skateboarding legend and videogame superstar Tony Hawk about his Tony Hawk's Pro Skater games, a series that reached its eighth major release in 2007 with Project 8. We asked him about the influence that games and their originating sports have on each other, and it is his firm belief that the games not only recruit new skaters but also increase the general

Anthony Frank Hawk, best known as Tony Hawk, was born in 1968 and is one of the world's most famous and influential professional skaters. Well known for his inventions of aerial skateboard tricks, he made himself a legend when he landed the 900 at the XGames in 1999. Hawk has used his proskater status to create multiple businesses such as Hawk Clothing and, with Powell Peralta and Per Welinder, Olistide Projects, now known as Birdhouse Skateboards. In 2000 he published a biography, HAWK: Occupation: Skateboarder, and he even has a roller coaster named after him at Six Flags Texas.. In 1999, Tony Hawk partnered with Acitvision to develop the Tony Hawk skateboard videogame, which immediately became one of the industry's topselling franchises. It is now in its 10th release. Hawk also created a nonprofit organization designed to build skateboard parks in low-income communities, and in cooperation with several other top athletes, founded Athletes for Hope. Although he has retired from the competitive skating world, he continues his charity work and still performs at demos and gaming conventions.

TONY HAWK'S PROVING GROUND

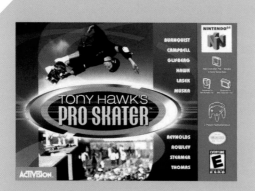

TONY HAWK'S PRO SKATER

The first ever Tony Hawk game was released in 1999 by Activision. The most recent game, *Tony Hawk's Pro Skater*, is divided into two parts. In the first, you skate through areas such as a shopping mall, warehouse, and school campus to complete a set of five challenges. The second part of the game has you skate three times through skate parks in order to get the highest scores. The game also features a range of songs that became famous after the game...who can honestly say they can't remember "Superman"?

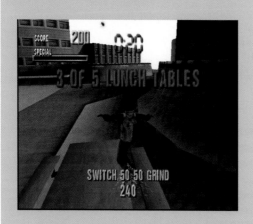

public's perception of the sport itself. Tony then added, -"hardcore skaters appreciate that there is a videogame that represents them authentically." In other words, it's a win-win situation, where both camps come together, enjoying new experiences.

"...we have now put the focus on the player as opposed to the pro. It is all about creating your own style now...."

-Tony Hawk

The season saw a host of games released. But the perhaps most exciting development was the release of the - arguably - most physical of the new games consoles, the Nintendo Wii. Not many sports games were specifically made for the console, but those that were, highlighted some of the possibilities with wireless, motion sensitive controllers. Both Wii Sports and the Wii version of the Tiger Woods PGA games showcased a new way of bridging the gap between the game screen and the playing field or course. It is expected that both the Playstation3 and the Xbox360 will follow suit with similar endeavours, using both camera and controller technologies. But games will always be games, unless they want to cross over into simulation territory. We asked Tony Hawk about the possibilities of virtual skateboards for games consoles, and his reply spotlights the differences: "It would be hard to make a virtual skateboard for our games that responds like the real thing. And if that was possible, our games would be as hard as the real thing." The game would then seize to be a game, and instead move into the simulation camp, possibly losing some of its appeal along the way, at least for the not-so-dedicated players. This is of course a constant balancing act the developers have to perform, weighing accuracy and authenticity against immediacy and playfulness. Tony Hawk's Pro Skater games have tried both sides of the fence, with quite different game experiences as a result:

-"We have such a diverse group of skaters and personalities that we wanted to highlight the characters more. Hence, there was more of a Jackass feel to the Underground series. But we have now put the focus on the player as opposed to the pro. It is all about creating your own style now."

This goes to show that there are a lot of concerns to take into account when creating a sports game. Should one cater to the hardcore fan where the onscreen performers can be sculpted, trained and customised down to the very last detail, or go for the pick-up-and-play factor? A lot of games try to cover both, where one can jump straight into

"...there was more of a Jackass feel to the Underground series. But we have now put the focus on the player as opposed to the pro."

-Tony Hawk

the action if that's what you want, or meticulously set up teams, equipment and schedules before even entering the virtual playing field. The gaming experience is therefore quite individual, with the same game being played very differently by different players. This is something that is quite evident in the season's games, their ability to appeal to sports and video game fans alike.

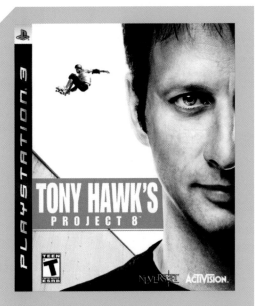

TONY HAWK'S PROJECT 8

Referring to the storyline where you join Tony Hawk's eight-member pro-skater team, Tony Hawk's Project 8 is also the eighth edition of the famous skating franchise. This newest version has made major improvements on the previous games with not only better graphics but also a more realistic gameplay, including the Nail the Trick Mode, where you can work on your tricks in slow motion and in great detail.

FIFA 08
(USA: FIFA Soccer 08)

SETTING

FIFA 08 allows soccer fans from around the world to step into the shoes of their favorite soccer players and compete with 515 teams in more than 30 leagues. If you can handle the constant pressure, you will experience the glory and fame of a real-life soccer player.

GAME SUMMARY

FIFA 08 builds on previous versions of the game, bringing some new features to the table. You can choose between 15,000 players and will take to the field in several glorious new stadiums. New this year is "Be A Pro" mode, where you take on the role of one player and must work specifically to improve certain aspects of your game. Through a series of assignments you must refine your positioning on the field, your dribbling, and your tackling. Helpful arrows on the field will direct you to your areas of responsibility, such as covering players on the opposing team. At halftime you will get feedback on your improvements that you can use throughout the rest of the game. Detailed ball handling animation requires you to consider the use of force and air resistance. Points are given for reacting to changes. For instance, sprinting will reduce your agility and makes it harder to find a target. As you perfect your skills on both offence and defense, only the tougher shots will cause the shooting meter to really fill up. The AI is better than ever, reacting to every change in the game.

CHALLENGES & HINTS

FIFA 08 finally gives you the opportunity to be your soccer hero and help him elevate the game of soccer to the next level. Remember that the new and detailed animation system makes ball control extremely responsive, forcing you to consider and react to all the changes that occur on the field.

AVAILABLE ON

- ✓ Nintendo DS
- ✓ Nintendo Wii
- ✓ PC Windows
-   PC Mac
- ✓ Playstation 2
- ✓ Playstation 3
- ✓ Playstation Portable
- ✓ Xbox 360

GAME FACTS *

PUBLISHER
Electronic Arts

DEVELOPER
EA Sports

FIRST RELEASED
2007-09-27

GAME GENRE	TIME PERIOD
Football	Present
THEME	**COMPLEXITY**
Sport	Low

SIMILAR GAMES

Winning Eleven: Pro Evolution Soccer 2007
FIFA 07
World Soccer Winning Eleven 9

RATING & MULTIPLAYER

USA	Europe	Network	Offline
		10 Players	6 Players

KEY GAMEPLAY ELEMENTS

Steer/Maneuver
Tactics/Plan
Administration

GAME WORLD SIZE — Small
YOUR ROLE — Football Player
REPLAY VALUE — Several Times

AVERAGE SCORE

8.6

out of 10

Data and images may vary on the various platforms

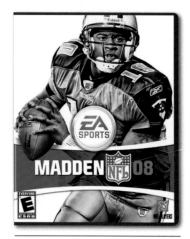

Madden NFL 08

SETTING

As the newest Madden NFL game, Madden NFL 08 gives you the chance to play in the big leagues. Play with the team of your choice or become a superstar with a character you create from scratch.

GAME SUMMARY

Be in control of the team and play like you've never played before in this all new Madden NFL game. Madden NFL 08 brings back old familiar teams and players and gets you deeper into the game than ever before. With the all new Superstar mode, you can create a player and train yourself to play as a single character in the NFL. You can also manage a team over three decades. You choose the players' salaries, positions on the field, and more. With the Receiver Spotlight option, you can also choose a specific player to focus on. The gameplay has improved a lot in Madden NFL 08. The players respond differently to tackles, depending on their weight and resistance. You can also improve on the physical skills and teamwork abilities of your team, which can be used to win matches. Play online, against a friend on the same console, or against the computer.

CHALLENGES & HINTS

Icons on the screen represent the type of player on the field, i.e. fast receivers, big hitters, defensive linemen, etc., and each position has more than one designation. This adds a whole new tactical dimension to the game. As this system makes the team's approach somewhat more transparent, the key to success is to vary your game as much as possible.

AVAILABLE ON

- ✓ Nintendo DS
- ✓ Nintendo Wii
- ✓ PC Windows
- ✓ PC Mac
- ✓ Playstation 2
- ✓ Playstation 3
- ✓ Playstation Portable
- ✓ Xbox 360

GAME FACTS *

PUBLISHER
Electronic Arts

DEVELOPER
EA Sports

FIRST RELEASED
2007-08-14

GAME GENRE	**TIME PERIOD**
Am. Football	Present
THEME	**COMPLEXITY**
Sport	Medium

SIMILAR GAMES

NCAA Football 08
All-Pro Football 2K8
NBA Live 08

RATING & MULTIPLAYER

USA	Europe	Network	Offline
	3+ www.pegi.info	Yes	1-2

KEY GAMEPLAY ELEMENTS

Steer/Maneuver
Administration
Tactics/Plan

GAME WORLD SIZE	Small
YOUR ROLE	Football Player
REPLAY VALUE	Several Times

Data and images may vary on the various platforms

TWO WAYS TO PLAY

FAMILY PLAY
Anyone can play like a pro. You perform basic moves like passing and juking while we handle the rest!

ADVANCED
Take total control. The Nunchuk adds the ability to control player movement & execute more advanced moves.

LOADING

2 Ways to Play Madden!

FAMILY PLAY
Wii Remote ONLY
Anyone can play like a pro. You can perform basic offensive and defensive moves while we handle the rest!

VS

ADVANCED
Nunchuk Style
Take total control. The Nunchuk adds the ability to control player movement & execute more advanced moves.

(A) CONTINUE

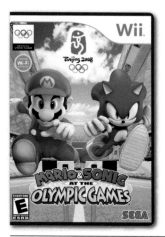

AVAILABLE ON

✓ Nintendo DS
✓ Nintendo Wii
   PC Windows
   PC Mac
   Playstation 2
   Playstation 3
   Playstation Portable
   Xbox 360

GAME FACTS *

PUBLISHER
Sega

DEVELOPER
Sega

FIRST RELEASED
2007-11-20

GAME GENRE	**TIME PERIOD**
Sport	Present
THEME	**COMPLEXITY**
Sport	Low

SIMILAR GAMES

Athens 2004
MLB Power Pros
NBA Live 08

RATING & MULTIPLAYER

USA	Europe	Network	Offline
		Yes	4 Players

Mario & Sonic
AT THE OLYMPIC GAMES

SETTING

For the first time in history, two of the world's biggest videogame heroes come together to compete for the gold medal at the Beijing 2008 Olympic Games.

GAME SUMMARY

Mario & Sonic at the Olympic Games features some of the most famous characters from the Mario and Sonic universes, including Luigi, Knuckles, Yoshi, Tails, and, of course, our two main heroes, Mario and Sonic. Each character has his or her own special talents. For example, Mario is an all-around strong athlete, Sonic is fast, and Knuckles is powerful. You can compete in many of the different games featured at the Beijing Olympics, such as track and field, swimming, archery, and more. Each sport is a mini game, where the controls are fitted to suit the specific type of event, giving you a varied experience. The game features an online leaderboard via the Nintendo Wi-Fi Connection and two gameplay modes: Tournament and Mission.

CHALLENGES & HINTS

Just like in the real Olympic Games, the challenge is to beat the records of everyone else by perfecting your skills. Players from around the world fight to reach the top of the online leaderboard, so be prepared for some fierce competition. Do you have what it takes to bring home the gold medal?

KEY GAMEPLAY ELEMENTS

Steer/Maneuver
Administration
Tactics/Plan

GAME WORLD SIZE	Small
YOUR ROLE	Athlete
REPLAY VALUE	Several Times

AVERAGE SCORE

NA

out of 10

*Data and images may vary on the various platforms

Sport

NBA Street Homecourt

SETTING
Step into the shoes of a future legend and do whatever it takes to gain respect and skills on the streets. You start in your home court with a self-made player that you place on the map by winning challenges from coast to coast.

GAME SUMMARY
Meet the best players from the NBA such as legends Mix Vince Carter and LeBron James on famous street courts. Start out in your own home court as an unknown player with big dreams and make a name for yourself in the professional street community. If you play well, sponsors will come, and along with them, new and better players for your team. With the ball in hand, you can show off your own style by creating tricks as you go along. Dunks as well as double dunks are possible as there is no limit to what you can accomplish as a player. If you make it to the NBA, it's your master skills that separate you from the competition.

CHALLENGES & HINTS
With the new Game Breaker feature, you can unleash some overpowered tricks, but be careful. Losing the ball will cost you, and your rivals will quickly rule the court. Only determination and confidence will get you from the streets to the courts of such stars as Carmelo Anthony and Richard Hamilton.

AVAILABLE ON

Nintendo DS
Nintendo Wii
PC Windows
PC Mac
Playstation 2
✓ Playstation 3
Playstation Portable
✓ Xbox 360

GAME FACTS *

PUBLISHER
Electronic Arts

DEVELOPER
EA Sports

FIRST RELEASED
2007-02-20

GAME GENRE
Basketball

TIME PERIOD
Present

THEME
Sport

COMPLEXITY
Low

SIMILAR GAMES

NBA 2K8
NBA Street V3
NBA Live 08

RATING & MULTIPLAYER

USA	Europe	Network	Offline
E	3+ www.pegi.info	2 Players	No

KEY GAMEPLAY ELEMENTS
Steer/Maneuver
Attack/Fight
Tactics/Plan

GAME WORLD SIZE	Small
YOUR ROLE	Basketball player
REPLAY VALUE	Several Times

AVERAGE SCORE

7.9
out of 10

Data and images may vary on the various platforms

Sport

NHL o8

SETTING

Get your skates on and suit up for another season of fast-paced, hard-action hockey. EA's NHL series has been immensely popular since its inception with NHL Hockey in 1991, which was then considered the most realistic videogame of its time. Like its predecessors, this year's edition brings us one step closer to the ultimate hockey simulator, both in terms of look and handling.

GAME SUMMARY

NHL o8 features a range of improvements, such as the new skate engine that features all new responses and animation. For the first time, all 29 teams of the American Hockey League are at your disposal, so that you can manage and develop the team of your choice. The game features an all-new Goalie mode, where you control the goalie in third-person perspective so that you can make all those important saves, be it with gloves or stick. Stick movement has also improved so that you can control the puck more easily, face one-on-one match-ups effectively, and shoot the puck with greater accuracy.

CHALLENGES & HINTS

Aiming your shot at high speeds while chasing a small black puck is a challenge. And hitting a net that isn't much bigger than the goalie is a real accomplishment! With realistic handling, it takes quite a bit of practice and skill to outplay your opponent. Play wide, pass frequently, and shoot when it's least expected.

AVAILABLE ON

Nintendo DS
Nintendo Wii
✓ PC Windows
PC Mac
✓ Playstation 2
✓ Playstation 3
Playstation Portable
✓ Xbox 360

GAME FACTS *

PUBLISHER
Electronic Arts

DEVELOPER
EA Sports

FIRST RELEASED
2007-09-12

GAME GENRE	**TIME PERIOD**
Hockey	Present
THEME	**COMPLEXITY**
Sport	Low

SIMILAR GAMES

NHL 07
FIFA o8
NBA Live 07

RATING & MULTIPLAYER

USA	Europe	Network	Offline
		Yes	Yes

KEY GAMEPLAY ELEMENTS

Steer/Maneuver
Trade
Administration

		AVERAGE SCORE
GAME WORLD SIZE	Small	
YOUR ROLE	Hockey Player / Manager	**8.8**
REPLAY VALUE	Several Times	out of 10

Data and images may vary on the various platforms

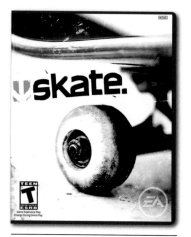

AVAILABLE ON

Nintendo DS
Nintendo Wii
PC Windows
PC Mac
Playstation 2
✓ Playstation 3
Playstation Portable
✓ Xbox 360

GAME FACTS *

PUBLISHER
Electronic Arts

DEVELOPER
Electronic Arts

FIRST RELEASED
2007-09-14

GAME GENRE	TIME PERIOD
Extreme Sport	Present
THEME	**COMPLEXITY**
Sport	Low

SIMILAR GAMES

Tony Hawk's Proving Ground
Tony Hawk's Project 8
Amped 3

RATING & MULTIPLAYER

USA	Europe	Network	Offline
	12+ www.pegi.info	4 Players	4 Players

SKATE

SETTING

As a bold skater in the city of San Vanelona, you can either impress or distress the city's citizens while you mingle with the pros. Play upcoming pros like Danny Way, Mike Carroll, and Chris Cole, or create your own skater and develop your own moves and style.

GAME SUMMARY

The new control system of SKATE is revolutionary to skateboard games. Instead of pressing buttons you use the right analog control to execute jumps and tricks and the left control for moving the skater around. Using the dynamic controllers makes it easier to mimic real skateboard movements. San Vanelona invites exploration, allowing you to skate freely around the city without loading screens. The main focus in the game is to gain sponsors by winning challenges. The map indicates various challenges that range from performing specific tricks to filming awesome combinations that can later be used to gain sponsor deals. As you progress through the game, you unlock new areas, including some indoor locations. You can also capture video and photos of your greatest skate moments and upload them to the game's website for everyone to envy.

CHALLENGES & HINTS

Take your game online and challenge skaters from around the world in timed Jam events. Although the new control system is more true to the real thing, your moves also have to be more precise! And turning the analog stick at random isn't going to help; a true skater masters the skill of precision.

KEY GAMEPLAY ELEMENTS

Steer/Maneuver
Build & Design
Explore

		AVERAGE SCORE
GAME WORLD SIZE	Large	
YOUR ROLE	Skater	**8.6**
REPLAY VALUE	Several Times	out of 10

Data and images may vary on the various platforms

AVAILABLE ON

Nintendo DS
✓ Nintendo Wii
PC Windows
PC Mac
Playstation 2
Playstation 3
Playstation Portable
Xbox 360

GAME FACTS

PUBLISHER
Electronic Arts

DEVELOPER
EA Sports

FIRST RELEASED
2007-03-13

GAME GENRE	**TIME PERIOD**
Skiing	Present
THEME	**COMPLEXITY**
Sport	Low

SIMILAR GAMES

SSX on Tour
Amped 3
NFL Street 2 Unleashed

RATING & MULTIPLAYER

USA	Europe	Network	Offline
		No	Yes

SSX
BLUR

SETTING
SSX Blur takes place on three different mountains, and the goal of the game is to become king of the mountain as you compete against other contestants.

GAME SUMMARY
Strap your boots on and head down the slopes in the all-new SSX Blur for the Wii. The main goal of the game is to win contests to unlock new courses and characters. SSX Blur puts the Wii's motion controllers to full use. The Nunchuk is used to control speed, movement, and jumping, while the Wii controller is used for performing tricks and throwing snowballs at opponents and targets. There are three mountain peaks and 12 tracks for racing, tricks, and the new slalom mode. At every level you can win prizes and unlock new stuff, including some of the 12 playable characters. Complete tricks successfully and build your boost meter up; once it's full you can perform Ubertricks, which are preformed by drawing shapes while jumping, such as hearts and clovers.

CHALLENGES & HINTS
Using the Wii remote can be a bit tricky. Turning right and left and performing Ubertricks is hard, but pulling them off will be rewarded with high scores and a much greater chance to watch your rivals eat dust, or in this case, snow.

KEY GAMEPLAY ELEMENTS
Steer/Maneuver
Build & Design
Trade

		AVERAGE SCORE
GAME WORLD SIZE	Medium	
YOUR ROLE	Skier / Snowboarder	**7.3**
REPLAY VALUE	Several Times	out of 10

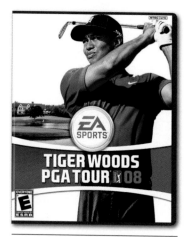

AVAILABLE ON

- ✓ Nintendo DS
- ✓ Nintendo Wii
- ✓ PC Windows
- ✓ PC Mac
- ✓ Playstation 2
- ✓ Playstation 3
- ✓ Playstation Portable
- ✓ Xbox 360

GAME FACTS *

PUBLISHER
Electronic Arts

DEVELOPER
EA Sports

FIRST RELEASED DATE
2007-09-11

GAME GENRE
Golf

TIME PERIOD
Present

THEME
Sport

COMPLEXITY
Medium

SIMILAR GAMES

Super Swing Golf
Hot Shots Golf Fore!
Wii Sports

RATING & MULTIPLAYER

USA	Europe	Network	Offline
	3+ www.pegi.info	4 Players	4 Players

Tiger Woods PGA Tour 08

SETTING

It is time for another PGA Tour and for you to bring your golfer to the top of the rankings. Much like its prequels, you start out as a rookie Tiger Woods or create a golfer of your choice and then work your way to worldwide professional tournaments where you compete against the world's best golfers.

GAME SUMMARY

Golf is a game of perfection, and only practice will bring you to the top of the charts. To accelerate your career, take on various skill challenges to improve your drives, putting skills, and rescue skills. The all-new Confidence Shot mode makes it easier to nail the perfect shot. The more confidence you have, the more accurately you hit the ball. Take part in long-drive contests and par-3 challenges, or play championships at the Westchester Country Club, Cog Hill, and 16 other courses from the FedEx cup. Record your best shots and post them online for others to challenge and beat. The game controls differ quite a lot on the various platforms. The Wii version even lets you perform an actual swing using the Wii remote as a club.

CHALLENGES & HINTS

Birdies and eagles don't come easily. Factors such as side wind, natural obstacles, the slope on the green, your choice of club, and more will affect your score. To play to perfection, you must take all of this into consideration and plan your shots. Perhaps a slight draw with your seven iron will place your ball on the green?

KEY GAMEPLAY ELEMENTS

Steer/Maneuver
Tactics/Plan

AVERAGE SCORE

GAME WORLD SIZE	Large
YOUR ROLE	Pro Golfer
REPLAY VALUE	Several Times

7.8

out of 10

Data and images may vary on the various platforms

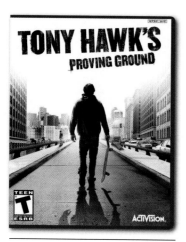

Tony Hawk's
PROVING GROUND

SETTING

Tony Hawk moves from the West Coast to the East Coast. Now you can work your way up the ranks on the streets of Baltimore, Philadelphia, and Washington, D.C.

GAME SUMMARY

You start out as one of many unknown skaters on the East Coast. Although you move along a very loose story-line, there are three skate classes: hardcore, riggers, and career. The hardcore mode is based on street skaters who skate for the rush, not for prizes and trophies. Riggers are the daredevils of Proving Ground, always trying new tricks and transforming their environments into skate parks, and the career class revolves around pro skaters who skate for a living. Within each class you are given the freedom to play how you like in order to reach your goals. Skate your way through nine episodes in any order. In addition to the Nail the Trick feature introduced in Project 8, you can also Nail the Grab and Nail the Manual. In your skater lounge, you can skate with your friends and display your trophies. Make your own skating movies by editing recorded footage of yourself and adding up to 50 songs.

CHALLENGES & HINTS

To reach your full potential, seek advice from someone who's been there before you, such as one of the many pro skaters you meet along the way including Jereme Rogers, Jeff King, Daewon Song, and Tony Hawk himself. They can teach your tricks and mechanics that will help you in all three skating classes.

AVAILABLE ON

- ✓ Nintendo DS
- ✓ Nintendo Wii
- PC Windows
- PC Mac
- ✓ Playstation 2
- ✓ Playstation 3
- Playstation Portable
- ✓ Xbox 360

GAME FACTS *

PUBLISHER
Activision

DEVELOPER
Neversoft Interactive, Page44

FIRST RELEASED
2007-10-15

GAME GENRE
Extreme Sport

TIME PERIOD
Present

THEME
Sport

COMPLEXITY
Low

SIMILAR GAMES

Tony Hawk's Project 8
Skate
Amped 3

RATING & MULTIPLAYER

USA	Europe	Network	Offline
		Yes	Yes

KEY GAMEPLAY ELEMENTS

Steer/Maneuver
Tactics/Plan
Explore

GAME WORLD SIZE	Large
YOUR ROLE	Skater
REPLAY VALUE	Several Times

AVERAGE SCORE

NA

out of 10

*Data and images may vary on the various platforms

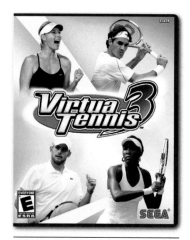

AVAILABLE ON

Nintendo DS
Nintendo Wii
✓ PC Windows
PC Mac
Playstation 2
✓ Playstation 3
✓ Playstation Portable
✓ Xbox 360

GAME FACTS*

PUBLISHER
Sega Europe, Sega of America

DEVELOPER
Sumo Digital

FIRST RELEASED
2007-03-20

GAME GENRE	TIME PERIOD
Tennis	Present
THEME	**COMPLEXITY**
Sport	Low

SIMILAR GAMES

Top Spin 2
Virtua Tennis
Tennis Masters Series 2003

RATING & MULTIPLAYER

USA	Europe	Network	Offline
EVERYONE	3+ www.pegi.info	4 Players	4 Players

Virtua Tennis 3

SETTING

Take on the world's greatest players as you practice diligently and work your way up the rankings to become the new world tennis champion. You begin your tennis career at rank 299 out of 300 (thank god you're not last!).

GAME SUMMARY

Create a player down to the tiniest detail, including a particular playing style. As soon as you start progressing in career mode, the difficulty level quickly increases, and you have to keep up by building skills through training sessions and minigames. You can also improve as a player by attending the tennis academy. Here you receive instructions on different styles and techniques that ultimately help you become a well-rounded player. Your main tasks, whether it be in a minigame or the finals of an important tournament, are relatively simple. Make sure the ball goes over the net and keep it within the lines on your opponent's side of the court. To win, you must be quick on your feet and strategically place the ball where it's difficult for your opponent to reach. Playing against legends such as Federer, Roddick, and Sharapova feels like a real-life match, as all their mannerisms and behaviors are absolutely authentic.

CHALLENGES & HINTS

Virtua Tennis 3 doesn't focus solely on playing but also on the player's health. Keep a healthy balance between rest and physical activity by taking time off to allow your body to recover, which helps you avoid injury and illness. Your stamina can quickly recover by consuming energy drinks, but in the long run, only rest will be the most help.

KEY GAMEPLAY ELEMENTS

Steer/Maneuver
Tactics/Plan
Build & Design

GAME WORLD SIZE	Small
YOUR ROLE	Tennis Player
REPLAY VALUE	Several Times

AVERAGE SCORE

7.9

out of 10

Data and images may vary on the various platforms

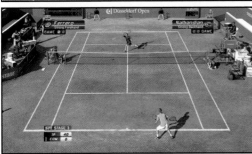

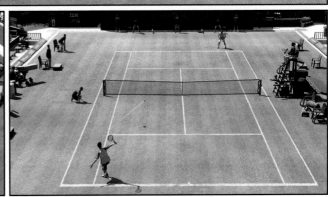

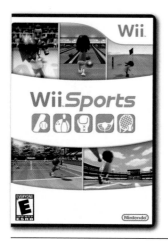

AVAILABLE ON

Nintendo DS
✓ Nintendo Wii
PC Windows
PC Mac
Playstation 2
Playstation 3
Playstation Portable
Xbox 360

GAME FACTS

PUBLISHER
Nintendo

DEVELOPER
Nintendo

FIRST RELEASED
2006-11-17

GAME GENRE	**TIME PERIOD**
Sport	Fantasy/Timeless
THEME	**COMPLEXITY**
Sport	Low

SIMILAR GAMES

MLB Power Pros
Brunswick Pro Bowling
Pangya! Golf with Style

RATING & MULTIPLAYER

USA	Europe	Network	Offline
	www.pegi.info	No	4 Players

Wii Sports

SETTING

Take your small Mii characters to the tennis court, golf course, bowling alley, baseball field, or boxing ring and break a sweat with fun and colorful games! Use the motion-controlled Wii remote, get off the couch, and move your body to perform the perfect strike, forehand, pitch, or upper-cut, depending on the sport you're playing.

GAME SUMMARY

Wii Sports is a collection of simple but fun sports games that include tennis, golf, baseball, boxing, and bowling. The game's simplicity is reflected in its stylized yet simple 3D graphics and bright colors. Although each game concentrates on the core mechanics of hitting a ball, swinging a racket, putting a golf ball, or punching your opponent, the games offer a fully simplified sports experience. This makes Wii Sports an easy pick-up-and-play game for everyone. Play often and hone your skills to become a pro, or try out the daily "fitness age" training, which calculates your fitness age based on three skills tests.

CHALLENGES & HINTS

Your main challenge is to continually top your results so that you can eventually become a pro—but an even bigger challenge will be keeping your parents and the rest of your friends and family away from the game! And no matter what you do, you can't cheat the fitness test. Trust us, we tried!

KEY GAMEPLAY ELEMENTS

Steer/Maneuver
Tactics/Plan
Attack/Fight

GAME WORLD SIZE	Medium
YOUR ROLE	Various
REPLAY VALUE	Several Times

AVERAGE SCORE

7.3

out of 10

Curveball
60 mph

246 ft

Fastball
68 mph

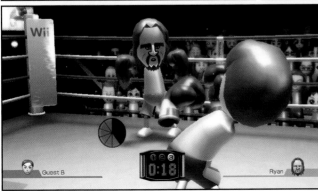

Guest B

Ryan

Strategy

GAMES

MEDIEVAL II: TOTAL WAR KINGDOMS

Armchair strategists have never had it this good. Previously a mainstay of desktop computers, the new wave of strategy gaming is handheld. Aspiring Roman emperors can test their skills on the PSP with *History Channel: Great Battles of Rome*, while budding city builders can play *SimCity* on the Nintendo DS. Strategy gaming sure has come a long way.

Even so, the basic premise of strategy games is the same as it was when they were played with pen, paper, and thick rule books: test your skills as a strategist and tactician in real or imagined conflict situations. If you lose, you can always start over. Thankfully, the computer has taken over the role of referee—not to mention custodian of all those tiny soldiers, vehicles, and game markers. If you lose a couple of troopers now, it's due to bad decisions, not sloppy housekeeping.

The main trends of the season are handheld and online. *Command & Conquer 3: Tiberium Wars* can be played both as a single-player campaign and online against other players around the world. You can even invite nonplayers to watch the battles, not unlike a live chess match. If the dark middle ages are more to your liking, *Medieval II: Total War Kingdoms* is equally hooked up. When you've battled your way through the Americas and the crusades, it's perhaps time to

DEFENDER OF THE CROWN

But the big push this season was toward hand-held strategy gaming. Helped by the earlier success of games such as *Advance Wars DS*, a large number of big strategy games were made into portable equivalents, while quite a few were designed especially for handhelds. Strategy game icon Sid Meier took his *Pirates!* to the PSP, and

"It's only a matter of time before we see commuters and bus riders engrossed in full-scale tactical warfare...."

test your commandeering skills against other human players, who can sometimes be a bit more unpredictable than computer opponents. Going offline, the old favorite *Defender of the Crown*, well loved in the 16-bit era, made a comeback this season with *Heroes Live Forever*. As always, it's about conquering England in medieval times, and yes, you can still call out to good old Robin Hood for help.

the old classic *Theme Park* arrived on the DS, as did the similarly themed *Thrillville* on the PSP. In true *Pokemon* style, *Yu-Gi-Oh!*, the *Marvel Trading Card Game*, and *The Eye of Judgment* used their obvious ties to physical trading cards to full effect. A welcome return for a lot of older players came in the shape of a heap of slightly aggressive

STARCRAFT 2 (2008)

earthworms with *Worms: Open Warfare 2* on both of the major handhelds. Also available on mobile phones, these bomb-throwing critters seem to be popping up all over the place.

When looked at as a whole, it is evident that handheld strategy gaming is still in its infancy. Not all games use the medium to its full potential, but many show a lot of promise. It's only a matter of time before we see commuters and bus riders engrossed in full-scale tactical warfare using the same device that they call home with.

In addition to pure strategy games, a few action games are close to trespassing on strategy's turf. The various Tom Clancy games, such as *Ghost Recon: Advanced Warfighter 2*, *Rainbow Six: Vegas*, and *Splinter Cell: Double Agent* all incorporate short- to mid-term tactical decision-making as key gameplay elements. Optimized

for consoles, they all bring the action-strategy hybrid to an audience not usually associated with strategy gaming's somewhat calmer modes of play. Then again, when one looks closely, all games contain strategy elements. Whether it's a first-person shooter or racing game, it's always decisions, decisions, decisions. And that's the beauty of it.

HISTORY CHANNEL: GREAT BATTLES OF ROME

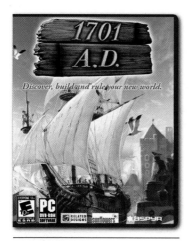

AVAILABLE ON

✓ Nintendo DS
  Nintendo Wii
✓ PC Windows
  PC Mac
  Playstation 2
  Playstation 3
  Playstation Portable
  Xbox 360

GAME FACTS *

PUBLISHER
Deep Silver, Disney Interactive

DEVELOPER
Keen Games, Sunflower

FIRST RELEASED
2007-04-01

GAME GENRE	**TIME PERIOD**
Strategy	Renaissance
THEME	**COMPLEXITY**
History	Medium

SIMILAR GAMES

The Settlers IV: Rise of an Empire
Ages of Empire III
Europa Universalis III

RATING & MULTIPLAYER

USA	Europe	Network	Offline
	3+ www.pegi.info	4 Players	No

1701 A.D.
(EUROPE: ANNO 1701)

SETTING
1701 A.D. takes you all the way back to the 18th century where you are assigned the task of building and controlling your own city. You are responsible for creating your town, arranging trade, and planning for its constant expansion.

GAME SUMMARY
Charged with the exciting mission of charting and conquering unexplored territory, you must first (with the help of seamless tutorials) source raw materials such as wood, stone, and ore to build your town. Use these resources to construct buildings and homes for your townspeople, and provide residents with food by building farms and mills. Your city's citizens will gradually grow and prosper, and will begin to demand more of you; consider levying taxes to fund further development. This game is totally addictive, and you will soon find yourself expanding your colony into foreign lands and exploiting their native inhabitants. As your empire grows you must defend it from ferocious invaders. The possibilities are limitless, and make for hours upon hours of thrilling gameplay.

CHALLENGES & HINTS
Make sure to build your pubs, churches, and other important buildings in your city centre to satisfy your residents. The more you develop your civilization, the more demanding your citizens become, which raises the difficulty level significantly.

KEY GAMEPLAY ELEMENTS
Explore
Gather
Build & Design

		AVERAGE SCORE
GAME WORLD SIZE	Medium	
YOUR ROLE	Various	**8.0**
REPLAY VALUE	Once or Twice	out of 10

Data and images may vary on the various platforms

AVAILABLE ON

Nintendo DS
Nintendo Wii
✓ PC Windows
PC Mac
Playstation 2
Playstation 3
Playstation Portable
✓ Xbox 360

GAME FACTS *

PUBLISHER
Eidos Interactive

DEVELOPER
Eidos Interactive

FIRST RELEASED
2007-01-30

GAME GENRE	TIME PERIOD
Strategy	Recent History
THEME	**COMPLEXITY**
War	Medium

SIMILAR GAMES

Silent Hunter: Wolves of the Pacific
Blazing Angels 2: Secret Missions of WWII
Command & Conquer 3 Tiberium Wars

RATING & MULTIPLAYER

USA	Europe	Network	Offline
TEEN T CONTENT RATED BY ESRB	12+ www.pegi.info	8 Players	No

Battlestations
MIDWAY

SETTING
Engage in World War II's infamous 'Battles of the Pacific' as you command submarines, planes, and battleships to victory.

GAME SUMMARY
Start off as the naval recruit Henry Walker in the famous battle of Pearl Harbor. Begin your career as a gunner man defending your fleet and go on to experience some of the Allies' most demanding Pacific campaigns. Through a series of 11 large-scale campaigns covering major WWII events, you get to play as both a Naval Commander and an Air Force pilot. Command huge, roaring battleships, navigate dangerous waters as part of a submarine fleet, and engage in old fashioned dogfights with classic Spitfire planes. Switch between a number of different units, enjoy a diverse arsenal and detailed military vehicles, and work your way through all kinds of weather conditions in real-life environments. Battlestations: Midway is a blend of different game genres that requires both tactical thinking and direct action. The game allows you to zoom out to the map and command AI units from afar, much like a strategy game, or you can dive into the action and personally engage in the battles. Up to you!

CHALLENGES & HINTS
The battles are happening in the air, at sea, and under the waves simultaneously! Every unit is of great importance to the survival of your fleet. You must continuously keep an eye on many aspects of the battle. There's a lot to be learned in this game, but tutorials will guide your way.

KEY GAMEPLAY ELEMENTS
Attack/Fight
Tactics/Plan
Steer/Maneuver

		AVERAGE SCORE
GAME WORLD SIZE	Large	
YOUR ROLE	Various	**7.5**
REPLAY VALUE	Once or Twice	out of 10

Data and images may vary on the various platforms

AVAILABLE ON

Nintendo DS
Nintendo Wii
✓ PC Windows
✓ PC Mac
Playstation 2
Playstation 3
Playstation Portable
✓ Xbox 360

GAME FACTS∗

PUBLISHER
Electronic Arts

DEVELOPER
EA Games

FIRST RELEASED
2007-03-28

GAME GENRE	**TIME PERIOD**
Strategy	Future
THEME	**COMPLEXITY**
War	Medium

SIMILAR GAMES

Act of War
Universe at War: Earth Assault
Emperor: Battle for Dune

RATING & MULTIPLAYER

USA	Europe	Network	Offline
		8 Players	No

Command & Conquer 3
TIBERIUM WARS

SETTING
When the original Command & Conquer game was released more than 10 years ago, it in many ways defined the RTS genre. In the long-awaited futuristic sequel, 17 years of peace are disrupted when the Brotherhood of Nod initiates a worldwide offensive against the Global Defense Alliance, starting the Third Tiberium War.

GAME SUMMARY
The game is set shortly after the attack of the Brotherhood, an attack led by the infamous Kane. Kane's ongoing mission: to destroy Earth's last remaining blue zones—hideouts where the vestiges of humanity take refuge. As the only person who can stop him, you must command your troops through a series of battles to try and save the world. The game requires you to not only destroy enemies, but to strategically ally with them, using engineers to capture buildings and preserve power plants. You are required to build a base, recruit soldiers, and develop weapons and technology quickly as there is little time to prepare for battle. Artificial intelligence will take strategic advantage of your flaws. The game will test your abilities as a commander, including your organizational skills. Be sure to build power plants and collect enough Tiberium to keep your base operative and running efficiently.

CHALLENGES & HINTS
The key to winning against the Brotherhood of Nod is effectively building and maintaining your offense and defense and strategically using them in war. Your resources will be scarce and your base will constantly be under enemy attack. Keep a cool head as you navigate through this dangerous world of technological warfare.

KEY GAMEPLAY ELEMENTS

Attack/Fight
Tactics/Plan
Administration

		AVERAGE SCORE
GAME WORLD SIZE	Large	
YOUR ROLE	Commander	**8.2**
REPLAY VALUE	Once or Twice	out of 10

∗Data and images may vary on the various platforms

AVAILABLE ON

Nintendo DS
Nintendo Wii
✓ PC Windows
✓ PC Mac
Playstation 2
Playstation 3
✓ Playstation Portable
Xbox 360

GAME FACTS ∗

PUBLISHER
Sega Europe, Sega of America

DEVELOPER
Sports Interactive

FIRST RELEASED
2007-10-19

GAME GENRE	**TIME PERIOD**
Strategy	Present
THEME	**COMPLEXITY**
Sport	High

SIMILAR GAMES

FIFA Manager 08
Premier Manager 08
Championship Manager 200

RATING & MULTIPLAYER

USA	Europe	Network	Offline
EVERYONE **E** CONTENT RATED BY ESRB	**3+** www.pegi.info	16 Players	Yes

Football Manager 2008
(USA: WORLDWIDE SOCCER MANAGER 2008)

SETTING
Forget the pain and physical strain of playing football and take charge of the entire team, dealing with everything from financing to talent scouting.

GAME SUMMARY
Football Manager 2008 plays like the previous manager games but is fully updated with the newest team transfers and players. There are a total of 100 new features, some small and some big, such as Match Flow, which enhances the feel of match day with match previews, team talks, the actual match, half time, and an after-match summary. As a football manager, you have to buy and sell players and find new talent to make the perfect team. Before each match you decide who should play which position in order to maximize the performance of your team. You can take your team to many of the largest events in the world, from the FIFA world cup to the Olympic games.

CHALLENGES & HINTS
Do you think you can be the next Alex Ferguson? Managing a football team is not as easy as it is to play football. You have to make sure you buy the right talent and sell the poor performers to make the perfect team, which is easier said than done.

KEY GAMEPLAY ELEMENTS

Tactics/Plan
Administration
Trade

GAME WORLD SIZE	Small
YOUR ROLE	Football Manager
REPLAY VALUE	Once or Twice

AVERAGE SCORE

NA
out of 10

*Data and images may vary on the various platforms

Supreme Commander

SETTING
It's far into the future, and humankind has the ability to travel through space. The human empire used to govern the colonies that were created by this new form of travel, but war has broken out between the humans and the Cybran Nation and Aeon Illuminate.

GAME SUMMARY
Supreme Commander lets you experience real-time strategic warfare on a massive scale, where you can deploy up to a thousand units at the same time and wage huge battles with all of your units simultaneously. Since the game is set on a large scale, a zooming feature allows you to get as close to your units as you need to, or you can zoom all the way out to see the entire map on screen. The game is oriented around the Armored Command Units, who build bases and upgrade and develop units in order for you to start gathering resources and developing attack units. The three different factions featured in the game have their own special strengths and weaknesses that can make or break your commanding decisions.

CHALLENGES & HINTS
At the end of the day, it's all about thinking like a commander and making life-and-death decisions. A strategic call you might have thought was a good one might come back and bite you later on.

AVAILABLE ON
Nintendo DS
Nintendo Wii
✓ PC Windows
PC Mac
Playstation 2
Playstation 3
Playstation Portable
Xbox 360

GAME FACTS

PUBLISHER
THQ

DEVELOPER
Gas Powered Games

FIRST RELEASED
2007-02-16

GAME GENRE	**TIME PERIOD**
Strategy	Future
THEME	**COMPLEXITY**
Sci-Fi	Medium

SIMILAR GAMES
Command & Conquer 3 Tiberium Wars
Starcraft II
Universe at War: Earth Assault

RATING & MULTIPLAYER

USA	Europe	Network	Offline
	12+ www.pegi.info	8 Players	No

KEY GAMEPLAY ELEMENTS
Tactics/Plan
Attack/Fight
Gather

GAME WORLD SIZE	Large
YOUR ROLE	Commander
REPLAY VALUE	Once or Twice

AVERAGE SCORE

8.5
out of 10

AVAILABLE ON

Nintendo DS
Nintendo Wii
PC Windows
PC Mac
Playstation 2
✓ Playstation 3
Playstation Portable
Xbox 360

GAME FACTS

PUBLISHER
SCEA, SCEE

DEVELOPER
SCEI

FIRST RELEASED
2007-10-23

GAME GENRE	**TIME PERIOD**
Strategy	Fantasy/Timeless
THEME	**COMPLEXITY**
Fantasy	Medium

SIMILAR GAMES

Magic: The Gathering
Etherlords II
Solitaire

RATING & MULTIPLAYER

USA	Europe	Network	Offline
TEEN T	12+ www.pegi.info	2 Players	2 Players

The Eye of Judgment

SETTING

A hybrid of a classic trading card game and a video-game, The Eye of Judgment is a revolutionary title. Using the PlayStation Eye camera and high-tech playing cards, this game creates an augmented reality by reading your game cards and bringing them to life in spectacular on-screen 3D fights.

GAME SUMMARY

To play the game, players lay down cards on the "9 field" battle mat in front of the PlayStation Eye. Once the cards are added, 3D characters appear above them and battle against each other on screen. The first one to gain control over five of the nine fields wins. Each of the 100 different characters has his or her own abilities and magic spells that can make or break any battle, so a good amount of tactical skill is needed. Different sets of new cards can be purchased, just like the popular card games Pokemon and Magic: The Gathering. There are four ways to play Eye of Judgment: single player versus the PS3, against a friend in two-player mode, against someone online, or letting the PS3 play the game for you.

CHALLENGES & HINTS

Eye of Judgment combines turn-based strategy videogames with classical trading card games, which makes it quite a strategy builder. You constantly need to figure out which card will do the most damage to your opponent in order to beat him.

KEY GAMEPLAY ELEMENTS

Tactics/Plan
Attack/Fight
Administration

GAME WORLD SIZE	Small	
YOUR ROLE	Card Player	
REPLAY VALUE	Several Times	

AVERAGE SCORE

NA

out of 10

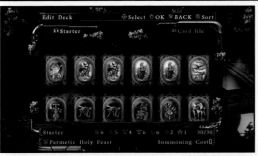

Edit Deck · Select · OK · BACK · Sort

Starter · Card file

Starter
Parmetic Holy Feast · Summoning Cost

Abilities · Scroll · BACK

Elven Berserker Maiden
Elf

While Elven Berserker Maiden has exactly 1 HP, she adds 2 to her Attack and gains a Dodge attempt.

Card Profile · Scope On · Back

Card Profile · World Map

Elven Rider

Elf

Affiliation
Til Vorg Monarchy
Ability
Unchallenged Joust

Orcs had been sighted in the eastern glade. The master blew his horn and the lancers spurred their mounts to a gallop.

Card Profile · ViewMode · BACK

Old Capital Tolicore

WATER CITY TINOA

SAND CITY VISVAR

These fearless elven riders spend their lives in the saddle, perfecting their horsemanship and jousting skills.

FOREST CITY BR

Sciondar Dragon's Attack is equal to 5 plus the number of other

AVAILABLE ON

Nintendo DS
Nintendo Wii
✓ PC Windows
PC Mac
Playstation 2
Playstation 3
Playstation Portable
✓ Xbox 360

GAME FACTS *

PUBLISHER
Sierra Entertainment, Vivendi

DEVELOPER
Massive Entertainment

FIRST RELEASED
2007-09-18

GAME GENRE	**TIME PERIOD**
Strategy	Present
THEME	**COMPLEXITY**
War	Medium

SIMILAR GAMES

Command & Conquer 3: Tiberium wars
Joint Task Force
Republic: The Revolution

RATING & MULTIPLAYER

USA	Europe	Network	Offline
		16 Players	No

World in Conflict

SETTING

World in Conflict takes place in 1989, the year when the Berlin Wall supposedly never fell. Instead, the Soviet Union has advanced into Western Europe and the west coast of the United States, and it becomes your task as a field commander to save your homeland. World in Conflict is said to be one of the best multiplayer games of its time.

GAME SUMMARY

The United States now faces combat on two fronts—the Soviet Union HAS attacked both Western Europe and major cities on the American west coast starting in Seattle. You work for the U.S. army as a company commander, and you take control of the country's most powerful military equipment and machines, all of which are period specific. The story is engaging and heartfelt as you see and hear everything from conversations between husbands and wives to heated debates between the president and his military advisers. As well as utilizing modern firepower on the battlefield, you experience combined arms warfare, bringing strategy to the forefront. Your reinforcement points can be used to accumulate units that are slowly refunded back into your reinforcement pool as they are destroyed. In head-to-head as well as team-based battles, you have to strategize to create tactical attacks on the enemy. Use your vast arsenal of weapons to destroy a bridge, which forces the enemy to take the long way!

CHALLENGES & HINTS

Some missions will be timed, raising the difficulty level of this game to new heights. You will, for example, be given an objective to capture a tower in 45 seconds, a mission that is great fun when using your military strength and very challenging when working under a deadline.

KEY GAMEPLAY ELEMENTS

Tactics/Plan
Attack/Fight
Administration

		AVERAGE SCORE
GAME WORLD SIZE	Large	
YOUR ROLE	Commander	**9.0**
REPLAY VALUE	Several Times	out of 10

Data and images may vary on the various platforms

ZSX3: NINJASTARMAGEDDON! BY SKA SOFTWARE

Indie
GAMES

WHAT IS AN INDIE GAME?

For film and music, the term Indie has been used to describe a departure from the mainstream, from the control of large companies, and from the creation of a product that mirrored that which came before it. These three characteristics also apply to today's thriving Indie videogame movement.

When a game is labeled as indie, it generally means most, if not all, of the following apply:

-Developed by a small team—Indie game teams often have three or fewer developers.

- Developed on a small, self-financed budget—Indie game teams frequently develop their games with little or no outside investment and are almost always funded by the developers themselves.

-Developed without external control—Indie game teams may be influenced by external factors, but the final decision for what goes into their games comes from the team itself.

SAVAGE: THE BATTLE FOR NEWERTH BY S2 GAMES

Of course, there are exceptions to these rules. For example, *Bang! Howdy*, a Wild West–themed multiplayer online tactical strategy game, was developed by the independent company Three Rings Design, Inc. The company is slightly larger than a typical indie game developer at 24 full-time employees, but the game is inarguably indie.

Bang! Howdy was an official entrant in the 2007 Independent Games Festival (IGF), where it was awarded the prize for Technical Excellence.

Another exceptional indie game is *Savage: The Battle for Newerth.*

This game was developed by S2 Games, LLC. Unlike most indie developers, S2 Games is purported to have received more than one million dollars in development funding for *Savage* from external sources.

This game, too, was an official entrant at the 2004 IGF, where it not only won several awards but walked away with the Seumas McNally Grand Prize.

BANG! HOWDY BY THREE RINGS DESIGN, INC.

As with *Bang! Howdy*, S2 Games had more resources than the average indie game developer, but they kept true to the indie game spirit by remaining in complete control of their game while contributing something new and innovative to the industry as a whole.

THE CONSOLIDATION OF THE VIDEOGAME INDUSTRY

A combination of factors have contributed to the development of the indie game movement. As the computer game industry evolved over the last 30 years, small companies began merging with and being consumed by larger companies, until the gaming industry was dominated by a small group of large companies, such as Electronic Arts, Nintendo, Activision, Sony, etc.

With large development, marketing, and distribution resources, these companies were able to produce high-quality games, disseminate those games into every corner of the globe, and contribute to the exponential growth of the industry with cutting-edge software and hardware platforms.

THE INDUSTRY STAGNATES

The large videogame companies did a lot of good for the industry, but by the late 1990s, drawbacks to the industry's consolidation became apparent. As the market became more competitive, these now publicly traded companies became risk averse, which led to a drop in innovation and a shift toward backroom control of game development teams.

"Obviously, something had to be done, but who was going to do it, and what were they going to do?"

As a result, game players started complaining that many of the new games being released were nothing more than old games wrapped in shiny new packages. The technology was advancing, but the gameplay and game content were not. Similarly, game developers found themselves no longer in control of the projects for which they were responsible and that innovation was often slapped down in lieu of tried-and-true formulas. "What worked yesterday, will work today and tomorrow"—or will it?

Obviously, something had to be done, but who was going to do it, and what were they going to do?

GROWTH OF THE HOBBYIST CULTURE

Hobbyists have been writing computer games as long as computers have existed, but in the 1990s, when computers became drastically more affordable and powerful, the game development hobbyist culture exploded. The introduction of the Internet further contributed to the growth of hobbyist game development as hobbyists were able to share information more rapidly and ex-

GARAGE GAMES: BEHIND TORQUE, A CHEAP GAME ENGINE.

tensively than ever before. Game development websites abounded, but even with all this help, hobbyists found that although they could make simple games, making anything as complex as a first-person-shooter or an online role-playing game was nearly impossible with the tools they had.

CHEAP GAME ENGINES

The catalyst for extensive indie game development arrived in 2001 and 2002. Up until then, hobbyists had been required to write their own game engines: the skeleton upon which games and game content lies. This was a technically challenging task, and often a hobbyist found him- or herself spending more time programming the engine than writing the game itself. Alternatively, a hobbyist could buy a game engine from an established company and build his or her game on top of it, but game engines were extremely expensive, costing upwards of half-a-million dollars or more—out of reach for most hobbyists.

Then, in 2000 and 2001, several inexpensive ($100 or less) but high-quality game engines became available. With these game engines, hobbyists and hobbyist teams could focus on what they had wanted to do all along: develop a great game.

THE INDIE REVOLUTION

Quickly, the results of these factors coalesced into a blooming indie game movement. Many hobbyists turned their "hobby" into a profession, building their own independent game studios. The indie revolution had begun. Indie games started showing up everywhere and on all kinds of gaming platforms.

Gish by Chronic Logic was released in May 2004. By May 2007, more than 4,500 copies were sold worldwide. Available on both Windows and Max OSX platforms, this game has won several awards since its release, including the 2004 Game Tunnel Game of the Year award, the 2005 IGF Seumas McNally Grand Prize, and the 2005 IGF Innovation in Game Design award.

Alien Hominid HD by Behemoth was released

MINIONS OF MIRTH BY PRAIRIE GAMES

in November 2004. It had the distinction of having one of the widest platform penetrations of any indie game on the market and is currently available on Game Boy Advance, the GameCube, PlayStation 2, the XBox, and the XBox360.

Minions of Mirth by Prairie Games was released in December 2005. Available in both Windows and Max OSX versions, the game saw sales of $80,000 by November 2006, with a registration of approximately 30,000 players. This game has the distinction of being one of the few independently developed MMORPGs.

THE INDUSTRY EVOLVES

Today, the computer gaming industry is in the midst of an evolution. Indie games are finding their niche in the market and new pathways for getting indie games onto alternative platforms such as consoles, hand-held devices, and even arcade games. All the while, more and more people are joining the ranks of indie game developers, invigorating the industry with new and innovative ideas.

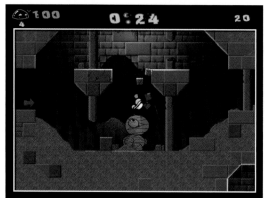

GISH BY CHRONIC LOGIC

ALIEN HOMID HD BY BEHEMOTH

GETTING INTO INDIE GAME DEVELOPMENT

If this discussion has piqued your interest, you might be interested in joining the indie game movement yourself. There is no time like the present and opportunities abound!

There are several game engines available. A good place to start your research is at DevMaster.Net. (www.devmaster.net) At this time, the most highly rated 3D game engine is the Torque Game Engine by GarageGames.

GarageGames (www.garagegames.com) is an all-encompassing provider of game development technology, offering four different game engines that can be used to develop 2D and 3D games for Windows, Mac OSX, Linux, and even the XBox360. Additionally, they are an online publisher and distributor of independent games. They host a thriving online community of independent game developers and are themselves a first-party developer that makes its own games.

If none of these opportunities interest you, don't worry, there are a myriad of other options and solutions available to assuage your particular wants and needs. A simple web search for "Indie Game Development" should get you started.

Good luck and happy gaming!

AVAILABLE ON

Nintendo DS
Nintendo Wii
✓ PC Windows
PC Mac
Playstation 2
Playstation 3
Playstation Portable
Xbox 360

GAME FACTS

PUBLISHER
RakeInGrass

DEVELOPER
RakeInGrass

FIRST RELEASED
2007-03-01

GAME GENRE	**TIME PERIOD**
Action	Future
THEME	**COMPLEXITY**
Sci-Fi	Low

SIMILAR GAMES

Galaga
Silkworm
1942

RATING & MULTIPLAYER

USA	Europe	Network	Offline
		No	No

Jets'n'Guns Gold

SETTING

You are a freelancer created by the old war, and the universe is in need of your skills again. Load up your spaceship with all kinds of weapons, from homing missiles to spreading laser guns. You will need all the firepower you can buy to get through the universe in one piece.

GAME SUMMARY

As a freelancer, you are contacted by your old commander and introduced to a big problem. The evil dictator Xoxx plans on destroying the universe, and to do so, he has kidnapped Professor Von Hamburger. The scientist was working on a quantum canon that, in theory, could end the universe in one shot. Throughout the game you gain access to different space vessels, which you can load up with all kinds of weapons before heading out on your mission. During your missions, you must survive oncoming waves of enemies, but destroying them earns you money that you can use to pick up different things along the way. More weapons and ships are unlocked as you play, but your enemies also become stronger as the game goes along. You can upgrade weapons as well as your ship parts to improve your chances of success.

CHALLENGES & HINTS

Choosing weapons before heading out on a mission is crucial. Keeping your old faithful gun or upgrading to a new big blaster isn't always going to result in success. Test out your weapons first. A shotgun can never do a machine-gun's work.

KEY GAMEPLAY ELEMENTS
Attack/Fight
Steer/Maneuver
Gather

GAME WORLD SIZE	Medium
YOUR ROLE	Futuristic Fighter Pilot
REPLAY VALUE	Once or Twice

AVERAGE SCORE

NA

out of 10

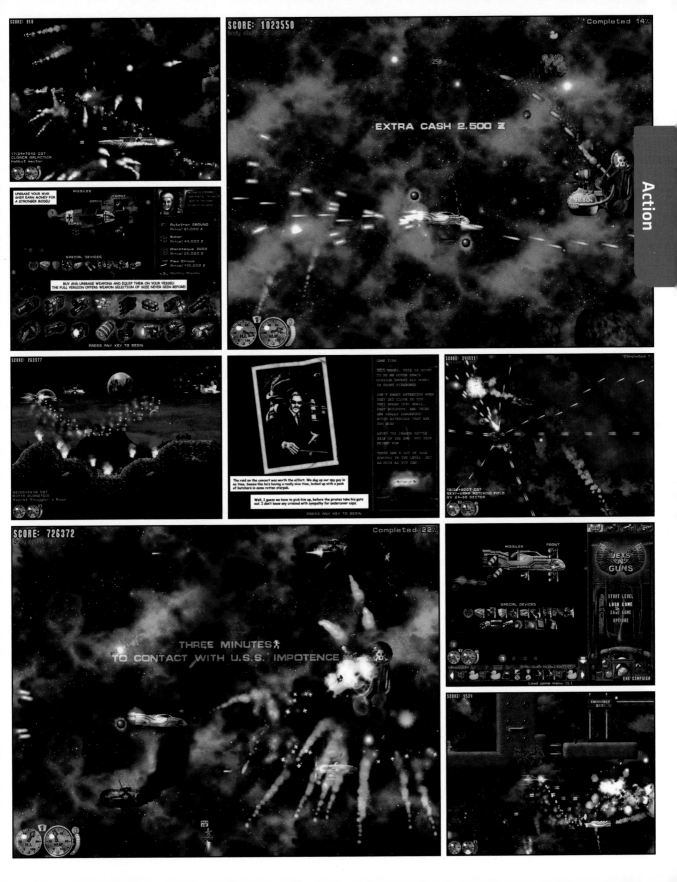

AVAILABLE ON

Nintendo DS
Nintendo Wii
✓ PC Windows
PC Mac
Playstation 2
Playstation 3
Playstation Portable
Xbox 360

GAME FACTS

PUBLISHER
Moonpod

DEVELOPER
Moonpod

FIRST RELEASED
2007-01-10

GAME GENRE	**TIME PERIOD**
Adventure	Future
THEME	**COMPLEXITY**
Sci-Fi	Low

SIMILAR GAMES

Lego Star Wars
System Shock 2
Space Quest

RATING & MULTIPLAYER

USA	Europe	Network	Offline
RP RATING PENDING	NOT RATED www.pegi.info		
		No	No

Mr. Robot

SETTING
Welcome on board the spaceship Eidolon, heading for an earth-like planet. As it gets close to its destination, weird things start to happen, and you, the low-ranked service robot Asimov, play a big role in figuring out what's causing this weirdness.

GAME SUMMARY
Take on the role of the robot Asimov on board the spaceship Eidolon headed for a planet to be colonized by mankind. While the humans are deep asleep, the ship is taken over by the program HEL's, which make the ship do strange things as it gets close to its destination. You are assigned several tasks to help fix the problem, which leads you to eventually learn new things like hacking terminals. allowing you to fight the defense programs in a turn-based style. Gain experience and get your hands on new equipment and upgrades by defeating the enemies and leveling up. But be careful, as there are also enemies outside the terminals—robots who want to fry your circuits. But don't worry, as you eventually get help from three other robots. You have to use your surroundings as well as your brain to get around in the ship, as you will encounter small puzzle-like problems. The game has a static third-person perspective.

CHALLENGES & HINTS
Find a balance between using and saving up extreme strikes, as you do not know when you will need some extra energy to defeat a strong enemy quickly. Nothing is more annoying than restarting from the last checkpoint because of a stupid mistake.

KEY GAMEPLAY ELEMENTS

Solve Puzzles
Gather
Explore

GAME WORLD SIZE	Large
YOUR ROLE	Robot Janitor
REPLAY VALUE	Once or Twice

AVERAGE SCORE

8.3

out of 10

I'm impressed 1138, you've actually managed to think something through for once.

DATA MASTER   2

	energy	power	extreme	
Asimov	61/63	24/33	100%	
Zelda	46/49	38/38	10%	
Orgus	29/29	30/47	100%	
Raistlin	41/41	47/64	0%	

ENIGMA   1

ADULT SCRAMBLER   2

GAL PS III

AVAILABLE ON

Nintendo DS
Nintendo Wii
✓ PC Windows
PC Mac
Playstation 2
Playstation 3
Playstation Portable
Xbox 360

GAME FACTS

PUBLISHER
Jowood, The Adventure Company

DEVELOPER
Telltale Games

FIRST RELEASED
2007-08-01

GAME GENRE	**TIME PERIOD**
Action	Present
THEME	**COMPLEXITY**
Comedy	Low

SIMILAR GAMES

Destination: Treasure Island
Nancy Drew: Legend of Crystal Skull
Escape from Monkey Island

RATING & MULTIPLAYER

USA	Europe	Network	Offline
TEEN T CONTENT RATED BY ESRB	NOT RATED www.pegi.info	No	No

Sam & Max
SEASON 1

SETTING
Follow Sam and Max through six bizarre episodes on their mission to fight crimes that keep popping up in humorous and unexpected ways. They battle a variety of crazy characters, preferably in a very violent manner.

GAME SUMMARY
Sam is a taller-than-normal canine that defends justice and is the leader of the super crime-fighting duo. Max is a hyperkinetic rabbit-like creature that likes to solve every problem using violence but always remains loyal to Sam. The game progresses through six episodes where situations that threaten the peace quickly arise. A bizarre conspiracy that hypnotizes child star Soda Poppers and talk show host Myra Stump is the target of an investigation for the freelance police duo. As you get deeper into the game, all the evidence points to Washington, D.C., more precisely, to the U.S. President's own office. In the final episodes of Season One, Sam and Max are led into the Internet itself before finding the mastermind Hugh Bliss, who is behind the mind-controlling plot to turn the world's inhabitants into followers of the Prismatologers cult. Hilarious cut scenes with outrageous dialog make this game not only fun to play but also fun to watch.

CHALLENGES & HINTS
Sam and Max: Season One is not particularly challenging. Rather, the game is entertaining because of its cynical humor and amusing situations. Enjoy and laugh along as the game pokes fun at American Idol and Oprah Winfrey.

KEY GAMEPLAY ELEMENTS

Attack/Fight
Explore
Steer/Maneuver

GAME WORLD SIZE	Medium
YOUR ROLE	Hero
REPLAY VALUE	Once pr Twice

AVERAGE SCORE

NA

out of 10

AVAILABLE ON

Nintendo DS
Nintendo Wii
✓ PC Windows
PC Mac
Playstation 2
Playstation 3
Playstation Portable
Xbox 360

GAME FACTS

PUBLISHER
GarageGames

DEVELOPER
21-6 Productions

FIRST RELEASED
2006-12-06

GAME GENRE Puzzle	**TIME PERIOD** Multiple/Timetravel
THEME Sci-Fi	**COMPLEXITY** Medium

SIMILAR GAMES

The Incredible Machine
Diner Dash
Bridge Construction

RATING & MULTIPLAYER

USA	Europe	Network	Offline
	NOT RATED www.pegi.info	No	No

TubeTwist
QUANTUM FLUX EDITION

SETTING
It is time to use your brain like your life depended on it, as you are sent across portals into other periods of time, and the only way back is to gather enough energy by using Macrotons.

GAME SUMMARY
Your professor Jaymour has gone missing, and the only thing she left behind are her experiments. And to find out the secret behind the project, you need to learn how to handle Macrotons. By using tube parts of all sorts, you guide the tiny energy spheres into small reactors. If you do this correctly, energy will be stored for later use. Be aware that the colors must match and there might be more than one sphere. As you complete the different levels, you gain access to new places with harder puzzles. You will also come across different types of parts that all give the puzzles a different twist. Some parts are not movable, and you must find a way to use those parts together with your own. There are multiple solutions to each puzzle and no time limit or score, so there is no need to rush. You can save your solutions to show them to your friends.

CHALLENGES & HINTS
The puzzles will become increasingly difficult as you progress, but if you like a challenge on the side, try out the experiment packs, some of which can be really tricky. Most importantly, don't give up! When you're stuck, reset and try from scratch.

KEY GAMEPLAY ELEMENTS
Solve Puzzles
Build & Design
Tactics/Plan

GAME WORLD SIZE	Small
YOUR ROLE	Scientist
REPLAY VALUE	Once or Twice

AVERAGE SCORE

NA
out of 10

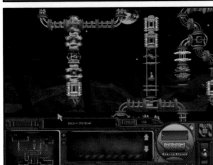

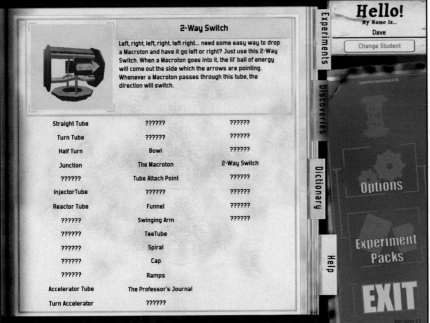

2-Way Switch

Left, right, left, right, left right... need some easy way to drop a Macroton and have it go left or right? Just use this 2-Way Switch. When a Macroton goes into it, the lil' ball of energy will come out the side which the arrows are pointing. Whenever a Macroton passes through this tube, the direction will switch.

Straight Tube	??????	??????
Turn Tube	??????	??????
Half Turn	Bowl	??????
Junction	The Macroton	2-Way Switch
??????	Tube Attach Point	??????
InjectorTube	??????	??????
Reactor Tube	Funnel	??????
??????	Swinging Arm	??????
??????	TeeTube	
??????	Spiral	
??????	Cap	
??????	Ramps	
Accelerator Tube	The Professor's Journal	
Turn Accelerator	??????	

Hello!
My Name Is...
Dave

Change Student

Experiments

Discoveries

Dictionary

Help

Options

Experiment Packs

EXIT

Version 1.1

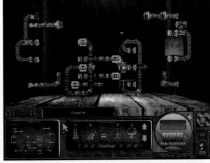

AVAILABLE ON

Nintendo DS
Nintendo Wii
✓ PC Windows
PC Mac
Playstation 2
Playstation 3
Playstation Portable
Xbox 360

GAME FACTS

PUBLISHER
Ska Software

DEVELOPER
Ska Software

FIRST RELEASED
2007-01-01

GAME GENRE	TIME PERIOD
Action	Future

THEME	COMPLEXITY
Sci-Fi	Low

SIMILAR GAMES

Freelancer
EV Nova
X3 Reunion

RATING & MULTIPLAYER

USA	Europe	Network	Offline
		No	No

Zombie Smashers X3
NINJASTARMAGEDDON!

SETTING

This is the latest of three games in the Zombie Smashers series, and in this game you take on the universe! Fight pirates, cyborgs, and other threats in space, and earn money by looting and completing missions.

GAME SUMMARY

The zombies and ninjas are separated on their respective side of the universe and have made peace thanks to the pterodactyl government. With your space vessel you travel through space-fighting enemies, trading and completing missions. You drive a space car with a companion, and it is up to you to choose weapons for both the ride and your partner. Pirates are a regular problem, and defeating opponents gives you a chance to take their wares as well as their money. Explore the different sectors of the universe, but keep your eyes open for dangers. You gain access to new ships and weapons as you acquire more money, which you get through looting, selling, and completing missions. How long will the peace last, and how will you survive?

CHALLENGES & HINTS

Pay attention and don't doze off. Before you know it there will be a pirate attack or you are suddenly stuck without gas in an abandoned sector of space. Good luck!

KEY GAMEPLAY ELEMENTS

Attack/Fight
Steer/Maneuver
Trade

GAME WORLD SIZE	Large
YOUR ROLE	Space Ace
REPLAY VALUE	Once or Twice

AVERAGE SCORE

NA

out of 10

About us

BENDIK STANG, Editor in Chief & Lead Designer, Founder of gameXplore

Bendik is the initiator of the *Book of Games* series. He is an extremely creative person who loves to invent and design things—just look at the beautiful design of this book! In addition to his many responsibilities at gameXplore, Bendik serves as coordinator for the Norwegian chapter of the International Game Developers Association. He holds a masters of science with a specialization in 3D animation and game design—in other words, he knows a lot about game composition. In 2003, he founded gameXplore together with Hans Christian Bjørne with a vision to guide people through the jungle of games. Bendik is an avid gamer and loves MMORPGs and strategy games. He is also an eternal optimist and is still waiting for the next Monkey Island. In his limited spare moments, Bendik spends time with his lovely and extremely patient wife, Charlotte, and their fantastic kids, Lea Aurora and August Emil.

MORTEN A. ØSTERHOLT, Editor & Chief Project Manager

As project manager for the *Book of Games*, Morten has kept, directly or in-directly, track of the more than 60 people working on this project and disciplined us all. Hence, he has played a significant role in the making of this book. With an MBA in marketing and broad business experience as category manager for Statoil Retail and project manager for Fastweb's software development, Morten has brought the sorely needed skill of project management to gameXplore. But Morten is no newcomer to videogaming. He grew up in a home filled with electronic gadgets and was only four when he got his first console in 1978, a Zanussi Play-O-Tronic. He has since worked his way through most platforms. Morten's favorite genres include racing, strategy, and FPS. He spends his scarce spare time time with his beautiful wife, Helene, and their one-year-old son, Oliver.

ERIK HOFTUN, Editor & Publisher

As the oldest member on the team, Erik has been around a fair bit. He came to gameXplore from the position as senior partner in Geelmuyden.Kiese, one of Scandinavia's leading public relations companies, and has varied international experience before that, both in Asia and the U.S. As the only one on the team with prior publishing experience, Erik knew a bit about the challenges facing the team. His warnings about the many pitfalls on the way from a brilliant idea to a great book now fall on more attentive ears. Erik is a latecomer to the world of videogaming with one important exception: always a pilot at heart, he has been playing *Flight Simulator* for many years and finds it an excellent substitute for not having the time any longer to keep his pilot's license current. Lately he has also taken a liking to *Motor Storm* on the PS3. As the father of five ranging in age from six to eighteen, Dad's newest project was well received at home, with everyone agreeing he is the coolest dad around. Mom, on the other hand, has, at times, expressed concern that the kids are a bit too involved in game testing, especially when *Guitar Hero* blasts from the speakers in the family room and a number of PSP and DS handhelds render their users deaf to any attempt at communication.

HANS CHRISTIAN BJØRNE, Editor

holds an MBA in business finance and is in charge of strategy and business development at gameXplore. Hans Christian has an eye for detail, and every page of this book has gone through his quality control. In addition to administrating day-to-day operations at gameXplore, he plays a significant role in product development management. Prior to founding gameXplore with Bendik in 2003, he worked as a product manager for Cantametrix Inc., a music search technology company in Seattle. In his limited spare time, Hans Christian loves to play games, golf, hit the slopes skiing, play jazz piano, and hang out with his friends and lovely girlfriend, Katrine. His introduction to the world of computer games was in 1986 when he played *Space Quest 1* with Bendik. (Back then, none of them had the faintest idea that they would be founding gameXplore 17 years later.) Hans Christian's favorite game genres are racing, sport, and entertainment.

ALF MARIUS FOSS OLSEN, System Developer

The only true hippie on the team—he looks like a hippie, walks like a hippie, and talks like one, too—Alf is also a great systems developer and by far the most structured on the team. A computer science engineer, Alf Marius does scripting and design work on our database and is responsible for quality assurance of game data. This year he has been responsible for rebuilding the database and designing our new publishing system for the *Book of Games* series. Working for gameXplore, he has become hooked on gaming, and when he does not compose techno music, he spends most of his nights with a PSP in his hands. Favorite games: *Fort Apocalypse* and *Master of Orion*.

MATTIS HENNING BØDTKER, Game Editor

Mattis is the newest and youngest addition to the team. He has studied media and communications and loves doing graphic design. Prior to joining gameXplore, Mattis was a freelancer for the Scandinavian Nintendo distributor, Bergsala AS, testing games and contributing to their game guides. He started playing videogames at the age of six, but the main turning point for him was when he received the Nintendo 64 title *The Legend of Zelda: Ocarina of Time*. Mattis has spent this year playing *The Legend of Zelda: Twilight Princess*, *Hotel Dusk: Room 215* and replaying one of his favorite games, *Shenmue*. Oh, in case you haven't figured it out yet, he loves Nintendo titles.

JØRGEN KIRKSÆTHER, Contributing Editor and Walking Videogame Encyclopedia,

has played with videogames for thirty years. Since his first encounter with microcomputers in the mid 1970s, he's enjoyed, programmed, researched, written, and talked about games and gaming as a gamer, journalist, analyst, lecturer, and academic. He is currently a games reviewer and journalist for a national radio and television network and a national newspaper in Norway and an expert adviser to the Norwegian government and the European Commission's network of awareness nodes, all while he finishes his PhD dissertation on the historic development of videogames. His all-time favorite game is *Pac-Man*.

About us continued...

ERIC V. SEGALSTAD, Contributing Editor
After he wrote the features for last year's *Book of Games*, Eric flew to Indian Kashmir and documented a season's worth of backcountry skiing for TheLineOfControl.com. He is currently finishing up a book about one of his other passions, music, so it's fitting that his article in Volume 2 is about the stuff we listen to while playing the games. What's his book about? Visit The27s.com for the scoop.

DAVID COLE, Contributing Editor
David Cole is the founder and president of DFC Intelligence. Since 1994, he has personally authored numerous reports on the videogame and interactive entertainment industry, spoken at leading industry conferences, and consulted with top companies in the entertainment, telecommunications, investment, and consumer electronics industries. Mr. Cole is one of the most widely quoted analysts on videogames, computer software, and the Internet. Mr. Cole has a BA in economics and industrial relations, as well as a JD from the University of North Carolina.

BARNEVAKTEN.NO (CHILDMINDER), Contributing Editors
ChildMinder is an organization that gives parents advice and knowledge about children and media. Their objective is to protect children from violence and other harmful influence in the media. ChildMinder helps parents to increase their knowledge about how children are using television, computer games, and the Internet. We thank ChildMinder, and especially Odd Arild Olsen and Øystein Samnøen for sharing their insights and research on gaming in schools.

LUKE NEWCOMBE, Contributing Editor
Born in Vancouver, B.C., Canada, Luke "Duke" Newcombe has lived all over the world and currently resides in London, England. He has been playing videogames since he was five years old and has many years of experience in the videogame industry. Luke has worked in communications, publicity, and marketing for companies like AlienPants, GameXplore, and Xequted, and he has freelanced as a writer for Official Xbox Magazine. His favorite game these days is *World in Conflict* on the PC and TimeShift on the Xbox 360. Read more about Luke at his blog: gameguru.tv/duke

GARETH WILLIAMS, Contributing Editor
Gareth Williams is a freelance journalist with lots of experience from the interactive entertainment industry. He was recently appointed news editor of 360 Gamer and has previously written for X360, Official Xbox Magazine, PSM2, P3Zine, PCGZine, CVG, and Pro-G. He has also worked with ATi, Nintendo, Game Network, Atari, and the Golden Joystick Awards 2005. As you might have guessed, Gareth is more than a little interested in games.

EDVARD R. MURENA III, Contributing Editor

Edvard lives in Oregon, U.S., and is an experienced indie game developer and associate of GarageGames, a company whose mission is to provide independent developers with tools, knowledge, and co-conspirators—everything needed to make great games. Edvard is the author of *The Game Programmer's Guide to Torque* (2006).

SPENCER SHERMAN, Contributing Editor

Ever since competing with his brothers to play Zelda on a portable black and white television, Spencer Sherman has been a gamer. His television set has received several upgrades since, but his passion for videogames and the videogame industry remains unchanged. After spending a year living and working in Tokyo, Spencer returned to Skidmore College to write a research paper on Microsoft's marketing strategies in Japan under the guidance of Professor Masami Tamagawa. He received a degree in English Literature and Asian Studies from Skidmore College, and began working as a Jr. Systems Engineer for Activision's highly anticipated *Call of Duty 4: Modern Warfare*.

ALLISON LUONG, Contributing Editor,

is cofounder and managing director of Pearl Research, a San Francisco– and China-based market research and consulting firm. Ms. Luong has a lot of experience in consulting, marketing, and market research for a wide array of high-tech clients. She leads Pearl Research's ongoing analysis of interactive entertainment, gaming, wireless, and Internet markets. Ms. Luong has been featured in Wired, the Economist, Red Herring, Smartmoney, BBC News, and the Financial Times. Ms. Luong is a graduate of University of California at Berkeley. Visit www.pearlresearch.com for more information.

SCOTT STEINBERG, Contributing Editor

is the author of Get Rich Playing Games (yours FREE at getrichgaming.com), publisher of technology supersite DigitalTrends.com, and managing director of Embassy Multimedia Consultants (embassymulti.com), which counsels game industry developers, publishers, and distributors worldwide. The biz's most prolific freelance author and radio/TV host, he's covered gaming/technology for 300+ outlets including CNN, the Los Angeles and New York Times, Playboy, Rolling Stone, USA Today, and TV Guide. Other ventures include software publisher Overload Entertainment and GamesPress.com, the ultimate resource for game journalists, as well as the groundbreaking books Videogame Marketing and PR and The Videogame Style Guide and Reference Manual.

ROBERT HOOGENDOORN, Contributing Editor

In 2003, he presented research on online game communities at the Level Up International Games Conference in Utrecht, Netherlands. Beyond his activities in the academic world of videogames, he is also a co-organizer of the World Cyber Games and editor in-chief of Ownage.nl. In 2006 he started his own company, focusing on the video and textual content of videogames and videogame culture. He now writes for several Dutch gaming magazines. For more information about Robert Hoogendoorn, visit gamefanatic.nl

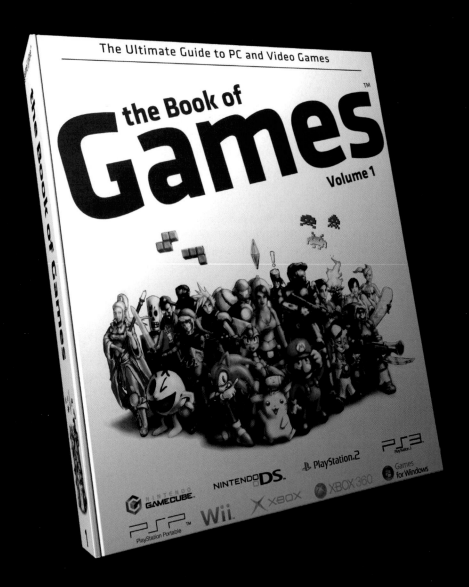

Next volume in the series
coming November 2008

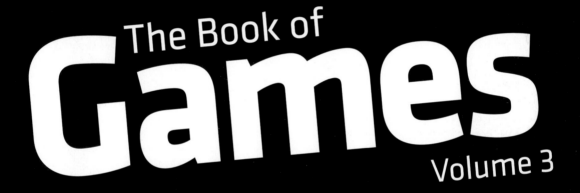
The Book of
Games
Volume 3

www.bookofgames.com

Glossary

3D Studio Max

One of the most popular software applications used by video game artists, it is used to create the 3D models that are the basis of nearly all modern video games.

ActiveX

A family of Microsoft object technologies. Originally named Object Linking and Embedding (OLE), it is commonly used to allow external applications like Windows Media Player to run inside of Internet Explorer.

Afk

'Away From Keyboard" is the sort of thing a player types before they run to the fridge to grab another soda. This lets the other players in their online group know that they shouldn't pick any fights they need the player's help to win.

AI

See *Artificial Intelligence*.

Alias Wave Front

Now a part of Autodesk, Alias's Academy Award–winning software Maya is a fully integrated modelling, animation, and rendering system. It is used by movie makers, video game developers, and others to create amazing visual effects.

Alienware

Computer manufacturer of systems designed with gaming in mind and a look that matches their name. Their purchase by Dell had many gamers awaiting the watering down of their image.

Amiga

Providing the ability to run more than one program at once (multitasking OS), stereo sound, and rich color graphics, the Amiga was a popular gaming computer in the 1980s. It was developed by Jay Miner and released by Commodore in 1985 as a successor to the Commodore 64.

Amstrad

British consumer hardware manufacturer, especially known for the Amstrad home computers in the 1980s.

Anti-Aliasing

A technique to smooth jagged edges from digital signals. Digital images are composed of tiny squares, and making those squares into a diagonal line is a little like trying to turn a stairway into a ramp. Anti-aliasing is an algorithm that uses shades of the line edge to effectively "squint" at the stairway until it looks like a ramp. You can see an example of the effect of anti-aliasing text on the right. The anti-aliased text is on the bottom line.

Artificial Intelligence

Refers to adaptive or learning behavior in computer game software.

Atari

Atari released the first video game console to have removable cartridges when it moved out of the arcades with the Atari 2600. Throughout the 1980s, Atari continued to release gaming consoles, with one of their last being the Lynx handheld that lost out to the success of Nintendo's GameBoy. Atari is also the creator of one of the most widely known games in video game history: *Pong*

Augmented Reality

Technology that aims to combine the benefits of Virtual Reality with the richness of real life. While Virtual Reality aims to submerge the user into a completely synthesized environment, Augmented Reality strives to augment the real world through layering some sensations from the virtual world, like smell, touch, or visual overlays, onto real-world sensations.

Binary

A system of numbers that has two possible values per digit.

Bit

A single digit in the binary (base-2) number system. These are those zeros and ones everyone is always talking about.

Bit Width (8 bit, 16 bit, 32 bit, 64 bit)

Bit width refers to the size of the information chunks that a computer chip can handle per operation it performs. Larger bit widths mean the processor doesn't have to split math computations into multiple instructions and also allows the computer to address larger amounts of memory. This typically results in richer graphics and sound due to the higher detail allowed by the large bit width. See also binary.

A 16 bit computer can process numbers up to 65,536 whereas a 32 bit computer can process numbers up to 4,294,967,296 in a single operation.

Bitmap

An image format that represents a picture by describing the location and color of each pixel in an image.

Blizzard Entertainment

Game development company that has captured the MMORPG genre with *World of Warcraft*. Their games often combine real-time strategy with player advancement and include #1 selling hits like the *Warcraft*, *Starcraft*, and *Diablo* series.

Bluetooth

A short-range wireless protocol that is used by handheld devices like game controllers and cell phones to communicate with computers and game systems.

Blu-ray

An optical media like the DVD or CD, Blu-ray uses a blue laser to make discs that hold up to 50 GB.

Boost

Enhancement of a player attribute or ability like speed or health. Some only last for a limited amount of time.

Brb

"Be Right Back" means exactly what it says and is used in all sorts of online messaging situations. Maybe the phone rang, maybe your conversation was getting boring. For whatever reason they left, the messager of "brb" does usually come back.

Byte

The most commonly used unit of storage in the computer world. Though they can be other sizes, in modern usage, all bytes are assumed to store 8 bits.

1 kilobyte (KB) = 1,024 bytes
1 megabyte (MB) = 1,048,576 bytes
1 gigabyte (GB) = 1,073,741,824 bytes
1 terabyte (TB) = 1,099,511,627,776 bytes
1 petabyte (PB) = 1,125,899,906,842,624 bytes

Cartridge

See *Game Cartridges*.

Case Modding

To customize computer cases for look or performance enhancement. Most case mods are purely decorative and modders add that special bling by painting designs, hooking up neon and LED lights, and cutting holes for see-through panels. Other case mods focus on heat dissipation for overclocked systems or on making that beastly computer as quiet as possible. In all cases, the extremes of the case modding community are engineering and artistic wonders.

Cathode Ray Tube

Display technology found in noflat panel TVs and computer screens.

Cell Chip

The main processing unit of Sony's PlayStation 3, manufactured by IBM. The chip has a controller core that manages the instructions for six additional processing units. These processing units do the heavy computation for the Cell and make the system perform like a six-CPU cluster on a single chip.

Central Processing Unit

The "brain" of the computer, it coordinates all the actions of the game and farms out tasks to specialized processors for video and sound.

Chat

Communicating through electronic networks by typing and reading. Can also include pictures, video, and sound.

Cheats

Cheating codes or commands are often leftovers from the development and testing stages of a game. There is no standard set of cheats but "no clip" and "god mode" are common.

Chipping

Allows gamers to bypass security features. Mainly used for running illegal copies of a game.

Cinematics

Scenes in a video game over which the player has no control.

Cinemaware

Game developer that was known for its excellent graphics during the 1980s and early 90s. Its game *Defender of the Crown* was ported from the Amiga to nearly every other platform available at the time.

CISC

See *Complex Instruction Set Computing*.

Clan

A group of friends who meet online on a regular basis to play and practice a particular game as an elite unit. A clan might meet other clans online to play against them or at competitions for prizes.

CMYK
Cyan Magenta Yellow Black is the color standard used for printing colors on paper. See also *RGB*.

Complex Instruction Set Computing
A general term for a family of instructions used on microchips. This style of instruction set allows software developers to write higher-level instructions at the expense of additional logic on the chip. For a time, this style was perceived to have lower performance than RISC-based processors. On today's large chips, however, the logic circuitry is comparatively small and both RISC- and CISC-style instruction sets have found a middle ground. The Pentium chip family is the most prominent example of a CISC chip. See also *Reduced Instruction Set Computing*.

Console
A dedicated gaming platform. Often referred to as a Nintendo by older generations, these are the PSs, Xboxes, and Gamecubes of the world. Their sole purpose is to play games and make people happy!

Controller
A piece of hardware like a joystick, directional pad, or steering wheel used by the player to control the actions in the video game.

Cooperative Play
Game play that involves playing with other human players as partners rather than adversaries.

CPU
See *Central Processing Unit*

CPU Cooler
This device cools hard-working CPUs by blowing air on the chip, but it can also use more exotic liquid or thermoelectric cooling systems.

CPU Fan
Fan attached directly to the CPU or CPU heatsink that uses air to cool the CPU.

CRT
See *Cathode Ray Tube*.

Cursor
The graphic used to mark the current location of the mouse pointer.

Database
A server or file that provides highly structured data storage for large amounts of data. You use Excel for your Christmas list; the National Security Agency uses a database.

DirectX
A set of interfaces provided by Microsoft that simplifies game programming for Windows.

Dreamcast
Sega's last console before becoming software-only, this was the first console of the sixth generation, released fifteen months before the PlayStation 2.

DS
A dual-screen portable gaming device released by Nintendo in 2004. Its ability to allow wireless interaction with other DS users was a unique feature.

DS Lite
A slimmer version of the Nintendo DS released in 2006.

EA
See *Electronic Arts*.

EGA
See *Enhanced Graphics Adaptor*.

Eidos (Interactive)
Games publisher. Major titles include the *Tomb Raider* series, *Hitman* and *Commandos*.

Electronic Arts
One of world's largest games companies. Established in 1982, they were pioneers of the computer game market. Major games include *The Sims*, *Skate or Die!*, *SimCity*, *Command & Conquer*, and *Medal of Honor*. Their sports subsidiary publishes a series of high profile game titles.

Emulator
One computer system pretending to be a different system. This allows modern computers to run arcade games from the 1980s or Windows games on a Macintosh.

Enhanced Graphics Adaptor
Old graphics technology most often found in 1980s PCs.

Entertainment Consumers Association (ECCA)
An American nonprofit membership organization established to

serve the needs of those who play computer and videogames. Formed in 2006, the ECA is an advocacy organization for consumers of interactive entertainment. According to the ECA, gamers represent nearly 50 percent of the U.S. population and spend $10 billion annually on gaming, yet as a group they are continually overlooked by both politicians and the mainstream press. The organization, which is headquartered in Connecticut, focuses its advocacy efforts on consumer rights, antigames legislation, and a host of other public policy concerns, as well as providing substantial community, educational, and affinity benefits to its members—from discounts on subscriptions, game rentals, and purchases to education, employment assistance, and insider access to industry news and events. Check it out at WWW.THEECA.COM.

Entertainment Software Rating Board

The ESRB is a non-profit, self-regulatory body that independently assigns ratings, enforces advertising guidelines, and helps ensure responsible online privacy practices for the interactive entertainment software industry.

EARLY CHILDHOOD
May be suitable for ages 3 and older. Contains no material that parents would find inappropriate.

EVERYONE
May be suitable for ages 6 and older. Titles in this category may contain minimal cartoon, fantasy or mild violence and/or use of mild language.

EVERYONE 10+
May be suitable for ages 10 and older. Titles in this category may contain more cartoon, fantasy or mild violence, mild language, and/or minimal suggestive themes.

TEEN
May be suitable for ages 13 and older. Titles in this category may contain violence, suggestive themes, crude humor, minimal blood, simulated gambeling, and/or infrequent use of strong language.

MATURE
May be suitable for ages 17 and older. Titles in this category may contain intense violence, blood and gore, sexual content, and/or graphical sexual content and nudity.

ADULTS ONLY
Should only be played by persons 18 years and older. Titles in this category may include prolonged scenes of intense violence and/or sexual content and nudity.

ESRB
See *Entertainment Software Rating Board.*

ESRB Content Descriptors

- *Alcohol Reference* - Reference to and/or images of alcoholic beverages
- *Animated Blood* - Discolored and/or unrealistic depictions of blood
- *Blood* - Depictions of blood
- *Blood and Gore* - Depictions of blood or the mutilation of body parts
- *Cartoon Violence* – Violent actions involving cartoon-like situations and characters. May include violence where a character is unharmed after the action has been inflicted
- *Comic Mischief* - Depictions or dialogue involving slapstick or suggestive humor
- *Crude Humor* – Depictions or dialogue involving vulgar antics, including "bathroom" humor
- *Drug Reference* - Reference to and/or images of illegal drugs
- *Fantasy Violence* – Violent actions of a fantasy nature, involving human or non-human characters in situations easily distinguishable from real life
- *Intense Violence* – Graphic and realistic-looking depictions of physical conflict. May involve extreme and/or realistic blood, gore, weapons, and depictions of human injury and death
- *Language* – Mild to moderate use of profanity
- *Lyrics* – Mild references to profanity, sexuality, violence, alcohol, or drug use in music
- *Mature Humor* - Depictions or dialogue involving "adult" humor, including sexual references
- *Nudity* - Graphic or prolonged depictions of nudity
- *Partial Nudity* - Brief and/or mild depictions of nudity
- *Real Gambling* – Player can gamble, including betting or wagering real cash or currency
- *Sexual Content* – Non-explicit depictions of sexual behavior, possibly including partial nudity.
- *Sexual Themes* – References to sex or sexuality
- *Sexual Violence* – Depictions of rape or other violent sexual acts
- *Simulated Gambling* – Player can gamble without betting or wagering real cash or currency
- *Strong Language* - Explicit and/or frequent use of profanity
- *Strong Lyrics* - Explicit and/or frequent references to profanity, sex, violence, alcohol, or drug use in music

• *Strong Sexual Content* – Explicit and/or frequent depictions of sexual behavior, possibly including nudity.
• *Suggestive Themes* - Mild provocative references or materials
• *Tobacco Reference* - Reference to and/or images of tobacco products
• *Use of Drugs* - The consumption or use of illegal drugs
• *Use of Alcohol* - The consumption of alcoholic beverages
• *Use of Tobacco* - The consumption of tobacco products
• *Violence* - Scenes involving aggressive conflict. May contain bloodless dismemberment
• *Violent References* – References to violent acts
When a content descriptor is preceded by the term 'Mild', it conveys low frequency, intensity or severity of the content it modifies.

ESRB Online Rating
Online-enabled games carry the notice "Online Interactions Not Rated by the ESRB." This notice warns those who intend to play the game online about possible exposure to chat (text, audio, video) or other types of content created by other players (e.g., maps, skins) that have not been considered in the ESRB rating assignment.

For the most up to date list of content descriptors and definitions, go to HTTP://WWW.ESRB.ORG/

EyeToy
Camera for Sony's PlayStation. Allows the body movements of the player to control the action of the video game.

First-Person Perspective
A game perspective that allows you to see through the eyes of the character you control. This is the perspective that most closely resembles the way we experience the outside world in real life.

First-Person Shooter
A game type where the player controls a single video game character. Usually the goal in these games is to shoot pretty much anything that moves.

Flash Memory Card
A storage device used by many video game consoles to store game progress, player statistics, and settings.

Floating Point Operations Per Second
A measure of CPU performance that looks at how many calculations a processor can do on real numbers per second. The Xbox360's CPU, for example, has a theoretical performance of 116 gigaFLOPS.

Floating Point Unit
A part of the CPU that does math operations on numbers with a decimal point.

FLOPS
See *Floating Point Operations Per Second.*

FPS
See *First Person Shooter* or *Frames Per Second.*

FPU
See *Floating Point Unit.*

FRAG
A unit for how many times you have killed an enemy or another player in a shooting game.

Frames Per Second
The number of images displayed on the screen per second. It is used as a common performance measure for graphics cards. Anything above 30 fps is considered acceptable.

Game Cartridges
Used on consoles like the Atari and Nintendo to store video game code. Getting these to work reliably often required blowing the dust out, holding them at a certain angle, and walking three circles around the console.

Game Engine
The software component at the core of a video game. The engine includes frameworks for 2D and 3D graphic rendering, a physics model and collision detection, sound, networking, and more. These frameworks can be reused across consoles and PCs and simplify the development process for game programmers.

Gameboy (GB/GBA)
From its release in 1989 to its current incarnation, the GameBoy is one of the most successful gaming systems ever released. It was originally bundled with *Tetris*, had a monochrome screen, and retailed for $109, cheaper than any other handheld gaming device at the time.

GameCube
Nintendo's fourth video game console, released just after the Nintendo64. Contemporaneous with the Sony PlayStation 2 and the Microsoft Xbox.

Game Play
Refers to the overall experience of playing the game, particularly

in reference to actions the player actually does in the game.

GarageGames
Game publisher that focuses on developing unique games while also providing tools and advice to help others develop new games. Tools by GarageGames include Torque Game Engine, Torque Shader Engine and Torque Game Builder.

Giga
1,000,000,000, or one billion, in Greek

God View
Refers to a view that looks down or allows a player to "fly" around the game location without regard to gravity.

GPU
See *Graphics Processing Unit.*

Graphics Processing Unit
A special processor that is dedicated to creating the 2D and 3D images displayed on a television or computer screen. These processors are customized to do graphics very well and allow the main processor to manage other aspects of the game.

Guild
A group of video game players that work cooperatively in online games.

Hacking
Using external programs or flaws in gaming software to gain an advantage. Often involves using glitches or bugs that developers fail to find during development or getting illegal access to computer systems.

HDMI
See *High Definition Multimedia Interface.*

HDTV
See *High Definition TeleVision.*

High Definition Multimedia Interface
Digital connection between a DVD player or video game device to a display that allows very high resolution, has built in copy protection, and also carries digital audio.

High Definition TeleVision
Television system that handles significantly higher resolution than standard systems like NTSC and PAL. Usually transmitted digitally, this television system is currently found mostly in flat panel televisions.

Infrared Connection
Connections that use the wavelength of light just below the visible spectrum and require a line of sight between connecting devices. It is commonly used for television remote controls.

Interlaced
Moving images, like standard television, that are drawn by refreshing every other horizontal line in a single cycle, then the skipped lines in the next cycle.

IR
See *Infrared Connection.*

Joypad
More commonly referred to as a game pad or controller, this device has buttons that a player uses to control the game.

Joystick
A control unit most prominently used on classic arcade games. A vertical stick, often with trigger and thumb-activated buttons, it is used to control the on-screen action. Features range from the dead simple Atari joystick—one button and the stick—to the positively baroque with twelve programmable buttons and eight-way position sensors.

Kilo
1,000 in Greek.

LAN
See *Local Area Network.*

LAN Parties
Can vary from two to thousands of people linking their computers together by an Ethernet cable. Big, sponsored events attract thousands of people and often last for several days.

LCD
See *Liquid Crystal Display.*

Learning Curve
Used to describe the difficulty of a player familiarizing themselves with the rules, environment, and game play of a game.

LED
See *Light Emitting Diode.*

Level(s)
Refers to advancement, either of the player's character or to a new stage of the game. With each new level players often get

additional abilities, while new stages or levels of a game offer different, usually harder, obstacles.

Light Emitting Diode
Extremely reliable electrical component that glows when a current passes through it. Red and amber have been the most common and cheap colors for decades, but recent advances have made blue, green, and even white LEDs commonplace in all kinds of consumer electronics.

Liquid Crystal Display
Used to create flat-panel displays. Some models are not suitable for gaming due to their slow refresh rate that leads to image blurring in fast-moving games.

Local Area Network
A network that allows connected computers to communicate without their communications crossing onto the Internet.

LOL
"Laughing Out Loud." The most commonly used expression to say that something is very funny.

Massive Multiplayer Online Game
A game where there is a large amount of players communicating and playing together.

Massive Multiplayer Online Role-Playing Game
A role-playing game that has tens of thousands to millions of other human players. The games are played over the Internet and include *World of Warcraft* and *EverQuest*.

Maya
Software for creating and rendering three-dimensional digital objects for use in games or movies. Made by AutoDesk.

Mega
1,000,000, or one million, in Greek.

Memory Card
Usually based on flash memory, these cards store game progress and player statistics, even while the console is powered off.

Microsoft
The largest software company in the world, a longtime game publisher, and a recent entrant into the game console manufacturing industry.

Microsoft Game Studio
A subsidiary of Microsoft that develops and publishes games for the PC and the Xbox family of consoles.

Millisecond
1/1000th of a second.

Minigame
A small game with differing rules played within the context of a larger game.

MMOG
See *Massive Multiplayer Online Game*.

MMORPG
See *Massive Multiplayer Online Role-Playing Game*.
Mocap
See *Motion Capture*.

Motion Capture
A technique that digitally records real-life motion, particularly of human bodies, and uses the information from the capture to aid developers in recreating lifelike movement.

Mod
A modification to the game that ranges from adding new weapons and locations to complete recreation of the storyline and game goals.

Modding
PC hardware modding is the most common form of modding where a computer's exterior is modified. Hardware modding is getting more common for consoles but is not as developed as PC modding. Software modders have the intention of providing new features or content to a game, such as a new map.

Modchip
By adding new chips to a game console, homebrew games and unique operating systems can be used on a traditional console. Often, these modchips are applied in order to allow gamers to play pirated games.

Motion Sensitive Controller
A game pad that measures the rotation and acceleration of the game pad to control the characters in the game.

Mouse
A device used with a computer to control a pointing cursor on the computer's display.

Nanosecond
One billionth of a second.

Nintendo
The oldest company in the games business, Nintendo got its start in 1895 manufacturing playing cards. Now the publisher of, among others, the *Zelda*, *Mario Bros.*, and *Donkey Kong* games, as well as the GameBoy, Wii, and DS games consoles.

Nitrous
Boost of potent fuel. Watch out when you use this, too much and you'll lose control!

Nonplayer Character
An in-game character controlled by the computer or console.

NPC
See Nonplayer Character

Non-Uniform, Rational B-spline
A mathematical model commonly used to represent curves in video game graphics.

Noob (as Newbie or New Beginner)
Is often used as an insult against others. It denotes that your play demonstrates that you don't know the rules and customs of the game you are playing.

NTSC
National Television System(s) Committee. The analog television system in use in North America.

Nurbs
See *Non-Uniform, Rational B-spline*.

OLED
See *Organic Light Emitting Display*.

Online
Connected to the Internet or a LAN.

Online Gaming
Playing games with other humans across the Internet or a LAN.

Open Graphics Library
A standard for graphics display that, due to its standardization, is commonly used across all gaming platforms.

OpenGL

See *Open Graphics Library*.

Organic Light Emitting Display
A flat display technology that provides bright crisp and bendable displays without a large power demand. They became common in 2005, especially on camera display screens and other handheld devices

Over Clocking
Turning up the speed of the CPU. Results in a faster computer, but the intense heat generated by over clocking may also damage the CPU.

P2P Peer-to-peer
Technology for connecting two or more computer systems directly, especially to aid the transfer of data between them.

PAL
See *Phase-Alternating Lines*.

Pan European Game Information
A European system for game rating. Its game ratings are based on the age groups for which a game is appropriate and includes six content warnings.

Bad Language
Game contains bad language

Discrimination
Game conatins depictions of, or material which may encourage discrimination

Drugs
Game refers to or depicts the use of drugs

Fear
Game may be frightening or scary for young children

Sex
Game depicts nudity and/or sexual behaviouror sexual contents

Violence
Game contains depictions of violence

PEGI Online
Logo granted by the PEGI Online Administrator

to any online gameplay service provider that meets the requirements set out in the PEGI Online Safety Code (POSC).

PC Personal Computer
Most often used to refer to computers that run Microsoft Windows, it can also be defined to include any computer owned for personal use.

PEGI
See *Pan European Game Information*.

Peripherals
Devices connected to a computer or game console that are not required but enhance the operating experience.

Phase-Alternating Lines
An analog television system in common use across much of Europe, Africa, and Asia.

Physical Interactivity
Describes how much you interact with the game. Games that require "button mashing" or lots of key combinations have higher physical interactivity.

Physics
In this context, the game's ability to calculate realistically the real-time physical interaction between objects, such as the gravitational forces and impact of collision between objects, resulting in a very realistic simulation of the real world.

Physics Engine
Portion of the game's software that is responsible for calculating the phyiscs acting on characters and projectiles in the game world.

Pixel
Smallest unit of display on a screen—a single dot.

Pk "Player Killing"
Used to refer to a human-controlled character killing another human-controlled character. Most commonly used in MMORPGs.

Plasma
Display technology used in flat screens that creates light by electrifying gases trapped in the screen.

Playtime
Total time spent playing a video game. In MMORPGs that track this, playtimes of over a month are not uncommon!

Polygon
A geometric shape like a rectangle or hexagon that is the building block of video game graphics.

Pong
The first video game to win widespread popularity. Available for the home and at the arcade, it is widely credited with creating the initial boom in the video game industry.

Pre-Rendered
Video game sequences that are modeled using computer software and changed into movie form before being put into the video game. This allows movies with a higher polygon count than a graphics card or system could normally produce, with the tradeoff being static game play and the requirement of large amounts of storage.

PlayStation (PS1)
Sony's orginial video game console. Competed with the Nintendo64 and Sega Saturn.

PlayStation 2 (PS2)
Sony's second-generation console. Competed with the Microsoft Xbox and Nintendo GameCube.

PlayStation 3 (PS3)
Sony's third-generation console. Competes with the Microsoft Xbox360 and Nintendo Wii.

PlayStation Portable (PSP)
Sony's handheld video game device.

PvP
"Player versus player" is an expression used when there are multiple human-controlled characters competing directly against each other.

Quest
Quests guide players to follow a series of clues, perform tasks, and often end with a difficult battle. Successful completion of the quest often delivers a powerful item or ability to be used in the game.

RAM

See *Random Access Memory.*

Random Access Memory

This is used as short-term memory for a computer. It does not retain the data stored in it when the power is shut off.

Rating

Category applied to a video game that advises consumers on the content and age-appropriateness of a game.

Read Only Memory

This memory is usually the location where a computer or video game console stores its permanent operating code. Read Only Memory can not be changed by the computer itself and is only useful for storing static information and instructions.

Real Time

Happening as fast as a human player can respond.

Reduced Instruction Set Computing

A simple set of CPU-level code that delivered higher performance in the early days of computing. See also Complex Instruction Set Computing.

Rendering

The process that turns a video game's mathematical model of an image into the image that is displayed on the screen.

RGB

Color model where every color is described by its red, green, and blue components. Used on computer screens. See also *CMYK.*

RISC

See *Reduced Instruction Set Computing.*

Rocket-Jumping

Firing a rocket at your own feet and jumping just as it explodes. This produces an extremely powerful jump at the cost of a portion of the player's health.

Rofl

"Rolling on Floor Laughing" is an expression used to say that something is hilarious.

Roflmao

"Rolling on Floor Laughing My Ass Off" is another expression used to say that something is hilarious. It gives the impression that something is funnier than Rofl.

ROM

See *Read Only Memory.*

RPG

See *Role Playing Game*

RTS

See *Real Time Strategy*

SCART

Cable connection standard consisting of a large plug with protruding cable "spades." Common in consumer video equipment.

SCEE/SCEA Sony Entertainment Sony Computer Entertainment

A subsidiary of Sony Corporation that handles the production, development, and publishing of video games and consoles. The extra letter refers to Europe or America.

Shader

Computer program that does the final processing on a 3D surface. It takes light absorption, shadows, reflection, and other factors in to account to create the final look of a surface.

Shooter

Video game that has direct operation of weapons, especially guns, as a core component of game play.

Sid Meier

Developer of some of the most commercially successful games of all time, including the *Civilization* series.

Side-scroller

Type of game where the characters move continually to the right to progress through the game.

Sierra (Entertainment)

Very successful publisher of games. Developed some of the first 3D games for the PC. Known for their King's Quest series.

Simulator

Type of game that attempts to replicate the experience of managing some aspect of the real world. This can be as a mayor as with *SimCity* or as a pilot in a flight simulator. These games have varying degrees of accuracy with some choosing to simplify certain aspects of a task in order to make the game play more enjoyable.

SoftImage

Canadian developer of animation software. Their most famous product is the SoftimageXSI, which was the first product to use inverse kinematics.

Spawn Point

Location at which players that has been fragged will reappear.

Spline

Mathematical representation of a curve used in computer graphics.

Split Screen

View displayed on the television when two players are using the same console and each requires her own perspective, as with a racing game.

Super Cooling

Chilling a liquid below its normal freezing point without it becoming a solid. This can be used when over-clocking the CPU.

Super Video Graphics Array

Analog computer display technology developed in the late 1980s.

SVGA

See *Super Video Graphics Array*. The term is often used as synonym for 1024x4768 pixels display resolution

Terra

1,000,000,000,000 or one trillion, in Greek.
Also the name of the first MMORPG.

Tetris

Released as the first game included with the GameBoy, this is a fast-paced puzzle game.

Texture

An image that is applied to the surface of a polygon in computer graphics. Using different textures can make a wall appear to be of stone, wood, or dripping alien goo.

TFT

See *Thin Film Transistor*.

Thin Film Transistor

Technology used in flat LCD screens.

Third-Person Perspective

A game perspective where you do not see the world through the eyes of the character you are controlling but rather as an observant. There are several types of third-person perspectives, but the most common is where you see your controlled character from behind or from the side.

Tk

"Team killing" is the expression used when one team member kills another member of the team.

Touch-Sensitive

A device that reacts to human touch.

TRS-80

Tandy Corporation's entry into the home computer market. It was sold through RadioShack and was a popular hobbyist computer.

Universal Serial Bus

A connection system used to connect peripherals and controllers to game consoles and computers.

USB

See *Universal Serial Bus*.

Vertex

The point at the corner of a polygon.

Vertex Shading

Manipulator of vertexes that can enable the glow of fog, flare of headlights at night, and realistic waves and reflections on water.

VGA

Video Graphics Adaptor. Analog computer display technology. The term is often used as synonym for 640x480 pixels display resolution.

Virtual Reality

Immersive computer generated experience that feels real to the person immersed in the environment.

Voxel

A combination of pixel and volumetric, a voxel is a unit of volume displayed in a 3D scene.

VRAM

Video-RAM. A type of DRAM used in graphics cards that allows two simultaneous accesses to the RAM data.

VUG

Vivendi Universal Games, a division of the French media conglomerate Vivendi. This division owns the Sierra and Blizzard game studios.

WAN

See *Wide Area Network*.

Warez

Pirated software.

Wi-Fi

A brand that denotes compatibility with the IEEE 802.11 wireless protocols. It allows devices to connect to each other and the Internet without the use of wires.

Wide Area Network

Networks that run across the Internet but use routing rules and security to maintain LAN-like connectivity and privacy.

Wii

Nintendo's seventh-generation video game console.

Wireless Controller

A controller that connects to the console without using wires usually using a radio device.

Xbox

Microsoft's first console released in competition with the GameCube and PlayStation 2.

Xbox Live

Microsoft Xbox's online system that enables online play between many Xboxes online. Works with Xbox and Xbox 360.

Xbox 360

Microsoft's successor to the Xbox, released in 2005.

XGA

eXtended Graphics Array, a display format often used as a synonym for 1024x768 pixels display resolution.

ZX Spectrum

Home computer built by Sinclair that used audio cassettes for data storage and was a popular gaming platform.

Index: Games by Platform

Games by ESRB Rating (USA)

Games by PEGI Rating (Europe)

Index: Games Alphabetical

Game Index: Book of Games Vol 1, Vol 2